From Home to Office
U.S. Women at Work,
1870-1930

Studies in American History and Culture No. 25

Robert Berkhofer, Series Editor

Director of American Culture Programs
and Richard Hudson Research Professor of History
The University of Michigan

Other Titles in This Series

From Home to Office

U.S. Women at Work, 1870-1930

by
Elyce J. Rotella

umi
RESEARCH PRESS

Produced and distributed by
UMI Research Press
an imprint of
University Microfilms International
Ann Arbor, Michigan 48106

Library of Congress Cataloging in Publication Data

Rotella, Elyce J
From home to office.

(Studies in American history and culture ; no. 25)
"A revision of the author's thesis, University of
Pennsylvania, 1977."
Bibliography: p.
Includes index.
1. Women—Employment—United States—History.
2. Clerks—United States—History.   I. Title.   II. Series.
HD6073.M392U57 1980   331.4'0973   80-29154
ISBN 0-8357-1163-3

For my mother
and
In memory of my father

Contents

viii   *Contents*

List of Figures

List of Tables

Acknowledgments

Any work is influenced by the intellectual and social forces which prevail in a particular time and place. This study owes much to developments in economic history, labor economics, and women's history. Without the accomplishments of many other scholars working in these fields, my work would not have been possible. This book and its author are also products of the modern feminist movement which has stimulated interest in and added urgency to questions about women's roles in society. I have benefitted greatly from my association with the growing field of women's studies, where I have found enthusiastic students and colleagues whose questions transcend disciplinary boundaries. A major portion of this research was funded by a Woodrow Wilson Fellowship in Women's Studies. Additional support was received from a California State Faculty Development Grant.

It would be impossible to name all the people who had a hand in getting me to the happy stage of writing these acknowledgments. Friends, colleagues, and students at the University of Pennsylvania, San Diego State University, and Tufts University have given me enthusiastic support and helpful feedback. Ann Miller and Richard Easterlin have been my mentors since I began my academic career. Both have contributed valuable suggestions, insightful comments, and constant encouragement.

I have received helpful comments from Marilyn Boxer, Stanley Engerman, Stefano Fenoaltea, Claudia Goldin, Joan Hannon, Janice Madden, Pamela Nickless, Michael Wachter, Anne Williams, and Mary Yeager. Earlier versions of some of this work have been presented at seminars and workshops at the University of Pennsylvania, the University of California at Berkeley, Stanford, Yale, Harvard, the University of Connecticut, and San Diego State University and at conferences of the

Social Science History Association, the Economic History Association, and the Organization of American Historians. I am grateful to the members of these workshops, seminars, and conferences for their comments and suggestions; many changes in the final version have resulted from these trial runs. Of course, I accept the blame for all errors and confusions which remain.

Much of chapter 3 appeared as an article in *Explorations in Economic History*, vol. 17, no. 2, pp. 95-117. I appreciate receiving permission to present it here.

Finally, I would like to express thanks to George Alter who has been my sounding board, my technical consultant, my unofficial editor, and my very best friend.

1

Introduction

Throughout U.S. history most women, whether married or not, worked at home. Many worked in their homes to produce goods and services which were sold in the market, but the major efforts of most women were directed toward producing goods and services for family consumption. Strong cultural norms prescribed a sexual division of labor in which the home was seen as the proper sphere for women's activities. In 1870, fewer than 15% of all women over age 15 were counted as "gainful workers" by census enumerators; the overwhelming majority were unmarried. Most employed women were poor and contributed their earnings to the support of their families. Black women had high rates of labor force participation, and the majority of employed white women were foreign-born or of foreign stock. Over 80% of women in non-agricultural jobs were domestic servants or operatives in textile or clothing factories.

During the 60 years covered by this study, there were important changes in the economic roles played by many American women. By 1930, over one-quarter of all women were employed. Married women had joined the labor force in unprecedented numbers, but single women still made up the great majority (72%) of female non-farm employees. Most women in the labor force were native born whites, many of them daughters of the respectable middle class whose families were not dependent on their wages. Over 40% of all female non-agricultural workers were in white collar jobs; half of these were in clerical occupations which had employed almost no women at the beginning of the period.

This study describes and analyzes the economic changes associated with the movement of women out of the home and into the office. Since most of the growth in the female labor force in this period was due to increased participation by unmarried women, the analysis will focus on determinants of labor supply decisions by young, single women. A great many of the women who joined the labor force in this period found work in offices. In 1870 only 1% of the total non-agricultural labor force was in clerical occupations, and women made up only 2.5% of all clerical workers. By 1930, nearly 10% of all U.S. non-agricultural employees were clerical workers, more than half of whom were women. Because of the important role played by office work in the history of the female labor force, this study examines the forces which contributed to growth and change in the sex composition of clerical employment. The rapid "takeover" of office work by women is all the more interesting because there are few instances of such dramatic change in the sexual division of labor.

Chapter 2 describes the pace and pattern of changes in women's participation in the labor force, paying particular attention to the demographic structure and occupational distribution of female employment. Chapter 3 uses a model based on standard economic theories of labor supply to analyze variation in female labor force participation in two cross-sections of American cities (1890 and 1930).

Chapters 4 through 7 focus on clerical work. In chapter 4 the growth of overall clerical employment from 1870 to 1930 is examined, and changes in methods of performing office work are described. Chapter 5 is concerned specifically with the expansion of female employment in office work and with the demographic characteristics of the female clerical labor force. The question of what caused the change in the sex composition of the clerical work force is addressed in chapter 6. Variation across cities in 1890 and 1930 in female participation in clerical occupations is analyzed in chapter 7.

This is a "new economic history" of women in the U.S. labor force from 1870 to 1930. When it has been most successful, the new economic history has contributed to the explanation of complex historical phenomena through creative use of economic theories and econometric techniques. Scholars from many disciplines are currently involved in examining women's changing role in American life. It is hoped that this study will contribute to this ongoing enterprise and will be seen as an example of the ways in which the tools of the economist can be put to good use by the student of history.

2

Women's Changing Role in the U. S. Labor Force

This chapter examines the pace and pattern of the expansion of women's role in the U. S. labor force from 1870 to 1930. An assessment is made of the relative importance of population growth, sectoral shift (from agriculture to non-agriculture), and changing participation for explaining the increased size of the female paid work force. Attention is focused on changing patterns of labor force participation and on particular decades which produced the most dramatic changes in participation. The demographic characteristics of the female labor force are examined, particularly changes in age and marital status. The occupational distribution of women workers is described with consideration given to the degree to which women's employment was concentrated in a number of sex-segregated occupations. Some occupations grew faster than others and therefore contributed disproportionately to the growth of the female labor force. Special attention is paid to clerical occupations which grew fastest and experienced a dramatic change in sex composition of employment from 1870 to 1930.

The Growth of Women's Employment

The period 1870–1930 was one of growing participation by women in the American labor force. As can be seen in table 2.1, 133 of every 1000 women ages 10 and over were working for pay in 1870; by 1930, 22% of all such women were gainful workers.[1] The figures for women ages 16 and over show an even more dramatic growth in participation. Women's share of the work force increased so that by 1930 women constituted 22% of all gainful workers.

TABLE 2.1

LABOR FORCE PARTICIPATION RATES FOR WOMEN AND MEN AGES 10 AND OVER AND AGES 16 AND OVER, 1870-1930.

WOMEN'S SHARE OF THE LABOR FORCE, 1870-1930.

	1870	1880	1890	1900	1910	1920	1930
LABOR FORCE PARTICIPATION RATES:							
Women (ages 10+)	13.3	14.4	17.4	18.8	21.5 (23.4)	21.4	22.0
Men (ages 10+)	74.9	78.7	79.3	80.0	80.8	79.9	76.2
Women (ages 16+)	14.8	16.0	19.0	20.6	24.0 (25.48)	24.2	25.3
Men (ages 16+)	88.7	90.6	90.5	90.5	91.1	91.0	88.0
WOMEN'S SHARE OF THE LABOR FORCE:							
Labor Force (ages 10+)	14.8	15.2	17.2	18.3	19.9	20.4	22.0
Labor Force (ages 16+)	14.1	14.5	16.5	17.7	19.6	20.2	21.9

Source: Alba M. Edwards, Comparative Occupation Statistics for the United States, 1870-1940. U. S. Bureau of the Census (Washington, D. C.: G. P. O., 1943) pp. 91, 92, 99.

The trend in women's labor force participation shown in table 2.1 is one of fairly steady growth throughout the period with the exception of the figure for 1910. The usual explanation for this irregularity is that changes in the instructions to enumerators in 1910 caused an overcount of gainful workers, especially women and children on farms. Alba Edwards in his 1940 census monograph[2] has dealt with this problem by adjusting the 1910 figure downward, assuming that the same proportion of women and children were employed in agriculture in 1910 as were so employed in 1900. Edwards' corrected figures are presented in table 2.1; the uncorrected census figures are presented in parentheses. There has been some disagreement with this method of adjustment. Robert Smuts has argued that the 1910 figures are most likely to be correct and that women gainful workers were under-enumerated in the other census decades.[3] He goes on to argue that the undercount gets progressively smaller over time (largely as women move from unpaid agricultural labor to wage employment) so that the increase in labor force participation seen in the reported figures is overstated. In order to avoid this problem the analysis in this study will concentrate on women in non-agricultural employment and in urban areas where census figures are more reliable and where it is certain that female participation did increase throughout the period.

Table 2.2 uses Edwards' corrected figures to document the shift of the U. S. labor force from predominantly agricultural to non-agricultural employment from 1870 to 1930. In 1870 fewer than half of all gainful workers were in non-agricultural pursuits. By 1930 nearly 80% were so employed. Women were always 10% or less of all enumerated agricultural workers so that the proportion of all female gainful workers employed in jobs outside of agriculture showed rather mild growth from 76.3% to 91.5% while the same figures for males are 41.9% to 74.9%. Clearly the sectoral shift from agriculture to non-agricultural employment was primarily a male phenomenon, at least so far as it is recorded in the census occupation statistics. It is interesting to note in table 2.2 that while women's share of the total labor force grew from 14.8% in 1870 to 22% in 1930, there was very little change in women's share of the non-agricultural labor force. This indicates that males were shifting from agriculture to non-agriculture at approximately the same rate that women were moving from being outside the measured labor force into non-agricultural gainful employment.

In table 2.3 calculations are performed which measure the importance of sectoral shift versus general labor force participation growth for explaining the observed increase in the percent of the total female population who were gainful workers in non-agricultural occupations (i.e.,

TABLE 2.2

PERCENT OF LABOR FORCE IN NON-AGRICULTURAL EMPLOYMENT AND WOMEN'S
SHARE OF THE LABOR FORCE (TOTAL, AGRICULTURAL AND
NON-AGRICULTURAL) 1870-1930

	1870	1880	1890	1900	1910	1920	1930
Percent of Labor Force (ages 10+) in Non-Agricultural Employment							
Total	47.0	50.6	57.4	62.5	69.0	73.0	78.6
Female	76.3	76.4	80.1	81.0	84.2	86.5	91.5
Male	41.9	46.0	52.7	58.3	65.2	69.6	74.9
Women's Share of Labor Force (ages 10+)							
Total	14.8	15.2	17.2	18.3	19.9	20.4	22.0
Agriculture	6.6	7.3	8.0	9.2	10.1	10.2	8.7
Non-Agriculture	24.1	23.0	24.0	23.7	24.3	24.1	25.7

Source: Percent of Labor Force in Non-agricultural Employment Calculated from Edwards, p. 100.

Women's Share of Labor Force from Edwards, p. 99.

female non-agricultural labor force participation rate = FNALFPR). Line 5 of the table calculates the number of women who would have been non-agricultural workers (no-shift FNALF) in each census year if the labor force had grown at the actual observed rate but workers had been distributed between the agricultural and non-agricultural sectors according to the percentages that prevailed in 1870. Line 6 is the percent of the actual number of non-agricultural workers represented by the no-shift FNALF. For example, we see that in 1900 the female non-agricultural labor force (FNALF) would have been 94.1% of the actual FNALF if there had been no change since 1870 in the percent of female workers employed on farms. The last three rows of table 2.3 compare the actual non-agricultural labor force participation rate (FNALFPR) to the rate which would have prevailed if non-agricultural employment had accounted for a constant 76.3% share of total female employment throughout the period. Line 10 shows the ratio of the no-shift FNALFPR to the actual FNALFPR. We can see that even in 1930, after the absolute number of women in agriculture had declined dramatically, the no-shift FNALFPR was over 83% of the observed rate. The corresponding figure for males is 57%.

The analysis in table 2.3 suggests that by far the largest portion of the growth in the female non-agricultural labor force in this period was due to the movement of previously non-employed women into non-farm gainful occupations. Little of the change reflected in these figures was accounted for by the shift of employed women out of agriculture into non-agricultural jobs. This is in marked contrast to the growth of male employment in non-farm work, which was closely related to sectoral shift. Because women employed in agriculture were undoubtedly undercounted by census enumerators, table 2.3 understates the importance of the shift out of agriculture for explaining female labor force growth. It is likely that the relative decline in agricultural activity and the attendant migration to urban areas were more important to women's labor market experience than is reflected in census-based figures. These data deficiencies make it impossible to take accurate account of the role of the shift out of agriculture. Therefore, this study focuses on participation by urban women in non-agricultural work, which is the area of most dynamic change in the female labor force in this period.

Table 2.4 shows the pattern of growth in the female non-agricultural labor force for the nation as a whole and for samples of the nation's most populous urban areas. Lines 2 and 4 present mean participation rates for the largest cities in each decade. Details of the urban sample will be described in chapter 3 and in appendix B. The urban sample will be used to carry out the regression analysis of female

TABLE 2.3

IMPORTANCE OF THE SHIFT OUT OF AGRICULTURE FOR EXPLAINING THE GROWTH IN
FEMALE LABOR FORCE PARTICIPATION, 1870-1930

FEMALE GAINFUL WORKERS (ages 10+) (in thousands)	1870	1880	1890	1900	1910	1920	1930	
Total	1917	2647	4006	5319	7445	8637	10752	(1)
Agricultural	455	626	796	1008	1176	1170	910	(2)
FNALF = Non-Agricultural	1462	2021	3210	4311	6269	7467	9842	(3)
Percent FNALF = (3)/(1)	76.3	76.4	80.1	81.0	84.2	86.5	91.5	(4)
No Shift FNALF = .763 x (1)	1462	2020	3057	4058	5681	6590	8204	(5)
No Shift FNALF/ACTUAL FNALF = (5)/(3)	100.0	99.9	95.2	94.1	90.6	88.3	83.4	(6)

TABLE 2.3 (Continued)

	1870	1880	1890	1900	1910	1920	1930	
FEMALE POPULATION (ages 10+) (in thousands)	14426	18026	23061	28246	34553	40449	48773	(7)
FEMALE NON-AGRICULTURAL LABOR FORCE PARTICIPATION RATES = FNALFPR								
Actual FNALFPR = (3)/(7)	10.1	11.2	13.9	15.3	18.1	18.5	20.2	(8)
No-Shift FNALFPR = (5)/(7)	10.1	11.2	13.3	14.4	16.4	16.3	16.8	(9)
No-Shift FNALFPR/Actual FNALFPR = (9)/(8)	100.0	100.0	95.7	94.1	90.6	88.1	83.2	(10)

Source: Lines (1), (2), (3) from Edwards, p. 100.
Line (7) from Edwards, p. 91.

TABLE 2.4

FEMALE NON-AGRICULTURAL LABOR FORCE PARTICIPATION
RATES FOR THE U. S. AND MEANS FOR URBAN
SAMPLE, 1870-1930

	1870	1880	1890	1900	1910	1920	1930	
U. S. National Female Non-Agricultural Labor Force Participation Rate (ages 10+)	10.13	11.21	13.91	15.26	18.14	18.45	20.18	(1)
U. S. Urban Female Labor Force Participation* Rate (ages 10+)			25.00	25.89	28.42	28.73	28.89	(2)
n=			(90)	(95)	(99)	(103)	(103)	
U. S. National Female Non-Agricultural Labor Force Participation Rates (all ages)	6.81	7.59	9.76	10.86	13.54	14.10	16.10	(3)
U. S. Urban Female Labor Force Participation Rates* (all ages) n=	15.87 (48)	17.85 (53)	20.02 (90)	20.82 (95)				(4)

*The urban participation rates are means of the largest U. S. cities. The number of cities included at each date are indicated in parentheses.

Source for urban data: U. S. Decennial Censuses of Population, 1870-1890. See Appendix B.

Source for national figures: Edwards, p. 100.

labor supply in chapters 3 and 7. Line 2 may be compared with the analogous national figures in line 1; line 4 should be compared with the national figures in line 3. It is readily apparent that the national and urban figures follow the same basic pattern of increased participation with the urban participation rates always being considerably higher than the national rates. In both the urban and national figures the decade 1880–1890 and the decade 1900–1910 show up as being particularly noteworthy for growth in women's participation in the non-agricultural labor force. The importance of these two decades is highlighted by the compound growth rates presented in table 2.5; they are the only periods which show growth rates notably above the long term (60-year) growth rate of 3.23%. For both decades the rate of female non-agricultural labor force growth is nearly twice the rate of female population growth. Clearly these two periods should be examined closely in an attempt to understand the factors contributing to the growth of female work force participation before 1930.

One conclusion that can be drawn from the preceding discussion is that even after removing the agricultural sector—which should be the major source of disparity—from the 1910 figures, the decade 1900–1910 appears to be one of dramatic growth in women's labor force participation. Partially because of lack of faith in the 1910 census figures, scholars have tended to ignore them and to treat 1900–1920 as one period. Most of the growth in the female labor force over this 20-year period has been attributed to the second decade, particularly the war years.[4] The figures presented here suggest that 1900–1910 may have been much more important for growth in labor force participation. However, as we shall see in later discussion of clerical work, the war years were important for increasing women's share of certain kinds of employment.

It is tempting to argue that the 1900–1910 increase in the size of the female labor force was due to the heavy immigration of foreign women who had a greater propensity to work for pay. However, the information presented in table 2.7 argues against this simple explanation—the percentage of females who were foreign-born remained virtually stable at 16.3% from 1900 to 1910, and the participation of native women increased at a faster rate than did that of the foreign-born. The result is that the portion of the total female non-agricultural labor force who were foreign born was smaller in 1910 than it was in 1900.

Demographic Characteristics of the Female Labor Force

Age. Table 2.6 shows the period 1870–1930 to be one of aging of the female population and the female labor force, with the labor force aging

TABLE 2.5

AVERAGE ANNUAL COMPOUND GROWTH RATES BY DECADE FOR FEMALE
POPULATION AND FEMALE NON-AGRICULTURAL
LABOR FORCE, 1870-1930

	1870–1880	1880–1890	1890–1900	1900–1910	1910–1920	1920–1930	
Growth Rates of Female Non-Agricultural Labor Force (Ages 10+) FNALF	3.28	4.73	3.04	3.77	1.77	2.80	(1)
Growth Rates of Female Population (ages 10+) pop	2.25	2.50	2.05	2.04	1.59	1.89	(2)
Ratio of Growth Rates FNALF/pop = (1)/(2)	1.45	1.89	1.48	1.85	1.11	1.48	(3)

Source for underlying figures: Edwards, pp. 91, 100.

TABLE 2.6

AGE DISTRIBUTION OF THE FEMALE POPULATION AND FEMALE NON-AGRICULTURAL LABOR FORCE, 1870-1930
FEMALE NON-AGRICULTURAL LABOR FORCE PARTICIPATION RATES, BY AGE, 1870-1930

		1870	1880	1890	1900	1910	1920	1930
PERCENT DISTRIBUTIONS								
Female Population Ages:								
I	10-15	19.79	18.18	17.79	16.85	15.52	15.35	14.51
	16-24	25.43	25.53	25.56	23.91	23.57	21.18	20.89
	25-44	35.29	34.95	34.81	36.11	37.11	37.20	36.73
	45+	19.49	21.34	22.18	22.87	23.80	25.63	27.73
		100.00	100.00	100.00	100.00	100.00	100.00	100.00
Female Non-Agricultural Labor Force Ages:								
II	10-15	8.29	7.50	7.12	6.33	3.62	2.12	.81
	16-24	} 91.71	} 92.50	47.23	43.28	} 81.00	39.34	36.08
	25-44			33.09	36.98		41.26	43.54
	45+			12.08	13.11	15.22	17.08	19.44
		100.00	100.00	100.00	100.00	100.00	100.00	100.00
NON-AGRICULTURAL LABOR FORCE PARTICIPATION RATES BY AGE								
	Women (Ages 10+)	10.13	11.21	13.91	15.26	18.14	18.45	20.17
	10-15	4.25	4.63	5.57	5.78	4.23	2.56	1.13
III	16-24	} 11.6	} 12.46	27.04	27.76	} 24.29	34.26	35.15
	24-44			11.86	15.79		20.20	23.92
	45+			7.64	8.81	11.61	12.30	14.12

Sources: Joseph Adna Hill, Women In Gainful Occupations, 1870-1920, U. S. Census Monographs, IX (Washington, D. C., G. P. O., 1929), p. 23.

Edwards, pp. 92, 100.

U. S. Bureau of the Census, 1930 Census of Population, Vol. 4, p. 40.

TABLE 2.7

RACE-NATIVITY DISTRIBUTION OF THE FEMALE POPULATION
AND FEMALE NON-AGRICULTURAL LABOR FORCE, 1890-1930
FEMALE NON-AGRICULTURAL LABOR FORCE PARTICIPATION
RATES BY RACE AND NATIVITY, 1890-1930

	1890	1900	1910	1920	1930
PERCENT DISTRIBUTIONS					
I Percent female population, (ages 10+)					
native white of native parentage	54.09	52.60	52.52	53.54	54.72
native white of foreign or mixed parentage	16.79	19.30	20.25	21.06	21.73
(total native white)	(70.88)	(71.90)	(72.77)	(73.79)	(76.45)
foreign-born white	17.36	16.30	16.27	15.07	12.58
black and others	11.74	11.70	10.65	10.02	10.96
II Percent female non-agricultural labor force, (ages 10+)					
native white of native parentage	35.71	36.99	39.61	44.95	
native white of foreign or mixed parentage	24.45	26.54	26.37	27.59	
(total native white)	(60.16)	(63.53)	(65.98)	(72.54)	(74.11)
foreign-born white	22.92	19.28	18.61	14.45	11.47
black and others	16.90	17.17	15.38	12.99	14.40

TABLE 2.7 (Continued)

	1890	1900	1910	1920	1930
PARTICIPATION RATES BY NATIVITY GROUP					
III Percent of total female population, ages 10+, employed in non-agricultural labor force:					
native white of native parentage	9.26	10.83	13.66	15.45	
native white of foreign or mixed parentage	20.43	21.07	23.59	24.25	
(total native white)	(11.91)	(13.58)	(16.43)	(17.93)	(19.56)
foreign born white	18.51	18.21	20.72	17.74	18.40
black and others	20.91	22.53	26.16	23.99	26.52

Sources: Computed from: U. S. Bureau of the Census,

1900 Census, Special Report on Occupations, pp. 10-11.

1910 Census of Population, Vol. 4, pp. 67, 302-308.

1920 Census of Population, Vol. 4, pp. 340-341.

1930 Census of Population, Vol. 4, p. 24.

more than the population. In 1890 43% of the female population and 54% of the female non-agricultural labor force were in the age group 10–24. By 1930 only 35% of the over-10 female population were under 25, and their share of the labor force had fallen to 37%. This change was due to (1) the almost total withdrawal of children under 15 from the work force and (2) the greater proportion of teenagers attending school, which contributed to the 11 percentage point drop from 1890 to 1930 in the share of the labor force represented by women ages 16-24. Correspondingly, the percentage of the female work force over 25 grew steadily during the period 1890–1930.

Participation rates (panel III, table 2.6) increased for women in all age groups except 10–15 throughout the period. Women ages 16–24 were more likely to be gainful workers than were women in other age groups in all decades, although the non-agricultural labor force participation rate grew faster for women in the two older groups. By 1930, 35% of women 16–24, 24% of women 25–44, and 14% of women over 45 were working for pay in non-agricultural occupations.

Race and Nativity. Table 2.7 presents information on the changing race and nativity structure of the female non-agricultural labor force from 1890 to 1930. Throughout the period the foreign-born share of the female population declined and the foreign-born share of the female non-agricultural labor force fell even more markedly. This was due largely to the slowing of immigration after 1914, which reduced the proportion of young women in the foreign-born population, and it was young women who were most likely to work outside the home. The effect of this aging of the foreign-born population can be seen in the participation rates in panel III; there is a decline in work force participation after 1910. Black women were more likely than white women to be working outside their homes at every date. However, their share of the total non-agricultural labor force declined over the period because of a slight decline in the relative size of the black population and because their participation rates grew more slowly than those of white women. The black non-agricultural labor force participation rate is a significant understatement of the propensity of black women to work for pay, because black women were more likely to be working in agricultural pursuits. As late as 1930 over 25% of all black female gainful workers were employed in agriculture, and the overall participation rate for black women was 38.9%.[5]

White, native-born women were responsible for most of the increase in female non-agricultural labor force participation. Among these, women born of native stock, though least likely to be employed, contributed most to the growing female non-agricultural labor force with a remarkable increase in participation from 9.26% to 15.45% (a 67% increase) over the period 1890–1920. Native white women of foreign or mixed parentage had higher participation rates at each census date; but they made up a much smaller share of the population, and their participation grew at a much slower rate. Unfortunately, the 1930 census does not provide information on the parentage of the work force. Therefore, it is not known if the most rapid growth continued to be among white women of native stock who contributed over 50% of the increase in the female non-agricultural labor force from 1890 to 1920. We can, however, be sure that the search for explanations for increased female participation in non-agricultural occupations should be concentrated on the experience of native-born white women.

Marital Status. Participation by married women in the non-agricultural labor force was low though increasing during the period 1890-1930. (See panel III, table 2.8.) By 1930, 11 of every 100 married women were gainful workers in non-farm occupations compared to 42 of every 100 single women. This represents a substantial increase for married women, particularly in the 1920s. Panel II shows that a progressively larger percentage of the over-15 female population were married at each successive census. This is due to (1) the aging of the female population to the extent that a larger proportion of women were over the age at which women commonly married and (2) the decline in the median age at first marriage as shown in panel I. Married women's share of the female non-agricultural labor force grew considerably faster than did their share of the population; from 12% in 1890 to over 28% in 1930. This reflects the more rapid increase in the participation rates of married women. Table 2.9 clearly demonstrates these trends. Over the 40-year period the married female non-agricultural labor force grew at an average annual compound growth rate of 5.2% (panel II) which was 2.4 times the growth rate of the married female population. By contrast, the growth rate for single, widowed, and divorced female workers was less than 1-1/2 times the population growth rate of that group (see panel III). There are marked differences among decades. The period 1900–1910 stands out as the decade of most rapid growth for both single and married women. The 1910 "overcount" may be partially responsible for the huge differences between the relative growth rates of married women workers in the first two decades of the century (panel III). Married women working in non-agricultural family establishments or doing piece-work for pay at home were more likely to be enumerated in 1910 than

TABLE 2.8

MEDIAN AGE AT FIRST MARRIAGE FOR FEMALES, 1890-1930, MARITAL STATUS DISTRIBUTION OF
FEMALE POPULATION AND FEMALE NON-AGRICULTURAL LABOR FORCE, 1890-1930
FEMALE NON-AGRICULTURAL LABOR FORCE PARTICIPATION RATES BY
MARITAL STATUS, 1890-1930

	1890	1900	1910	1920	1930
I MEDIAN AGE AT FIRST MARRIAGE – Females	22.0	21.9	21.6	21.1	21.3
PERCENT DISTRIBUTIONS					
Percent female population, (ages 15+)					
II married	56.75	56.95	58.86	60.60	61.01
single, widowed, divorced, unknown	43.09	43.49	41.14	39.40	38.91
Percent female non-agricultural labor force, (ages 15+)					
III married	12.1	13.4	19.43	20.90	28.42
single, widowed, divorced, unknown	87.9	86.5	80.57	79.10	71.58

TABLE 2.8 (Continued)

	1890	1900	1910	1920	1930
PARTICIPATION RATES BY MARITAL STATUS					
Percent of total female population, ages 15+, employed in non-agri- cultural labor force					
IV married	3.3	3.9	6.77	7.26	10.66
single, widowed, divorced, unknown	31.2	36.42	40.19	42.31	42.17

Sources: Median Age at First Marriage from U. S. Bureau of the Census, Historical Statistics of the U. S. from Colonial Times to the Present (Washington, D. C., G. P. O., 1957), p. 15.

Hill, pp. 76, 77.

U. S. Bureau of the Census, 1930 Census of Population, Vol. 4, p. 68.

TABLE 2.9

AVERAGE ANNUAL COMPOUND GROWTH RATES BY DECADE FOR THE FEMALE POPULATION
AND FEMALE NON-AGRICULTURAL LABOR FORCE BY MARITAL STATUS, 1890-1930
PERCENT OF DECADE GROWTH IN FEMALE NON-AGRICULTURAL LABOR FORCE
CONTRIBUTED BY MARITAL STATUS GROUPS, 1890-1930

		1890-1900	1900-1910	1910-1920	1920-1930	1890-1930
I	Growth rates of female population (ages 10+) (pop)	2.15	2.16	1.59	1.99	1.97
	Married	2.19	2.50	1.89	2.07	2.16
	Single, widowed, divorced, unknown	2.13	1.70	1.15	1.86	1.71
II	Growth rates of female non-agricultural labor force (ages 10+) (FNALF)	3.09	4.24	1.86	2.85	3.01
	Married	4.06	8.16	2.60	6.06	5.20
	Single, widowed, divorced, unknown	2.94	3.50	1.67	1.83	2.48
III	Ratios of compound growth rates FNALF/population	1.43	1.96	1.17	1.43	1.52
	Married	1.85	3.26	1.38	2.93	2.41
	Single, widowed, divorced, unknown	1.38	2.06	1.45	1.01	1.45
IV	Percent of change in female non-agricultural labor force contributed by:					
	Married	16.80	31.08	28.17	51.58	35.55
	Single, widowed, divorced, unknown	83.20	68.92	71.33	48.42	64.35
		100.00	100.00	100.00	100.00	100.00

Sources: See Table 2.9

in 1920. For single women the impressive growth shown in the figures
for the 1900–1910 period is more likely to be accurate.

The twenties were unquestionably very important for the movement
of married women into the work force. Married women's non-agricultural
labor force participation rate increased from 7.26% to nearly 11%, while
participation by unmarried women declined slightly. Married women's
share of the female non-agricultural labor force increased from 21% to
over 28%, and they contributed over 50% of total female non-agricultural
labor force growth for that decade (see panel IV, table 2.9). However, it
should be remembered that single women made up the overwhelming
majority of all female gainful workers throughout the period. At any
point in time up through 1930, single women, because of their much
higher level of participation, dominated the female labor force.

Certain data allow a more detailed examination of changes from
1920 to 1930 in the work force experience of women by marital status.
Table 2.10 presents labor force participation rates for women in various
age, race/nativity, and marital status categories for 1920 and 1930. The
rates refer to the total female labor force participation rate (agriculture
plus non-agriculture).   In general there is a pattern of decreasing
participation with age for married women in all groups, the one
exception being married women 15–19 in 1930 who had lower
participation rates than did married women 20–24.   Work force
participation was higher in 1930 than in 1920 for all married white
women except the youngest group. Black married women showed little
increase in participation overall, and for the oldest and youngest groups
participation actually fell.   In 1920 married foreign-born women were
more likely to be working for pay than were native women in each age
group. This remained true for the two youngest age groups in 1930; but
because the share of young women in the foreign-born population
declined over the decade, the overall participation rate of native-born
married women was higher in 1930. Over the decade dramatic increases
in married women's participation occurred in the age groups 20–24 and
25–44, most notably among native women.   Increased participation by
married women ages 25–44 accounted for 24% of the total increase in the
female labor force from 1920 to 1930.[6]

Table 2.10 shows that there was an overall one percentage point
decline in the participation rate for unmarried women over the decade.
Examination of the various age groups shows a pronounced decline in
participation by young, unmarried women, most notably among native
white teenagers. This undoubtedly reflects longer school attendance by
women prior to entering the job market. For unmarried white women in
the other age groups the decade saw increases in participation that were

TABLE 2.10

LABOR FORCE PARTICIPATION RATES, BY AGE, MARITAL STATUS, RACE-NATIVITY, 1920-1930

	1920	1920 Married	1920 Single Widowed Divorced	1930	1930 Married	1930 Single Widowed Divorced	1930 Single & Unknown	1930 Widowed & Divorced
All women (ages 15+)	21.1							
All women (ages 15+)		9.0	46.4	21.3	11.7	45.4	50.5	34.5
Native-born white		6.3	52.1		9.8	44.2	48.7	31.9
Foreign-born white		7.2	45.6		8.5	43.6	73.8	21.1
Black		32.5	58.8		33.2	57.7	52.1	65.0
Women ages 15-19		12.5	35.6		12.9	28.6	28.5	47.8
Native-born white		11.3	49.5		10.2	27.0	27.0	39.4
Foreign-born white		11.4	58.8		13.3	52.5	52.6	41.7
Black		28.0	40.6		25.1	36.1	47.5	60.1
Women ages 20-24		11.4	67.3		16.3	70.3	70.5	64.4
Native-born white		7.9	65.9		14.0	69.5	69.8	59.6
Foreign-born white		9.6	82.6		15.1	87.1	87.4	67.7
Black		31.1	67.0		31.5	68.1	44.9	73.6

TABLE 2.10 (Continued)

	1920	1920 Married	1920 Single Widowed Divorced	1930	1930 Married	1930 Single Widowed Divorced	1930 Single & Unknown	1930 Widowed & Divorced
Women ages 25-44		9.6	68.3		13.1	73.2	75.4	68.2
Native-born white		6.6	65.4		10.7	71.5	73.9	64.6
Foreign-born white		8.2	75.2		10.7	78.5	87.2	59.5
Black		34.1	80.4		35.9	79.9	58.6	81.6
Women ages 45+		6.6	28.0		7.8	29.4	47.5	23.9
Native-born white		4.9	26.4		6.6	28.5	44.9	22.4
Foreign-born white		5.0	22.5		5.4	23.0	58.6	16.0
Black		30.5	55.1		29.4	53.4	61.7	52.5

Sources: 1920 – U. S. Bureau of the Census, 1920 Census, Abstract, p. 562.

1930 – U. S. Bureau of the Census, 1930 Census, Abstract, p. 379.

TABLE 2.11

PERCENT URBAN IN TOTAL POPULATION BY REGION 1890-1930.
FEMALE NON-AGRICULTURAL LABOR FORCE PARTICIPATION RATE
BY REGION, 1900-1930.
CORRELATION BETWEEN PERCENT URBAN AND FEMALE
NON-AGRICULTURAL LABOR FORCE PARTICIPATION, 1900-1930.

		1890	1900	1910	1920	1930
Percent Urban =	Urban population					
	Total population					
Total U. S.		36.1	40.5	46.3	51.4	56.2
	North East	75.8	79.9	83.3	79.2	77.3
	Mid Atlantic	57.7	65.2	71.0	74.9	77.7
	East North Central	37.8	45.2	52.7	60.8	66.4
	West North Central	25.8	28.5	33.3	37.7	41.8
I	South Atlantic	19.5	21.4	25.4	31.0	36.1
	East South Central	12.7	15.0	18.7	22.4	28.1
	West South Central	15.1	16.2	22.3	29.0	36.4
	Mountain	29.3	32.3	36.0	36.4	39.4
	Pacific	42.5	46.4	56.8	62.4	67.5
Female Non-agricultural labor force participation rates (ages 10+)						
Total U. S.			17.3	20.7	21.3	23.4
	North East		27.3	31.5	32.0	31.0
	Mid Atlantic		22.1	26.4	26.9	27.8
	East North Central		15.8	19.6	20.8	23.1
	West North Central		13.9	17.0	17.7	19.9
II	South Atlantic		16.8	19.2	19.7	22.9
	East South Central		12.4	14.6	14.2	16.8
	West South Central		10.1	13.0	13.8	17.2
	Mountain		14.0	17.0	16.6	19.3
	Pacific		16.4	20.4	22.2	25.5

TABLE 2.11 (Continued)

	1890	1900	1910	1920	1930
Simple Correlation Coefficients					
III Percent Urban with Female Non-agricultural Participation Rate		.93	.93	.92	.89

Sources: Panel I, 1890, 1900, 1910, <u>1910 Census Abstract</u>
p. 56.

1920, 1930, <u>1930 Census Abstract</u>
p. 15.

Panel II, 1900, 1910, 1920, Hill, p. 30.

1930, <u>1930 Census of Population</u>, Vol. 6
<u>General Report on Occupation</u>, p. 53.

less dramatic than those of married women. The greatest increase was a jump from 65.4% to 71.5% (a 9% increase) for native white single women 25–44. However, despite the rapid increase in participation by married women, at the end of the period single women still dominated the total female labor force. For example, in 1930 native-born, white, never-married women made up 44% of all female gainful workers over 15 although they accounted for only 22% of the female population.[7]

Geographical Distribution and Urbanization. Over the 60 years prior to 1930 the population of the U. S. grew and redistributed itself across the continent. The average annual population growth rate over these 60 years was almost 2%, with the most rapid growth taking place in the early decades. The western regions of the country experienced the most rapid growth rates while the share of population living in the older areas of the East and South declined.

At the same time that the population was spreading out over the continent, it was also showing an increasing tendency to concentrate in urban areas. While there was no close relationship between regional population growth and female work force participation, there was consistently high correlation between the proportion of a region's population living in urban areas and the percentage of women at work in non-agricultural occupations. The size of the urban area was also important in determining women's likelihood of becoming gainful workers. In 1920 32.5% of women over 16 worked for pay in cities of populations over 100,000, 31% worked in cities of 50,000 to 100,000, 29.4% in cities of 25,000 to 50,000, and 18.8% in smaller cities and rural areas.[8] Table 2.11 shows the proportion of the population in urban areas for every region from 1890 through 1930 and the non-agricultural labor force participation rates of women over 16. The correlation coefficients presented in panel III show how closely urbanization was associated with female non-agricultural labor force participation. Because of the strength of this association, the analysis in subsequent chapters will focus almost exclusively on urban areas.

Occupational Structure

In this section attention turns to the changing occupational distribution of the non-agricultural labor force in order to discover those occupational groups which were most important for the growing female labor force. Additionally, we will examine the degree to which women were concentrated in a small number of occupations and the tendency for occupations to be segregated by sex.

The Changing Distribution of the Female Non-Agricultural Labor Force.
Table 2.12 presents information on the occupational distribution of non-
agricultural employment and on the growth rates for the 9 occupational-
industrial classifications used in the 1930 census. Alba Edwards has redistributed occupational information in earlier censuses to conform to the
1930 classification scheme.[9] While there are obvious problems in any
attempt to devise consistent occupational categories across 60 years of
changing census definitions and changing historical context, the
information in table 2.12 allows some conclusions to be drawn
concerning changes in the occupational structure. Many of the categories
used are actually industrial rather than occupational groups, but this
problem will have to be ignored here and the term occupational category
will be used.

For the total non-agricultural labor force the primary industries of
forestry, fishing, and mining were small and generally declining shares of
the work force. Manufacturing and domestic/personal service had
growth rates lower than the average rate for the non-agricultural labor
force and therefore had declining shares of total employment over the
period. This reversed for the service category in the 1920s. Despite this
decline, 37% of all gainful workers were in manufacturing jobs in 1930.
All other occupational categories showed growth rates above the national
average and expanding shares of total employment. Clearly, the most
spectacular growth was in the clerical occupations which grew from 1.3%
to 10.5% of the total non-agricultural labor force in just 60 years—the
fastest growing occupational category in every decade.

The bottom panel of table 2.12 shows the changing distribution of
the female non-agricultural labor force. Forestry, fishing, mining, and
public service employed negligible numbers of women at all dates. As
with the total non-agricultural labor force, the manufacturing and service
categories showed overall declines in labor force shares. There was an
initial large increase in the share of female employment in manufacturing
from 1870 to 1880. After this, the manufacturing share remained nearly
constant till 1900 when it began declining at a steadily increasing rate to
1930. Domestic and personal service showed a much more precipitous
decline from 67% of all female non-agricultural employment in 1870 to
32% in 1930. This is largely a reflection of the decrease in the
proportion of females employed as domestic servants in private
households.[10] The absolute number of personal/domestic service workers
declined from 1910 to 1920 but increased again by 1930.

Transportation and communication, trade, professional, and clerical
occupations all exhibited growing shares of female non-agricultural employment with growth rates far above the average. Again it was clerical

TABLE 2.12

OCCUPATIONAL DISTRIBUTION OF TOTAL NON-AGRICULTURAL LABOR FORCE AND
FEMALE NON-AGRICULTURAL LABOR FORCE, 1870-1930

	1870	1880	1890	1900	1910	1920	1930	Compound Growth Rates 1870-1930
Percent of Total Non-agricultural Labor Force in:								3.12 (U.S.)
Forestry and fishing	0.99	1.10	1.36	1.15	0.94	0.87	0.65	2.40
Mining	3.07	3.38	3.34	3.82	3.74	3.52	2.57	2.81
Manufacturing and mechanical industries	43.51	43.62	41.30	39.64	41.34	41.51	36.79	2.83
Transportation and communication	8.89	9.40	10.42	10.75	10.34	10.02	10.02	3.32
Trade	14.46	15.57	15.33	16.98	14.09	13.74	15.85	3.28
Public Service	1.48	1.57	1.52	1.56	1.67	2.38	2.23	3.83
Professional Service	5.63	6.24	6.55	6.50	6.64	7.01	8.48	3.83
Domestic and Personal Service	20.62	17.30	16.70	15.52	14.57	10.91	12.91	2.32
Clerical	1.34	1.82	3.50	4.06	6.67	10.04	10.49	6.71
	100.00	100.00	100.00	100.00	100.00	100.00	100.00	
Percent of Female Non-agricultural Labor Force in:								3.23 (U.S.)
Forestry and fishing	0	0	0.01	0.02	0.01	0.01	0	3.76
Mining	0	0	0.02	0.03	0.02	0.04	0.01	4.44
Manufacturing and mechanical industries	24.90	32.54	32.65	31.87	29.04	25.85	19.17	2.78
Transportation and communication	0.07	0.18	.55	0.97	1.84	3.00	2.86	9.77

TABLE 2.12 (Continued)

	1870	1880	1889	1900	1910	1920	1930	Compound Growth Rates 1870–1930
Trade	1.28	2.82	4.41	6.88	7.54	9.00	9.78	6.79
Public Service	0.01	0.03	0.05	0.07	0.77	0.14	0.18	8.32
Professional Service	6.44	8.74	9.74	10.07	11.72	13.62	15.50	4.79
Domestic and Personal Service	67.12	55.32	50.17	45.30	40.36	29.29	32.31	1.98
Clerical	0.13	0.35	2.40	4.32	9.39	19.04	20.19	12.28
	100.00	100.00	100.00	100.00	100.00	100.00	100.00	

Source: Calculated from Edwards, p. 100.

employment which exhibited the most spectacular growth. By 1930, 20
of every 100 members of the female non-agricultural labor force were
working in clerical occupations which had employed almost no women
only 50 years before.

Concentration of Female Employment. It has often been pointed out that
female employment is highly concentrated in a small number of
occupations.[11]   In fact, crowding models of discrimination are based on
this empirical reality.[12]   For the time period covered by this study, one
can develop an understanding of the high degree of concentration of
female employment by examining the information presented in table
2.13.   Edwards's detailed occupational distributions for 1870 through
1930 were used to identify the occupations in which women were most
likely to be employed.   Nine occupational categories were found to
contain the bulk of the female labor force at each of the seven census
dates. A list of the detailed occupations which make up these categories
can be found in appendix A.   The nine categories are: clothing
manufacture, textile manufacture, telephone operators, saleswomen and
clerks in stores, teachers and professors, trained nurses, laundry workers,
servants (largely domestic workers in private households), and clerical
workers.   The number of detailed occupations into which economic
activity is divided increases with time as does the number of detailed
occupations which compose the nine major categories of female
employment.   However, in all cases the number of detailed occupations
in the nine categories comprise less than 20% of the total number of
detailed occupations.

Table 2.13 demonstrates the degree of concentration of women
workers into these nine categories of major female employment. Panels 1
and 2 present total female employment in the non-agricultural labor
force and in the nine categories; in parentheses is the percentage of
employees who were female. Panel 3 shows proportions of total female
and male labor forces that were employed in the nine categories of major
female employment.   At each date, over 77% of all female non-
agricultural employees were in these categories.

Even though female employment was overwhelmingly concentrated
in the same categories throughout the period, there were some important
changes within this group. In 1870 women's jobs were almost entirely in
manufacturing or in domestic/personal service, with 86.6% of all women
non-agricultural workers being so employed.[13] Over the period the proportion of employed women working in the white collar occupations expanded tremendously.   Beginning in 1900 telephone operators appear in
the list of occupations, and by 1930 2.4% of all women non-agricultural

TABLE 2.13

CONCENTRATION OF FEMALE WORKERS IN NINE MAJOR CATEGORIES OF
FEMALE EMPLOYMENT, 1870–1930

	1870	1880	1890	1900	1910	1920	1930	
Female non-agricultural labor force (FNALF) in thousands	1463	2021	3210	4311	6269	7467	9842	
% female	(25.7)	(24.1)	(24.3)	(23.7)	(24.0)	(23.0)	(24.1)	(1)
Females employed in 9 categories (in thousands)	1363	1810	2771	3506	5042	5810	7766	
% female	(71.1)	(68.3)	(69.8)	(69.2)	(69.5)	(68.5)	(68.2)	(2)
% of female NALF in 9 categories	93.2	89.6	86.3	80.9	80.4	77.8	78.9	
% of male NALF in 9 categories	14.7	13.8	13.6	13.9	14.1	14.6	15.9	(3)
MANUFACTURING Clothing % of FNALF	13.5	17.4	18.6	16.2	13.8	8.2	5.9	
% of female	(71.6)	(77.1)	(79.4)	(77.9)	(72.7)	(66.1)	(65.5)	(4)

TABLE 2.13 (Continued)

	1870	1880	1889	1900	1910	1920	1930	
MANUFACTURING								
Textiles								
% of FNALF	7.43	9.2	7.3	6.8	6.4	6.3	4.6	(5)
% of female	(43.9)	(50.9)	(49.4)	(49.9)	(50.9)	(49.1)	(47.3)	
TRANSPORTATION & COMMUNICATION								
Telephone operators								
% of FNALF	0	0	0	.4	1.4	2.4	2.4	(6)
% female				(80.0)	(90.2)	(93.8)	(94.5)	
TRADE								
Saleswomen and clerks in stores--% of FNALF	0.6	1.6	3.1	4.2	5.8	7.1	7.2	(7)
% female	(3.7)	(8.2)	(16.0)	(20.5)	(28.6)	(34.2)	(29.5)	
PROFESSIONAL SERVICE								
Teachers & professors								
% of FNALF	5.8	7.6	7.6	7.5	7.7	8.7	9.0	(8)
% female	(65.9)	(67.9)	(70.9)	(73.5)	(78.2)	(81.7)	(78.3)	

TABLE 2.13 (Continued)

	1870	1880	1890	1900	1910	1920	1930	
PROFESSIONAL SERVICE								
Trained Nurses								
% of FNALF	0.9	0.9	0.1	0.3	1.2	1.9	2.9	(9)
% female	(95.9)	(95.3)	(91.7)	(93.6)	(92.9)	(96.3)	(98.2)	
PERSONAL & DOMESTIC SERVICE								
Laundry workers								
% of FNALF	4.0	5.4	6.8	7.7	9.5	6.3	5.3	(10)
% female	(90.7)	(87.7)	(86.0)	(85.5)	(90.0)	(88.1)	(82.9)	
PERSONAL & DOMESTIC SERVICE								
Servants, housekeepers, waitresses								
% of FNALF	61.7	48.0	40.6	33.0	25.5	18.2	21.8	(11)
% female	(88.1)	(84.1)	(84.2)	(83.6)	(78.3)	(75.4)	(77.2)	
CLERICAL OCCUPATIONS								
% of FNALF	0.1	0.3	2.3	4.9	9.2	18.7	20.0	(12)
% female	(2.5)	(4.4)	(19.3)	(30.2)	(37.6)	(49.2)	(52.5)	

Source: See Appendix A.

workers were employed as phone operators. The proportion of women working as saleswomen and clerks in stores grew from less than 1% in 1870 to over 7% in 1930. Professional employment for women increased as the categories of teaching and nursing grew. Clerical occupations expanded from almost nothing to become the employment of 20% of all working women in 1930.

Returning to the question of female labor force growth in the first two decades of the century, we can conclude that 1900-1910 was the most important decade for movement of women into the labor force while 1910-1920 was characterized by significant occupational redistribution with declining numbers of women employed in manufacturing and domestic services and massive movement of women into white collar occupations.

Sex Segregation of Occupations. The occupations in which women are concentrated tend to be occupations in which they make up a disproportionately large share of total workers (i.e., women account for a larger share of total employment in these occupations than they do in the overall non-agricultural labor force). The outcome of this is that the work force is largely segregated by sex into "women's jobs" and "men's jobs." At any point in time the overwhelming proportion of women workers are employed in "women's jobs."

There are many empirical studies of this phenomenon of occupational segregation by sex.[14] Only two will be reviewed here because they provide some information for this period.

Valerie Oppenheimer looked at those occupations in which women made up at least a majority of workers during the period 1900–1960.[15] In the 1900–1930 period over 60% of all women workers were in jobs in which the majority of workers were women, and between 42 and 48% were in occupations in which 80% or more of all employees were female.

Edward Gross was interested in the question of whether the degree of occuptional segregation had decreased over time. He computed an Index of Segregation using census data on 300-400 occupations from 1900–1960.[16] His index shows a high degree of segregation by sex and virtually no change in the degree of segregation in the occupational structure over the first 60 years of the century. The index indicates, for example, that in 1930 68.4% of female workers would have had to move out of female dominated occupations and into male dominated occupations in order for the sexes to be distributed among all occupations in the same way. Gross went on to argue that some of the persistence of segregation may be due to the possibility that it was the most segregated occupations which grew fastest. He then re-computed a "Standardized Measure of Differentiation" holding size of occupation constant. Using this measure he found some small decline in segregation from 1900 to 1930, but he attributed the decline to the movement of men into women's occupations.

By returning to table 2.13 we can learn something of the segregated nature of the labor force from 1870 to 1930. The level of detail in the occupational breakdown greatly affects the degree of segregation revealed by the figures; the finer the breakdown, the more segregation seen.[17] Some of the categories aggregate data on jobs which are overwhelmingly female with jobs in which men predominate. For this reason the data in table 2.13 disclose a smaller degree of segregation than actually prevailed in these occupations. Despite this problem, the table shows a very high degree of segregation.

Over the whole period, women's share of employment in these nine categories remained quite stable between 68% and 72%. In manufacturing, women's employment was highly concentrated in clothing production, where between 65% and 79% of all workers were female, and in textile production, where the female proportion varied between 43% and 51%. These figures understate the segregation because of the degree of aggregation. As an example, in 1930 women constituted 93% of operatives in corset factories and 100% of dressmakers, while they made up only 13% of all tailors and tailoresses.[18] In textile manufacture in 1930 women were 67% of all operatives in knitting mills but only 2% of all dyers,[19] and there is evidence that occupations within textile mills were segregated by sex to a higher degree than is shown by the largely industrial classification used by the census.[20]

Telephone operators first appear on the list in 1900. The occupation was a women's job almost from the beginning.[21] By 1930 2.4% of all women employed in non-farm work were telephone operators, and 95% of all operators were women.

In the sales category the figures mask a high degree of segregation. While there seems to have been a real movement of women into sales occupations over the period, it is likely that female sales workers were doing different kinds of work from men. "E. W. Bloomingdale declared in 1895 that there was not a woman in Bloomingdale Brothers who did the same work as men. Women sales clerks were usually found in the bargain basement, in other departments which carried low-priced items and did not require wide knowledge of the stock, and in departments which sold women's clothing and accessories."[22]

In the category of teachers, professors, and college presidents, women in 1930 were 81% of all teachers and 33% of all college presidents

TABLE 2.14

PERCENT OF TOTAL FEMALE NON-AGRICULTURAL LABOR FORCE GROWTH
FROM 1870 TO 1930 ATTRIBUTABLE TO GROWTH OF NINE
MAJOR CATEGORIES OF FEMALE EMPLOYMENT

Change from 1870 to 1930 in female non-agricultural labor force (in thousands)	8380
Change from 1870 to 1930 in female employment in 9 categories	6403
percent of growth due to growth of 9 categories	76.41
MANUFACTURING	
clothing	4.51
textiles	4.10
TRANSPORTATION AND COMMUNICATION	
Telephone operators	2.81
TRADE	
Saleswomen and clerks	8.32
PROFESSIONAL SERVICES	
Teachers	9.50
Trained nurses	3.43
PERSONAL AND DOMESTIC	
Laundry	7.20
Servants, housekeepers, waitresses	14.83
CLERICAL OCCUPATIONS	23.43
BREAKDOWN OF CLERICAL	
Bookkeepers, Clerks, Accountants	5.76
Clerks	8.42
Stenographers and typists	9.25
	23.43

Source: See Appendix A.

and professors.[23] It is certain that more segregation would appear if we could break down the category by level of teaching and type of school.

Domestic service occupations were the major employers of women throughout the period. In the field of laundry work the percentage female declined somewhat over time because the category includes workers employed in commercial laundries, many of whom were male, and commercial laundries increased over time. In the detailed category, "launderers and laundresses (not in laundry)," 99% were female. The servant class was the largest employer of women at all dates. The proportion female is lower than it would be if we were looking only at domestic servants employed in private households. In 1900, 97% of private houehold workers were women.[24]

In clerical occupations the pattern is different. In 1870 women made up only 2.5% of all workers in clerical jobs; by 1930 nearly 53% of all clerical workers were women and 20% of all women in the non-agricultural labor force were employed in clerical jobs. This pattern of female takeover of clerical work continues up to the present. In 1979, women were 80% of all clerical workers, and 35% of all employed women were working in clerical jobs.[25] The movement of women into clerical occupations will be examined in detail in later chapters.

Relationship Between Occupational Distribution and Growth of the Female Non-Agricultural Labor Force. Table 2.14 shows the percentage of total female non-agricultural labor force growth from 1870 to 1930 that is attributable to growth in employment in the nine occupational categories of major female employment. Twenty-six percent of total non-agricultural labor force growth over this period was due to the growth of female employment.[26] From table 2.14 we see that 76.41% of the total growth in the female non-agricultural labor force is attributable to growth in employment in the nine categories of major female employment. Most of this growth was associated with increased employment in occupations that could be characterized in 1870 as "women's jobs," i.e., clothing and textile manufacture, teaching, nursing, laundry, and domestic service employment. An additional 2.8% of total female non-agricultural labor force growth was due to the employment of women as telephone operators. Only in sales and clerical employment can growth in the female labor force be seen as due to the movement of women into occupations formerly held by men. In the case of clerical work the period 1870–1930 witnessed the massive growth of an occupational group which changed from "men's work" to "women's work." The movement of women into clerical employment contributed 23.43% of total female non-agricultural labor force growth over the period. Clearly, an examination of the takeover by women of clerical occupations is vital to an understanding of the growth of the female labor force.

Summary

This chapter has described the growth of women's employment in the United States over the period 1870 to 1930 and examined changes in the structure of the female labor force. The major cause of the growth of women's employment was increased participation by women in non-agricultural occupations. The demographic characteristics of the female labor force changed over the period. The average age of women workers rose as school attendance increased and as older women's participation grew. The share of black women and foreign-born women in the work force declined as the participation rates of native white women rose relative to both groups. Married women made up a small portion of the female labor force in every decade up through 1930, but married women's share of total employment increased because of their greater increases in participation, especially from 1920 to 1930.

One of the most striking and well-documented features of female employment in all time periods is the tendency for women workers to be found in a small number of sex-segregated occupations. This was found to be true for the period 1870–1930. For this reason most of the growth in the size of the female labor force came about through increased employment in occupations which were "women's jobs" as early as 1870. The most notable exception to this was the clerical sector which contributed nearly one-quarter of the 60-year growth in female employment and experienced a dramatic change in the sex composition of its work force at the same time.

3

Analysis of Women's Labor Force Participation in U.S. Cities in 1890 and 1930

Chapter 2 demonstrated that increased participation by women in the non-agricultural labor force was the major cause of growth in the female labor force from 1870 to 1930. In this chapter standard theories of labor supply are used to analyze women's labor force participation in urban areas at two points in time. The literature of female labor force participation is reviewed and the basic features of the theory are outlined. Since most work on women's labor force participation has focused on decisions made by married women, the existing theory places heavy emphasis on household production and earnings of other family members. This marital/family context of women's labor market decisions will be reexamined in light of the fact that unmarried women made up the overwhelming majority of female gainful workers throughout the period.

Participation equations will be estimated using ordinary least squares regression techniques for samples of American cities at two dates (1890 and 1930). Independent variables used include women's earnings, men's earnings, school attendance, child-woman ratios, demographic controls, and value added in the manufacturing industries that were the largest employers of female labor. Determinants of participation will be investigated for the overall female labor force and for various age and marital status groups.

The Economics of Labor Force Participation

The dramatic increase in women's participation in the American labor force has stimulated considerable effort by economists to identify and measure the determinants of this source of growth in labor supply. Nearly all of this work has focused on the post World War II period when the female labor participation rate jumped from 31.8% in 1947 to 50.1% in 1978.[1] The overwhelming portion of this increase was due to the greater propensity of married women to work for pay so that, in the quarter-century following 1947, 46% of the total growth in the civilian labor force was due to the increased presence of working wives.[2] Understandably then, most of the theory developed to explain women's labor force participation has been directed toward explaining the determinants of labor supply decision made by married women.

The earliest work in the development of the modern economic theory of labor supply was directed toward explaining decisions made by men.[3]. In this theory individuals are seen as making allocation decisions between two alternative uses of time: market work and leisure. The long-run decline in the supply of male labor is understandable within this framework in terms of the usual income and substitution effects which have opposite signs. The income effect outweighs the substitution effect yielding a backward bending supply curve for labor. This explanation did not, however, provide enlightenment in the case of the secular increase in the participation of women.

In an attempt to explain the phenomenon of increased female labor force participation, Jacob Mincer expanded the simple work-leisure model to include productive uses of time outside the market.[4] Studies of married women's participation in the paid work force have generally followed Mincer's pioneering study in which the family context of work and leisure decisions is stressed. Women are seen to divide their time among leisure, market work, and home work. The total number of hours worked is related to family income, but the distribution of work time between home and market will depend on the individual's relative productivities in the two sectors. Increased family income will have its accustomed negative effect on market work by increasing the demand for leisure and perhaps for home production as well. In this model there will be two substitution effects because an increase in the market wage increases the price of leisure time and raises the value of market work relative to home work. Both will tend to increase the amount of time devoted to market work as wages rise. Mincer found that the positive effect of increased women's wage was more powerful than the negative effect of greater family income thereby providing a plausible explanation for the observed growth in women's labor force participation.

Most studies of married women's work force participation decisions have used the model outlined above and have confirmed Mincer's basic finding (though Cain found a dominant income effect for some groups),[5] and have gone on to examine the importance of other variables: education, household production variables, labor market conditions, tastes.[6] To date little work has been done which uses the standard theory of labor supply derived from household utility maximization to investigate patterns of women's work force participation prior to 1940.

Two early studies examined the relationship between earnings and female labor force participation. Both of these used male earnings and found a negative relationship in cross-sectional data. Erika Schoenberg and Paul Douglas found for 1920 and 1930 "a slight tendency for cities with higher-than-average earnings (of males in manufacturing) to have a smaller-than-average proportion of adult women employed."[7] However, they did not look at the effect of women's own wages. Clarence Long, puzzled by the failure of female labor force participation to fall over time as average earnings (of males) rose, examined the simple relationship in cross-sections of U.S. cities for census dates from 1890 through 1950. He found a negative correlation in all but the 1950 cross-section. He made some effort to investigate the effect of female wages for 1939, but found no simple relationship.[8] Two recent studies in economic history have investigated the determinants of married women's labor force participation in the United States. Claudia Goldin used data from the manuscript censuses for seven southern cities in 1870 and 1880 to analyze racial differences in women's work force participation.[9] In a recent article, Martha Fraundorf used budget studies to estimate labor force participation models for married women at the turn of the twentieth century. She found that the presence of older children had a negative effect on mothers' participation because they could substitute as wage earners.[10]

In the next section we will use the framework of the standard theory of female labor supply as developed by Mincer to extend the analysis of the determinants of women's labor force participation back to the period 1890-1930 and to simultaneously measure the effect of male wages and females wages for the earlier period. The marital-family context of the model must be re-examined in light of the fact that the overwhelming majority of women who worked for pay were unmarried. Little research has been done on the determinants of labor force participation by unmarried women. The proportion of single women who work for pay has been relatively stable since 1947.[11] The variation of work force participation with age for single women is uni-modal like the pattern displayed by men.[12] This pattern leads to the expectation that the model which explains participation by unmarried women should be similar to that which explains male participation and which finds little effect of wage variation on the propensity to work for pay. The utility maximization model which generates these relationships is that in which non-market production constitutes a relatively unimportant use of time.

Bowen and Finegan, in the one major study which uses a similar model to investigate the determination of labor force participation for many demographic groups, have produced results which support the expectation that for the recent period unmarried women make labor supply decisions in a manner similar to that in which men make these decisions. They find that the signs and magnitudes of most explanatory variables are similar for single women and for men[13] and that "the participation rates of single women tend to be considerably less sensitive to labor market conditions than the participation rates of married women . . . . Many single women have no real alternative to participation in the labor force, either in terms of other sources of money income or in terms of an implicit 'home wage,' and therefore there should be a smaller (relative) number of single women whose participation decisions are influenced by any given change in labor market conditions".[14] Support for the same conclusions about single women's participation can be drawn from the findings of Schoenberg and Douglas for a 1930 sample of 41 cities in which the correlation between men's earnings and labor force participation was negligible for males between the ages of 16 and 54 and for females between 16 and 24.[15] Similar results were found by Douglas for 1920.[16]

As we have seen (tables 2.8 and 2.9), over the time period covered by this study there was a substantial increase in labor force participation by unmarried women so that 64% of the growth in the female non-agricultural labor force from 1890 to 1930 was due to increases in the numbers of unmarried women employed. For this reason our study must pay particular attention to participation decisions of unmarried women. The model tested will be the household choice model developed by Mincer to explain married women's actions. If it is seen that the model which explains well the actions of married women in the recent period also explains the actions of unmarried women in the past, we will argue that this is evidence that single women were making labor force participation decisions in a household choice context similar to that of married women. This is, we will argue that single women provided essential labor services to their families such that non-market production constituted an important alternative use of their time.

This view of the household in which time allocation decisions of children and young unmarried adults are determined by economic variables in their parents' family is consistent with the concept of a "family economy." Much recent historical research has focused on changes over time in the institution of the family and on the degree to which economic decisions were made on the basis of family rather than individual considerations.[17] Of particular relevance to this investigation are studies which point to the importance of family economic variables in determining labor market behavior of children and young adults. Claudia Goldin found evidence of substitution between mothers and daughters in the family economy in Philadelphia in 1880.[18] Work by Michael Haines on industrial families in 1889 to 1890 demonstrates that most of these families were dependent on their children to produce a sustantial portion of family income during long periods in the family life cycle. He finds evidence of substitution between adults and children in work effort in the market.[19] Leslie Tentler examined the role of daughters in working class families in the early twentieth century. She found that these young women made labor force decisions in a family economy context but suggests that the attachment of daughters to the family economy was less at later dates, saying that "during the 1920's the custom of giving the entire wage to the mother was probably abandoned in many families, even for daughters."[20] Other studies have raised questions about the timing of various transitions within the life cycle, particularly the transition from identification with the family of origin to individual adult status[21]

It appears that economic relations within the typical nineteenth-century family were close, with children making significant economic contributions to their parents' family. Labor supply decisions of these children were made within a household decision-making framework. If this is so, then unmarried daughters would be influenced in their labor force participation decisions by the same factors which affected married women. Any decline in the strength of family economy attachment by daughters would result in divergence between the factors determining participation of married and single women.

The Model

A simple estimatable model of labor supply for cross-sections of cities may be specified as:

$$L/P = \beta_0 + \beta_1 W_F + \beta_2 W_M + \beta_3 T + \beta_4 H + \beta_5 D + \beta_6 I + \beta_7 U$$

where

L/P = labor force participation rate (WFGW, FSINGW, FMARGW)

W_F = average annual earnings of female workers (FWAGE)

W_M = average annual earnings of male workers (MWAGE)

T = variable(s) to control for difference in tastes (FSC1617, FSC1014)

H   = proxy variable(s) for household productivity (CHILD)
D   = variables to control for differing demographic structure
        and regional location of cities (PF25, WPFNW, XPOP,
        PMAR, PWHITE, REGION)
I   = demand for female workers as reflected in occupational-
        industrial structure (VALFMFG)
U   = tightness of labor market (UNEMP)

Equations of this type will be used to estimate labor force participation of women in two cross-sections of American cities. Fifty-six cities are included in the sample for 1890; 72 cities are included in 1930. Discussion of the independent variables follows.

Female Earnings. The relationship between "own wages" and willingness to work in the market is the net outcome of two countervailing forces: (1) a substitution effect which would lead to more market work as alternative uses of time (leisure and home production) become more expensive and (2) an income effect which would encourage less market work and more consumption of leisure and home-produced goods. Studies of married women in the post World War II era have regularly found a positive relationship between women's wages and their work force participation implying the dominance of the substitution effect.[22] This has been attributed to the change for the family in the relative price of home-produced to market-produced goods and is contrary to the findings of a backward bending supply curve for males. The relationship is unclear for single women, who might be expected to be closer to the male pattern. We cannot, therefore, *a priori* predict the sign of the own wage effect for a time period in which the actions of single women dominated the female labor supply. However, if the single women were living in family homes (either daughters, or divorced or widowed mothers) and were contributing significantly to the family economy, we would expect that the effect of their own wages on their market work effort would be similar to that currently found for married women, i.e., the coefficient should be positive and significant.

The specification of this variable used in the regression analysis is a weighted average of female earnings in manufacturing and female earnings in clerical employment. Detailed description of wage data is presented in appendix B.

Male Earnings. Most studies have used men's wages as a proxy for family income exclusive of wives' earnings and have found a strong negative effect of increased male wages on women's market work effort.

Since the vast majority of working women in this period were unmarried, we might expect to find no effect of male wages. However, to the degree that a large percentage of single working women were parts of a family economy, we would expect the coefficient on male wages to indicate the income effect related to father's or brother's income. In this case we would expect a strong negative effect similar to that found in studies of married women in more recent times.

Male earnings may also represent income levels of potential husbands. We would expect that in cities with higher male earnings young couples would be able to marry earlier and young women (both married and unmarried) would be less likely to be in the labor market due to financial need. Simple correlations for both cross-sections, 1890 and 1930, reveal that in cities which had higher males wages, a larger proportion of women were married.

The male earnings variable is constructed as a weighted average of male earnings in manufacturing and male earnings in clerical employment (see appendix B for details).

Tastes. It is of course extremely difficult to devise ways of directly assessing tastes for market work relative to other uses of time. The prevailing nineteenth-century attitude was condemnation of women working outside the home. The reasons for this condemnation are varied: respected physicians argued that physical or mental labor destroyed women's reproductive organs; moralists argued that women were coarsened by encounters with the workshop and office so that employment threatened to destroy their femininity and the institution of the family; the courts held that women's proper place was in the home; economic observers and the Bureau of Labor found that women's employment threatened men's jobs and wages; the employment of wives and daughters was regarded as a sign of masculine failure.[23] Within this social framework it is unlikely that many women engaged in market work because of preferences for being in the paid labor force. Such negative attitudes toward women working did change substantially during the early part of the twentieth century so that by the era of the "flapper" it was no longer regarded as socially disgraceful for unmarried women to work for pay and to lead much more independent lives.[24]

Studies of women's labor force participation in the post World War II era have uniformly found a positive effect of educational attainment on women's inclination to work for pay. The effect of education is expected to increase labor force participation through two avenues: (1) more schooling increases the market wage; (2) schooling may be correlated with greater preferences for non-home activities or may

engender such preferences.[25] If schooling does reflect or cause greater
tastes for market work, we would expect to see a positive coefficient on a
variable measuring education. However, in light of the general
disapproval of working women in this period we might expect to see
little independent effect of education on women's work force
participation. We might even find a negative effect because education
may have been a luxury which could best be afforded by people in the
social class most likely to be able to conform to the prevailing ideal of
keeping women in the home, and many kinds of higher education
(especially before 1900) seem to have been designed to educate well-off
young women for domesticity.[26]

The variable used as a proxy for educational attainment in the
regression equations is the proportion of females of a given age group
who were enrolled in school. The group is ages 16–17 in 1930 and ages
10–14 in 1890. Different age groups are used for the two time periods in
recognition of the secular increase in school enrollment over the period.
While these variables measure school enrollment rather than educational
attainment, it is expected that cities which had a high percentage of
women currently enrolled in school would also have had a high level of
educational attainment on the part of the female population.

Household Productivity.   A women's choice to allocate time between
home production and market production will depend on her relative
productivity in the two sectors. For a woman who engages in work for
pay, the wage will reflect her productivity in the market sector.
Productivity in home work is difficult to assess, though we may assume
that for a woman who is not in the work force, the marginal value of her
output in the home exceeds her market wage. A major use of women's
time in the home is child care. It is well known that labor force
participation by women in recent periods is closely related to the number
and age of children in the home so that married women with young
children are less likely to work for pay.[27] We expect that the presence of
children increases a woman's productivity in the home and reduces the
probability that she will be in the labor force. Therefore, the ratio of
children under 10 to married women will be used as a proxy for average
family size and thus the child care burden. We expect that married
women's participation will be closely related to this variable.   If
unmarried women were also responsive to the child-woman ratio, this
will be taken as evidence that unmarried women made decisions of a
family economy type.

Demographic Variables. Variables will be employed to control for differences among cities in age structure, nativity structure, proportion of the female population who were married, and women's share of the population. In most cases the dependent variable will refer only to the white population so that a control for race will not usually be employed. The study focuses on the white population because the participation rate of black women remained quite stable over the period. A dummy variable is included to control for North-South differences.

Demand for Female Workers as Reflected in the Industrial-Occupational Mix. The industrial-occupational structure of the city determined the availability of jobs that were commonly filled by women. In some cities, especially those which had considerable textile and clothing manufacturing, jobs for female workers were readily available; search costs were consequently lower, and many women migrated to such cities. The extreme example of such a city was Fall River, Massachusetts, which in 1920 had a female labor force participation rate of 41.6 with 76% of all women earners employed in manufacturing. Various methods were tried in this study to control for industrial-occupational structure. In the results presented here the variable used to control for availability of manufacturing employment for women is constructed by dividing the value added in industries that were the major employers of women by the total population in the area. Details of the construction of this variable are presented in appendix B.

Unemployment. The net effect of unemployment on labor force participation of women is unclear. There is much literature on the question of whether high unemployment rates cause wives to seek employment (additional worker effect) or cause them to withdraw because jobs are harder to find (discouraged worker effect). Bowen and Finegan (1966) find support for the dominance of the discouraged worker effect in their 1960 cross-section of SMSA's.[28] Unemployment data are only available for 1930 and are of doubtful value because the census used the gainful worker rather than the labor force concept. When participation equations which included the unemployment rate among the independent variables were estimated, the sign was negative, which lends support to the discouraged worker hypothesis. However, the coefficient was small and insignificant, and adding the unemployment variable did not substantially change the coefficients on any of the other variables. Therefore, results which include an unemployment variable have not been reported here.

TABLE 3.1

MULTIPLE REGRESSION ANALYSIS OF INTERCITY DIFFERENCES
IN FEMALE LABOR FORCE PARTICIPATION, 1890 AND 1930
DEPENDENT VARIABLE = WFGW

	1930	1890	
FWAGE	.204 (.161)	.446*** (.093)	
MWAGE	-.200 (.159)	-.606*** (.178)	
FSC1617	-.018 (.125)	.499 (.348)	FSC1014
PF25	-.195 (.175)	-.345 (.290)	
WPFNW	-.079 (.087)	-.335*** (.089)	
XPOP	.379 (.656)	-.203 (.416)	
PMAR	-.740*** (.272)	-.873*** (.226)	
VALFMFG	.047*** (.016)	.087*** (.020)	
REGION	-.012 (.018)	-.085*** (.025)	
Constant	-.791	-.655	
R^2	.510	.834	
n	72	56	

(Standard errors in parentheses)

***Significant at .01
 **Significant at .05
  *Significant at .10

Variables defined next page

TABLE 3.1 (Continued)

Variable definitions: (all variables, except REGION, in logarithmic form)

Dependent variable: WFGW = $\dfrac{\text{white female gainful workers ages 10+}}{\text{all white females ages 10+}}$

Independent variables:

FWAGE (1930) = annual earnings of employed females, computed as a weighted average of women's wages in manufacturing occupations and in clerical occupations, corrected for cost-of-living differences

FWAGE (1890) = annual earnings of employed females, computed as a weighted average of women's wages in manufacturing occupations and in clerical occupations in manufacturing establishments

MWAGE (1930) = annual earnings of employed males, computed as a weighted average of men's wages in manufacturing occupations and in clerical occupations, corrected for cost-of-living differences

MWAGE (1890) = annual earnings of employed males, computed as a weighted average of men's wages in manufacturing occupations and in clerical occupations in manufacturing establishments

FSC1617 (1930) = $\dfrac{\text{women ages 16-17 attending school}}{\text{all women ages 16-17}}$

FSC1014 (1890) = $\dfrac{\text{women ages 10-14 attending school}}{\text{all women ages 10-14}}$

PF25 = $\dfrac{\text{women ages 10-24}}{\text{all women ages 10+}}$

WPFNW = $\dfrac{\text{native white women ages 10+}}{\text{all white women ages 10+}}$

XPOP = $\dfrac{\text{women ages 10+}}{\text{total population ages 10+}}$

PMAR = $\dfrac{\text{married women ages 15+}}{\text{total female population ages 15+}}$

VALFMFG = $\dfrac{\text{value added in manufacturing industries that were major employers of women}}{\text{total population in area}}$

REGION = 1 if city located in the South

Data

The data employed to estimate the above model are for two cross-sections of the largest American cities in 1890 and 1930. Fifty-six cities are included in 1890 and 72 are included in 1930. Information about the sample and the construction of variables can be found in appendix B. Demographic data is from the published schedules of the *U.S. Decennial Census of Population.* Wage variables were constructed from data published in the *1890 Census of Manufactures* on wages paid and persons employed, by sex. Data were available for both wages paid in manufacturing occupations and wages paid to clerical workers in manufacturing establishments. Wage variables for 1930 were constructed using data from a survey conducted by the U.S. Personnel Classification Board of clerical wages in cities and from manufacturing wage data in the 1930 census. Methods used by Erika Schoenberg and Paul Douglas to estimate male and female wages from the data presented in the manufacturing census[29] were extended to the 72 cities in the sample to obtain manufacturing wages by sex. Wage data for 1930 is corrected for differences between cities in cost of living. Value added in manufacturing was collected from the *U.S. Census of Manufactures* for 1890 and 1930.

Findings

Results are presented in this section for regression equations (OLS) which estimate female labor force participation for 1890 and 1930. Construction of variables used in estimating equations is explained following the tables. All variables are in logarithmic form so that coefficients may be interpreted as elasticities.

In table 3.1 results are presented that show the effect of earnings and schooling on the propensity of white women to work for pay. Control variables are employed for various demographic factors and for the availability of women's employment in manufacturing. Unemployment, the presence of children, and the possible economic contribution of children are not considered in these equations. We see that the effect of women's own earnings in both years is positive, extending back to 1890 the finding of the dominance of the substitution effect on market work effort by women. For 1890 the effect of men's wages is negative, highly significant, and of greater magnitude than the positive effect of women's own wages. In 1930 male wages have a negative but not significant effect. This finding probably points to a decline in the family context of female labor force decisions over the period. Single women constituted the vast majority of wage-earning women in both years (the mean value of single women's share of the female urban labor force was 88% in 1890, 74% in 1930) so that their actions dominate the relationship. The results are consistent with the hypothesis that as it became more acceptable for daughters to work outside the home before marriage the negative income effect attributable to fathers' wages would decrease. Also working in this direction is the decline in fertility and increased mechanization of the home which reduced the necessity of employing daughters in home production.

For both years the coefficient on the education variable is insignificant. This finding is consistent with the suggestion that for this time period there was no independent effect of education on tastes for market work (at least for education below the college level). We might expect some change in this result when the sample is stratified into age groups so as to eliminate the portion of the population still attending school. Results for 1930 will be presented which show a positive effect of education for some demographic groups.

The demographic control variables generally have the expected signs. PMAR, percent of women who were married, has a strong negative effect in both years. Interesting is the decline in the effect associated with the percentage native-born. Over the period the nativity structure of the female labor force changed (mean values = 35% foreign-born in 1890, 17% in 1930) as immigration was reduced and the foreign-born population aged. The change in the coefficient from being large, negative, and significant in 1890 to being small and insignificant in 1930 reflects this development. The sign on the age structure variable (percentage of the female population ages 10–24) is somewhat confusing. Since young women were more likely to work for pay, we might expect a positive sign. However, the variable is constructed for women ages 10-24 and therefore also captures the negative effect of school attendance. An equation estimated for 1930 using percentage ages 18–24 as the control yielded a positive sign.

It should be noted that the model explains a much larger proportion of the variation in 1890 than in 1930, which is consistent with the suggestion that household production concerns are more important in explaining overall female labor force participation in 1890 than they are in 1930.

In table 3.2 we look at the effect of children on female labor force participation. The first two columns relate to the importance of children as demanders of women's services in the home. The variable CHILD is the ratio of children under 10 to all married women; it is proxy for average family size. We see that in both 1890 and 1930 the effect of

TABLE 3.2

MULTIPLE REGRESSION ANALYSIS OF INTERCITY DIFFERENCES IN
FEMALE LABOR FORCE PARTICIPATION, 1890 and 1930--THE EFFECT
OF THE PRESENCE OF CHILDREN AND CHILD LABOR
DEPENDENT VARIABLE = WFGW

	1930	1890	1890	
FWAGE	.019	.403***	.442***	
	(.168)	(.103)	(.116)	
MWAGE	-.158	-.569***	-.564***	
	(.152)	(.182)	(.188)	
FSC1617	-.005	.401	.308	FSC10104
	(.119)	(.364)	(.413)	
PF25	.311	-.153	-.069	
	(.251)	(.380)	(.397)	
WPFNW	-.203***	-.395***	.400***	
	(.095)	(.109)	(.111)	
XPOP	.614	-.187	.246	
	(.631)	(.417)	(.430)	
PMAR	-.902***	-.886***	-.836***	
	(.266)	(.227)	(.236)	
VALFMFG	.033**	.082***	.087***	
	(.016)	(.021)	(.022)	
REGION	-.015	-.081***	-.080***	
	(.018)	(.025)	(.026)	
CHILD	-.446***	-.214	-.250	
	(.167)	(.225)	(.289)	
CWAGE			-.118	
			(.133)	
PCMFG			-.010	
			(.024)	
Constant	-.131	-.582	-.431	
R^2	.562	.837	.840	
n	72	56	56	

TABLE 3.2 (Continued)

Variable definitions: (all variables, except REGION, in logarithmic form)

CHILD   = $\dfrac{\text{children ages } 0\text{-}10}{\text{maried women}}$

CWAGE   =   Annual earnings of children employed in manufacturing

PCMFG   = $\dfrac{\text{children employed in manufacturing}}{\text{all manufacturing employees}}$

All other variables are defined in Table 3.1

(Standard errors in parentheses)

***Significant at .01
 **Significant at .05
  *Significant at .10

TABLE 3.3

MULTIPLE REGRESSION ANALYSIS OF INTERCITY DIFFERENCES IN LABOR
FORCE PARTICIPATION OF UNMARRIED WOMEN, 1890 and 1930
DEPENDENT VARIABLE = FSINGW

	1930	1930	1890	1890	
FWAGE	.301*	.292*	.379***	.442***	
	(.157)	(.175)	(.085)	(.102)	
MWAGE	-.186	-.185	-.491***	-.506***	
	(.147)	(.148)	(.003)	(.164)	
FSC1617	-.127	-.127	.312	.057	FSC1014
	(.118)	(.119)	(.312)	(.369)	
PF25	.111	.131	-.063	.076	
	(.166)	(.240)	(.281)	(.343)	
WPFNW	-.125	-.132	-.265***	.267***	
	(.166)	(.105)	(.084)	(.100)	
XPOP	.912	.928	.140	-.052	
	(.570)	(.590)	(.342)	(.352)	
VALFMFG	.033**	.032**	.075***	.080***	
	(.015)	(.016)	(.018)	(.019)	
PWHITE	-.200	-.203	-.433***	-.416***	
	(.191)	(.194)	(.141)	(.143)	
REGION	-.034	-.034	-.041	-.041	
	(.022)	(.023)	(.027)	(.027)	
CHILD		-.019		-.080	
		(.162)		(.205)	
CWAGE				-.190	
				(.115)	
PCMFG				-.026	
				(.021)	
Constant	-.449	-.415	-.048	.189	
R^2	.277	.277	.711	.737	
n	72	72	56	56	

TABLE 3.3 (Continued)

Variable definitions: (all variables, except REGION, in logarithmic form)

Dependent variable: FSINGW = $\dfrac{\text{unmarried female gainful workers ages 10+}}{\text{unmarried females ages 10+}}$

Independent variables: PWHITE = $\dfrac{\text{white women ages 10+}}{\text{all women ages 10+}}$

All other variables as defined in Tables 3.1 and 3.2.

(Standard errors in parentheses.)

***Significant at .01
 **Significant at .05
  *Significant at .10

TABLE 3.4

MULTIPLE REGRESSION ANALYSIS OF INTERCITY DIFFERENCES IN LABOR
FORCE PARTICIPATION OF MARRIED WOMEN, 1890 AND 1930
DEPENDENT VARIABLE = FMARGW

	1930	1930	1890	1890	
FWAGE	.072 (.079)	-.222*** (.076)	.089*** (.025)	.055* (.029)	
MWAGE	-.118* (.070)	-.097) (.064)	-.145*** (.046)	-.115** (.046)	
FSC1617	.070 (.059)	.078 (.051)	.113 (.090)	.106 (.103)	FSC1014
PF25	-.227*** (.084)	.124 (.104)	-.015 (.082)	.086 (.096)	
WPFNW	-.015 (.044)	-.135*** (.046)	-.073*** (.024)	-.113*** (.028)	
XPOP	-.217 (.287)	.058 (.255)	.031 (.099)	-.086 (.099)	
VALFMFG	.013* (.007)	.003 (.006)	.012** .005	.009* (.005)	
PWHITE	-.254*** (.096)	-.296*** (.083)	-.390*** (.041)	-.390*** (.040)	
REGION	.023** (.011)	.016* (.010)	-.006 (.008)	-.002 (.008)	
CHILD		-.329*** (.070)		-.122*** (.057)	
CWAGE				.024 (.032)	
PCMFG				.006 (.006)	
Constant	.454	1.059	.184*	.197**	
R^2	.567	.682	.878	.896	
n	72	72	56	56	

TABLE 3.4 (Continued)

Variable definitions: (all variables, except REGION, entered in logarithmic form)

Dependent variable: FMARGW = $\dfrac{\text{married female gainful workers}}{\text{married females ages 10+}}$

Dependent variable entered as [−log(1−FMARGW)]

All independent variables as defined in Tables 3.1, 3.2 and 3.3.

(Standard errors in parentheses.)

*** Significant at .01
 ** Significant at .05
  * Significant at .10

children on female labor force participation was negative, though the coefficient was significant only in 1930 when married women made up a substantial part of the female labor force.

In the third column of the table we examine the effect of children's other possible role, that of breadwinner. Child labor was quite low by 1890 according to historical standards, but it is still possible that children's earnings substituted for earnings of other family members and could therefore produce a negative income effect on women's work force participation analogous to the expected effect of male earnings. For 1890 we have average annual earnings of children in manufacturing employment (CWAGE) and the percentage of the manufacturing work force who were children (PCMFG). The information is from the *U.S. Census of Manufactures*; children are defined as persons under age 15. The mean value for PCMFG is 2.5%. As can be seen, the effect of both variables, though in the predicted direcion, is insignificant, indicating that children's presence in the labor market was not an important deterrent to female work force participation.

Tables 3.3 and 3.4 report findings for the samples broken down by marital status. More detailed breakdowns are available for 1930 and will be presented shortly. Results are presented both with and without the child-related variables included. Because the dependent variables in these equations relate to women of all races, a control for the racial structure of the city (PWHITE) is included among the independent variables.

We see in table 3.3 that in 1890 single women responded positively to their own wage and negatively to male earnings. This, particularly the large significant response to male earnings, suggests a family economy explanation for single women's participation in 1890. The family size variable, though negative, is not significant.

By 1930 single women were no longer nearly so responsive to the variables included in these equations. The same variables explain in 1930 less than one-half the variation which they explained in 1890. The coefficient of FWAGE is less significant and the coefficient on MWAGE has declined in magnitude and is no longer significant. This decline in responsiveness of unmarried women to male earnings is the most persuasive piece of evidence to support the contention that single women were less closely tied into a family economy in 1930 than they had been in 1890. The importance of race and nativity declined over the period both in terms of size and significance of the coefficients. The availability of manufacturing employment for women, though still significant, was a less important determinant of single women's participation in 1930 than it was in 1890.

TABLE 3.5

MULTIPLE REGRESSION ANALYSIS OF INTERCITY DIFFERENCES IN
LABOR FORCE PARTICIPATION BY WHITE WOMEN IN
DETAILED AGE-MARITAL STATUS GROUPS, 1930
DEPENDENT VARIABLE = WFGW (AGE-MARITAL STATUS GROUPS)

	Married			Unmarried		
	20-24	25-34		15-19	20-24	25-34
FWAGE	.001	.011		-.517**	-.135*	-.028
	(.111)	(.097)		(.222)	(.078)	(.091)
MWAGE	-.266***	-.218***		.565***	.161**	-.010
	(.104)	(.091)		(.207)	(.073)	(.084)
FSC1617	.136	.134*		-1.52***	-.130**	.120*
	(.085)	(.074)		(.169)	(.059)	(.069)
VALMFG	.029***	.021**		.079***	.019**	.003
	(.011)	(.010)		(.022)	(.008)	(.009)
REGION	-.016	-.003		-.093***	-.030***	-.019*
	(.012)	(.011)		(.025)	(.009)	(.010)
Constant	.912	.713		-.979	-.243	.053
R^2	.254	.199		.760	.492	.173
n	72	72		72	72	72

Variable definitions: (all variables, except REGION, in logarithmic form)

Dependent variable: WFGW = $\dfrac{\text{white female gainful workers}}{\text{all white females}}$ (age-marital status groups)

Entered as $[-\log(1-\text{WFGW})]$ in married women equations.

All independent variables as defined in Table 3.1.

(Standard errors in parentheses.)

*** Significant at .01
 ** Significant at .05
  * Significant at .10

The equations for married women (table 3.4) show the expected signs on the wage variables with the exception of the negative sign on FWAGE in the 1930 equation children. Male earnings had a negative effect on married women's work force participation in both 1890 and 1930. The presence of children was a strong deterrent to married women's participation in both years as was the proportion of the city's population who were white.

Table 3.5 provides breakdowns of the 1930 cross-section into age-marital status groups. For married women in both age groups the effect of male earnings is strongly and significantly negative on labor force participation. This association does not hold for any group of unmarried women. There is no significant response of married women to own wages, and the signs on this variable for single women are negative. Labor force participation for teenagers was determined above all by school attendance as an alternative use of time. For married women and for older single women there appears to be some independent positive effect of schooling by 1930. It is most important to notice that for no age group is there evidence of significant negative response by single women to male earnings. The conclusion seems warranted that, by 1930, unmarried women were no longer making the same kinds of family economy decisions about labor force participation that they did in 1890.

Summary

In this chapter standard labor supply theory was used to develop a model of female labor force participation. Cross-sectional data from U.S. cities in 1890 and 1930 were used to estimate participation equations for the total female labor force and for various age-marital status groups. The major finding of the exercise was that the standard household production oriented model of female labor supply worked best to explain the actions of married women in 1930 and single women in 1890. It was argued that these results reflect the development of the modern pattern of labor force participation with married women becoming more responsive to household variables and single women becoming less responsive to the same variables. This is consistent with the decline of the institution of the family economy which typified the nineteenth century.

4

The Rise of the Clerical Sector

The importance of clerical employment in the expanding female labor force was discussed briefly in chapter 2 where it was learned that nearly one-quarter of the growth from 1870 to 1930 in the female non-agricultural labor force was accounted for by increased employment of women in office jobs (see table 2.14). In this chapter attention turns to a detailed examination of clerical work in this period. We will describe the rate and pattern of growth in clerical employment, examine changes in office technology and the nature of clerical work, and use census data on the industrial distribution of clerical employment to analyze historical developments which contributed to the growth of demand for clerical services. The emphasis in this chapter will be on total clerical employment and on factors which increased demand for clerical workers. The following three chapters will focus on the supply of women to the clerical labor market.

Overview of the Growth in Clerical Employment

The six decades covered by this study were ones of extremely rapid growth in clerical employment. Table 4.1 presents information on the change in total non-agricultural employment and in clerical employment from 1870 to 1930. The clerical sector grew much more rapidly than did the non-agricultural labor force as a whole so that the share of clerical workers in the non-agricultural labor force increased from about 1% in 1870 to almost 10% in 1930. Coincident with this dramatic rise in the importance of the clerical sector was the even more rapid increase in the number of women employed as clerical workers. In 1870 less than .2% of all women in the non-agricultural labor force were employed as clerical workers: by 1930 this had risen to 20%. The consequence of this

TABLE 4.1

NON-AGRICULTURAL EMPLOYMENT AND CLERICAL EMPLOYMENT BY SEX, 1970-1930
CLERICAL SHARE OF NON-AGRICULTURAL EMPLOYMENT BY SEX, AND
WOMEN'S SHARE OF CLERICAL EMPLOYMENT, 1870-1930

		1870	1880	1890	1900	1910	1920	1930
I	NON-AGRICULTURAL LABOR FORCE (NALF) (in thousands)							
	Total	6075	8807	13380	18161	25779	30985	38358
	Female	1463	2021	3210	4311	6269	7466	9842
	Male	4613	6786	10170	13850	19510	23518	28516
II	CLERICAL LABOR FORCE (CW) (in thousands)							
	Total	74.2	150.4	380.8	708.2	1523.9	2837.7	3738.8
	Female	1.8	6.6	73.4	214.2	573.1	1396.0	1964.4
	Male	72.4	143.8	307.4	494.0	950.8	1441.7	1774.4
III	PARTICIPATION IN CLERICAL LABOR FORCE = CW /NALF							
	Total	1.22	1.70	2.84	3.89	5.91	9.15	9.74
	Female	0.13	0.33	2.29	4.94	9.15	18.75	19.96
	Male	1.73	2.11	3.02	3.56	4.87	6.13	6.22
IV	FEMALE SHARE OF CLERICAL LABOR FORCE	2.46	4.40	19.27	30.24	37.60	49.19	52.54

Sources: Non-agricultural labor force from Alba M. Edwards, Comparative Occupation Statistics
for the United States (Washington, D.C.: G. P. O., U. S. Bureau of the Census,
1943) p. 100.

Clerical labor force is defined as the aggregate of three census categories:
bookkeepers, cashiers and accountants; clerks (except in stores); stenographers
and typists

All data on clerical labor force except clerks in 1900 are from Edwards pp. 112, 121,
129. Clerks in 1900 estimated to correct for inclusion of clerks in stores by fitting
equation: log (clerks) = a+b(time) using Edwards data for 1880, 1890, 1910 and 1920.
Males and females estimated separately.

TABLE 4.2

PERCENT OF DECADAL INCREASE IN NON-AGRICULTURAL LABOR FORCE DUE TO INCREASE IN NUMBER OF CLERICAL WORKERS, BOTH SEXES AND WOMEN, 1870–1930

	1870–1880	1880–1890	1890–1900	1900–1910	1910–1920	1920–1930	1870–1930
I BOTH SEXES							
Change in non-agricultural labor force = ΔNALF (in thousands)	2732	4573	4781	7618	5206	7373	32283
Change in clerical labor force = ΔCW (in thousands)	76.2	230.4	327.4	815.7	1313.9	901.2	3664.6
ΔCW/ΔNALF	2.79	5.04	6.85	10.71	25.24	12.22	11.35
II FEMALES							
ΔFNALF (in thousands)	559	1188	1101	1958	1197	2376	8380
ΔFCW (in thousands)	4.8	66.8	140.8	359.0	822.9	568.4	1962.6
ΔFCW/ΔFNALF	.86	5.62	12.78	18.33	68.73	23.92	23.43
III FEMALE SHARE OF CHANGE IN CLERICAL LABOR FORCE = ΔFCW/ΔCW	6.29	28.98	43.00	44.01	62.63	63.08	53.56

Sources: See Table 4.1.

TABLE 4.3

AVERAGE ANNUAL GROWTH RATES BY DECADE FOR THE NON-AGRICULTURAL
LABOR FORCE AND THE CLERICAL LABOR FORCE, BY
SEX, 1870-1930

	1870–1880	1880–1890	1890–1900	1900–1910	1910–1920	1920–1930	1870–1930
I GROWTH RATES OF NON-AGRICULTURAL LABOR FORCE (NALF)							
Total	3.78	4.27	3.10	3.56	1.85	2.16	3.12
Females	3.28	4.73	3.04	3.77	1.77	2.80	3.23
Males	3.94	4.13	3.14	3.49	1.89	1.95	3.08
II GROWTH RATES OF CLERICAL LABOR FORCE (CẆ)							
Total	7.31	9.73	6.40	7.96	6.41	2.80	6.75
Females	13.74	27.20	11.31	10.34	9.31	3.47	12.34
Males	7.10	7.89	4.85	6.77	4.25	2.10	5.48
III RATIOS OF GROWTH RATE CẆ/NALF							
Total	1.93	2.28	2.06	2.24	3.46	1.30	2.16
Females	4.19	5.75	3.72	2.74	5.26	1.24	3.82
Males	1.80	1.91	1.55	1.94	2.25	1.08	1.78

Source: See Table 4.1.

very rapid increase in women's participation in clerical employment is seen in the bottom line of table 4.1: an increase from 2.5% to 53% in women's share of total clerical employment over the 60-year period

From table 4.2 we are able to learn the relative importance of clerical employment for explaining the change in the size of the non-agricultural labor force in each decade. From 1870 to 1930 the size of the non-agricultural labor force increased by over 32 million; more than 3.6 million (11.35%) of these additional workers were in clerical pursuits. Up until 1920 the clerical share of additional workers increased each decade. The most dramatic change took place from 1910 to 1920 when fully one-quarter of all added workers went into clerical occupations. For women the clerical sector was even more important for non-agricultural labor force growth, with 23.43% of the 60-year increase coming in the clerical sector. For women in clerical work the second decade of the century shows up as being particularly important. During that decade nearly 69% of the change in the female non-agricultural labor force was due to an increase in the number of women employed in clerical occupations.

Although the clerical sector grew at an impressive rate over the entire period, the pattern of growth was not constant throughout. Table 4.3 presents average annual compound growth rates by decade for the non-agricultural labor force and for the clerical labor force. Panel I shows growth rates, by sex, for the non-agricultural labor force. For males, the fastest growth took place in the earliest decades of the period, whereas for women the 1880s and the first decade of the century saw the fastest growth in the numbers of non-farm gainful workers.

Panel II presents growth rates for the clerical sector of the work force. Here is evidence of the phenomenally rapid pace of growth sustained by the clerical sector with an average annual growth rate over the 60-year period of 6.75%. In every decade except the 1920s the growth rate was over 6%, with the fastest increase in the number of clerical workers coming in the periods 1880–1890 and 1900–1910. Again we see the much more rapid increase in the numbers of women employed in clerical positions.

The third panel of table 4.3, which is constructed as a ratio of the figures in panel II to the figures in panel I, shows how fast the clerical sector grew relative to the entire non-agricultural labor force. Over the entire period the number of clerical workers grew more than twice as fast as did the non-farm labor force. In the period prior to 1900, the 1880s were notable for the fastest increase in clerical workers relative to total non-farm employment. Over that decade the total clerical labor force grew at 2.28 times the rate experienced by the non-agricultural labor force as a whole, and the female clerical labor force grew at 5.75 times the growth rate of the female non-agricultural labor force. It is, however, the decade 1910–1920 which bears the distinction of the most rapid growth in the clerical sector relative to the non-agricultural labor force. Over that 10-year period the number of clerical workers increased at a rate almost 3.5 times the growth rate experienced by the total non-agricultural labor force. The rate for female clerical workers was again over 5 times the rate for all female non-farm workers.

The Nature of Clerical Work

During this period of rapid growth in clerical employment, the nature of the tasks performed by clerical workers changed drastically as offices became larger and more complex, and as mechanical and organizational innovations were adopted which substantially altered the technology of the office.

The Early Office. We have limited information about the organization and nature of tasks performed in offices in the mid-nineteenth century. Many of the best descriptions of the early office come from literature and pamphlets. Descriptions by Dickens in *Bleak House* [1] and *David Copperfield* [2] and by Melville in *Bartleby, the Scrivener* [3] provide much of what we know of the pre-modern office. Probably the best description of the early office has been written by David Lockwood in a study of the social status of clerical workers entitled *The Black-Coated Worker.*[4] Lockwood constructed his description from early pamphlets and periodicals. While his work is concerned with clerical occupations in Great Britain, it is likely that most of what he writes can be applied to the U.S. as well. The description of the early office which follows is based in large part on Lockwood's account.

The pre-modern office was generally small and the relationships between clerks and employers were close and personal. Financial, mercantile, and manufacturing concerns were sure to employ a bookkeeper; but except in large firms, business correspondence was conducted through letters written in longhand by the managers themselves. Very large offices might employ a stenographer who took dictation and then copied from his notes. An office copy of correspondence could be achieved by using a copybook where the original letter was dampened and pressed against light-weight paper to make the copy,[5] but multiple copies required printing or the services of a copyist. Lawyers hired copyists (also called scriveners or amanuenses) to make multiple copies of legal documents. Professional stenographers were used to make records of court proceedings or meetings. The government and trade and transportation sectors hired comparatively large numbers of clerks to handle routine record keeping.

Virtually all clerical workers were men, and clerical positions often served as entry points into management careers. While many who entered the business world as clerks never rose above that position, pamphlets of the day make it clear that most who entered clerical positions did so with the hope of rising through the ranks to become managers or partners.[6] The distinction between clerical and managerial functions was not as clearly drawn as it is today, and clerks and bookkeepers were regularly expected to assume responsibilities that would now be classified as managerial. Office practices and bookkeeping systems were usually particular to firms. General principles of bookkeeping and management had not yet received wide publicity so that although clerks may have received some instruction in shorthand, penmanship, and business arithmetic in a private business school, most clerical training necessarily took place on the job. An 1878 description of the training necessary for the aspiring young clerk read, "A little instruction in Latin, and probably a very little in Greek, a little in Geography, a little in Science, a little in arithmetic and bookkeeping, a little in French, with such a sprinkling of English reading as may enable a lad to distinguish Milton from Shakespeare . . . ."[7]

Before 1870 the tools of the clerk and bookkeeper were the quill pen, the ledgerbook, the letter press, and the green eyeshade. The most valued qualities were the ability to write neatly and add accurately, ambition, and the likelihood of long and loyal service to the firm during which the clerk would learn the many particular details of the business and perhaps advance to management.

Technological Advances That Changed the Nature of Clerical Work. During the six decades around the turn of the twentieth century clerical work underwent dramatic changes in the types of work performed, the organization of the work, and the kinds of tools used by clerical workers. Offices became larger and began to resemble factories in the ways that the work was organized. Machines of all sorts replaced the pen and ledgerbook. The ranks of clerical workers swelled enormously and the possibilities of rising from clerk to executive became much more remote. The old tiny office composed of a bookkeeper-cashier, a general clerk, and the executive was soon an anachronism.

It was the typewriter—which, along with the telegraph and the telephone, revolutionized the transmittal of information—that was the single most important source of technological change in the office. The first workable typewriter was patented by C. Latham Sholes of Milwaukee, Wisconsin in July 1868. In early 1874 the first shipment of Sholes model writing machines produced by E. Remington and Sons was ready to be offered for sale at a price of $125.[8] The first advertising circular promised that the machine was a "perfect and practical substitute for pen and ink" and that "One person can do the work of two, and in some kinds of work three to five . . . . The machine will more than pay for itself in every three months that it is used."[9] There was some difficulty at first in marketing the new invention; some businesses found that their customers objected to the impersonality and implied rudeness of "machine-made" letters.[10] Nevertheless, the typewriter was adopted quickly in all lines of endeavor. One early organizational innovation was the formation of independent typewriting agencies to which lawyers, writers, and businesses could send their work to be typed.[11] However, it was not long until typewriters became common in business and government offices. In 1875 Dun, Barlow and Co. became the first large business firm to equip its offices with typewriters.[12] An advertisement by Densmore, Yost and Company (sole agents for typewriter sales) was issued in conjunction with an exhibit at the Centennial Exposition. It noted that 1005 machines had been sold by June 30, 1875 and predicted that the Type-Writer was "destined to become as popular and of as universal use in the counting room and office as the sewing machine is in the dwelling—for the simple reason that it will save as much time and labor in our business houses as the sewing machine saves in our dwellings."[13]

Use of the typewriter spread quickly so that demand for the machine increased. In 1881, 1200 Type-Writers were produced by Remington, the only manufacturer.[14] By 1890, 30 establishments were producing the writing machine and the vaue of their output was $3,630,126[15] (at least 36,000 machines). Typewriter production was highly competitive; by 1909 there were 89 manufacturers.[16] Prices fell as more firms entered the field, and many improvements were made in the design and operation of the machine.

The spread of the typewriter led to a rise in demand for trained operators. At first operating a typewriter was simply a matter of becoming familiar enough with the keyboard to be able to work it quickly. The 10 finger touch system was not invented until 1882 and was not popularized till 1888. The early typewriter companies trained operators and sent them along when machines were sold. The first formal instruction in typing was instituted by the New York City branch of the Y.W.C.A. in 1881. There was considerable debate at the time over the possible dangers to young women's delicate constitutions of training them for such work. However, the eight students were quickly placed in good jobs with no observed ill effects on their health, and schools which taught typing sprang up throughout the country.[17]   Two surveys on shorthand instruction were made in the 1880s by Julius Ensign Rockwell, the head stenographer of the U.S. Bureau of Education. He found that in 1882 there were 276 schools offering shorthand instruction to 12,470 students;   21% of these schools also offered instruction in typing. By 1889–90 there were 1310 such schools with 57,375 students; all offered typing instruction.[18] Shorthand writing and typing were complementary skills, and by 1890 the new job of stenographer-typist was established in the American occupational structure with over 33,000 people employed.

Though there was no other single technological change that transformed the office so much as did the typewriter, the period from 1870 to 1930 saw the invention and adoption of many other devices, large and small, which changed the way that clerical output was produced. Carbon paper was patented in 1869 and did much to enhance the usefulness of the typewriter.[19]   Many new machines incorporated typewriter-like mechanisms.   Among these were accounting machines, addressing machines, calculating machines, billing machines, Linotypes, cash registers, check writing machines, and stenotypes. Some machines, such as   the Dictaphone and its competitor, the Ediphone, were developed to complement the typewriter.

There was a wave of invention of new office machines in the 20 years following the first commercial use of the typewriter. The cash register was patented in 1879, dictating machines and stenotypes in the 1880s, the mimeograph machine in 1890, the Hollerith machine which was used to tabulate the 1890 census, a full-listing adding machine by Burroughs in 1892, and the first front strike typewriter in 1895.[20]   A second great wave of office machine invention took place in the second decade of the twentieth century. This seems to have been associated with the spread of scientific management ideas as developed by Frederick Taylor and his followers. "In the six or seven years before 1921 at least a hundred new office machines a year were put on the market."[21]   In 1919 the editors of the journal *Modern Business* produced the following list of machines commonly found in the American office:[22]

    typewriter
    dictating machine
    stenotype
    copy press
    automatic typewriter (these worked like player pianos)
    stencil or gelatin duplicators
    typesetting machines

printing presses
photographing machines
telephone
TelAutograph
dictagraph
mechanical messenger boys:
   pneumatic tubes
   overhead carriers
adding machines
calculating machines
billing machines
bookkeeping machines
cash register
statistical machines (card punch and reader)
mailing machines
addressing machines
letter openers
letter folder
envelope feeders
time clocks
paper cutters
padding machines
binding machines
bailing machines

Larger clerical labor forces and adoption of mechanical devices went hand-in-hand with innovations in the organization of clerical tasks. Many of the new methods involved greater specialization of labor and standardization of tasks. Some machines required adoption of more standard practices by businesses which used them. For example, bookkeeping machines were developed which used standardized forms and therefore required that the firm use conventional bookkeeping practices. By the early years of the twentieth century clerical work, which had been described in 1871 as requiring "knowledge of languages, skills in accounts, familiarity with even minute details of business, energy, promptitude, tact, delicacy of perception"[23] had become, for the majority of office workers, routine and mechanical.

The overall effect of these technological advances was to lower the unit cost of producing clerical output of a given quality, thereby increasing the supply of such output. Mechanized, routinized clerical work allowed cheaper labor to be substituted for the more expensive time of managers who in the past had had to write letters and other paperwork in longhand. Much business communication that previously had been conducted in person could be done through dictated letters or memos. The telephone allowed for similar saving in the time of managers.

The Occupational Distribution of Clerical Employment. The clerical occupations reported in the U.S. census may be sub-divided into three broad categories: bookkeepers, accountants, and cashiers; clerks (except clerks in stores); stenographers and typists. The number of gainful workers in each sub-occupation and the percent distribution of clerical workers over sub-occupations is presented in table 4.4. The fastest growing clerical category was that of stenographers and typists. Those employed in that category in 1870 were all professional stenographers. In 1890, the first year for which the census collected information on stenographers and typists, there were over 33,000. This was nearly 9% of all clerical workers. Over the 40 years from 1890 to 1930 employment in this sub-occupation grew at an average annual compound growth rate of 8.3%, the fastest growth taking place in the early years. In 1920 and 1930 almost 22% of all clerical workers were stenographers and typists. The functions performed by typists are similar to those of copyists who had been enumerated with clerks in the earlier years.

Bookkeepers, cashiers, and accountants experienced impressive numerical growth over the period but declined as a percentage of total clerical workers. This probably does not indicate a decline in bookkeeping activities as a percent of all clerical activities but rather reflects a change in organization of bookkeeping functions such that tasks were routinized and divided among a larger number of less skilled clerks under the supervision of a skilled bookkeeper. For example, this observation was made by one of the authors of a 1913 study of women clerical workers in Boston: "In one of the large down-town stores, 131 women are employed in the bookkeeping department but no one could be called a bookkeeper, although 5 earned $18 or more a week. A man combines the results of the women's work and does the only real bookkeeping in the department."[24]

Throughout the entire period the largest group of clerical workers was in the large amorphous category of clerks. It is difficult to know the full range of functions being performed by workers identified as clerks. From 1900 on, some information is available about one sub-group of clerks because the census listed shipping clerks separately from general clerks. In 1900, 10% of all clerks were working as shipping clerks: the proportions who were shipping clerks in the succeeding years were 11% in 1910; 8% in 1920; and 7% in 1930.[25] The great majority of all shipping clerks were employed in trade and manufacturing, and these jobs probably had a large manual component. The 1930 census listed office appliance operators as a separate category of clerks; 2% of all clerks were enumerated in this category though we know that the use of office appliances was more widespread than this would indicate. In 1930

TABLE 4.4

GAINFUL WORKERS IN CLERICAL SUB-OCCUPATIONS 1870-1930

	1870	1880	1890	1900	1910	1920	1930
NUMBER IN EACH SUB-OCCUPATION							
Bookkeepers, cashiers, accountants	31485	78484	159374	255526	486700	734688	930648
Clerks (except clerks in stores)	42609	71926	187969	340165	720498	1487905	1997000
Stenographers and typists	154*	n.a.	33418	112464	316693	615154	811190
Total Clerical	74248	150410	380761	708155	1523891	2837747	3738838
PERCENT OF CLERICAL WORKERS IN SUB-OCCUPATIONS							
Bookkeepers, cashiers, accountants	42.4	52.2	41.9	36.1	31.9	25.9	24.9
Clerks (except clerks in stores)	57.4	47.8	49.4	48.0	47.3	52.4	53.4
Stenographers and typists	0.2*	n.a.	8.8	15.9	20.8	21.7	21.7
	100.0	100.0	100.0	100.0	100.0	100.0	100.0

*Stenographers only.

Source: See Table 4.1

a government survey found that 30% of all women workers in offices used machines other than typewriters in at least part of their work.[26]

Increased Demand for Clerical Labor

The rapid growth in clerical employment in the 60 years from 1870 to 1930 reflects in part increased demand by employers for providers of clerical services. This section will consider determinants of the demand for clerical labor and causes of changes in this demand over time.

Theory of the Demand for a Productive Factor. The demand for a factor of production is a derived demand; that is, it is determined in part by the demand for the good which the factor is used to produce. In addition, the demand for a productive input is determined by the ways that the input is used in production and on the substitution possibilities available in the known production processes—a relationship that is formalized as the production function. The amount of clerical labor demanded at any one time will then depend on (1) the final demand for goods which are produced using clerical labor and (2) the ways in which clerical labor is used in the production process, which are determined by the technical realities of production.[27]

There is some difficulty in talking about the demand for clerical labor because of the problems of specifying the nature of the output produced by such labor and because of the fact that most clerical labor does not directly produce an output for final demand but rather produces an intermediate good. For example, in the manufacturing industry the final demand is for the good which is manufactured and the output of the clerical labor (e.g. the typed letters, purchase orders and bills, filed documents, bookkeeping ledgers) constitutes an intermediate good used in producing the final manufactured good. For purposes of clarity we will define a good called *clerical output* which is an intermediate good, the demand for which is derived from the demand for the final good and related to the production function for that good. We are then talking of two levels of derived demand: (1) the demand for clerical labor and (2) the demand for the intermediate good—clerical output.

The Demand for Clerical Labor as an Input Used to Produce Clerical Output. The demand function for clerical services may be written as:

$$D_{CL_i} = f(W_{CL}, P_{CK}, T, D_{co_i}).$$

where

D_{CL_i} = demand for clerical labor in industry i.

FIGURE 4.1

EFFECT OF A TECHNOLOGICAL ADVANCE ON THE DEMAND CURVE FOR CLERICAL LABOR

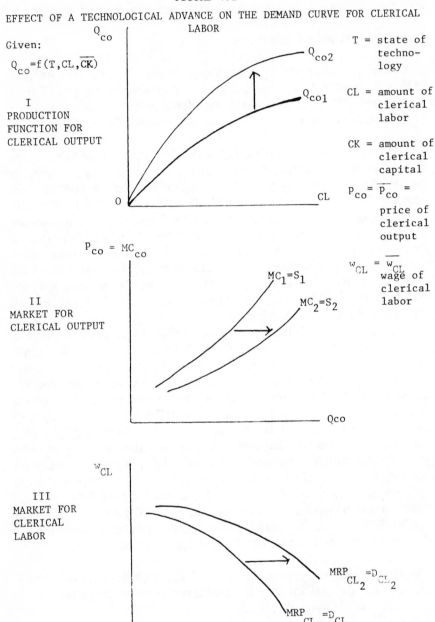

Given:

$Q_{co}=f(T,CL,\overline{CK})$

I
PRODUCTION
FUNCTION FOR
CLERICAL OUTPUT

II
MARKET FOR
CLERICAL OUTPUT

III
MARKET FOR
CLERICAL
LABOR

T = state of technology

CL = amount of clerical labor

CK = amount of clerical capital

$P_{co}= \overline{P_{co}} =$ price of clerical output

$w_{CL} = \overline{w_{CL}}$ wage of clerical labor

W_{CL} = wage of clerical labor. In a competitive industry producers will choose to hire labor to the point that $W_{CL} = VMP_{CL}$.

P_{CK} = price of capital used in the production of clerical output. Conceptually the equation would include the prices of all substitutable or co-operating factors.

T = the state of technology in the production of clerical output including substitution possibilities between CL and CK.

D_{co_i} = demand for clerical output in industry i which is derived in part from the demand for the final good being produced by the industry and is related to the production function for the industry.

We expect that the demand curve for clerical labor will be downward sloping to the right, reflecting a downward sloping marginal product curve. The shape of the demand curve (elasticity of demand) will be determined by (a) the technical possibilities of substituting capital or other kinds of labor for clerical labor; (b) the elasticity of demand for clerical output; and (c) the relative importance of clerical labor costs in the total cost of producing clerical output. Changes in the price of capital, the state of technology and the demand for clerical output will act to shift the demand curve for clerical labor.

Changes in technology and changes in the price of capital may be analyzed together. Many of the technological changes which took place in the clerical sector over this period were embodied in capital equipment and had the effect of reducing the price (raising the quality) of the capital used in the production of clerical output. Other technological advances were organizational and tended to raise the productivity of labor through increased division of labor and rationalization of tasks.

In a production process in which labor is the only variable input (so that there are no substitution possibilities), the effect of a technological advance is unambiguous: each unit of labor will be more productive, the supply curve (MC) of clerical output will shift to the right and the demand curve (VMP) for clerical labor will shift to the right. Therefore, more clerical output will be produced and more clerical services will be hired. The effect of such a technological advance is illustrated in figure 4.1. In panel I a technological advance shifts the production function upward leading to a greater total output for every level of labor input. The effect on the market for clerical output is shown in panel II. The marginal cost curve shifts rightward, indicating the now lowered cost of producing each additional unit of output. The result is that more clerical output is supplied at every price of such output. For any given

FIGURE 4.2 THE RELATIONSHIP BETWEEN CLERICAL EMPLOYMENT GROWTH AND PRODUCTION OF OFFICE EQUIPMENT

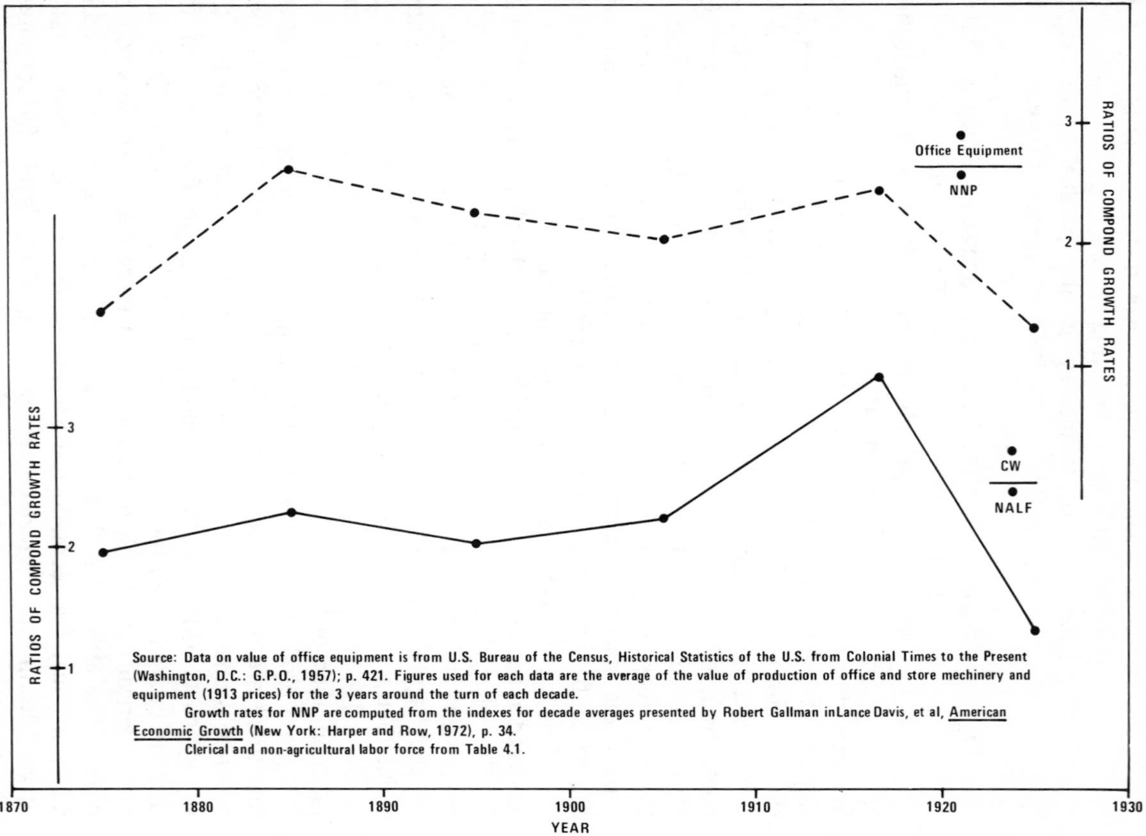

Source: Data on value of office equipment is from U.S. Bureau of the Census, Historical Statistics of the U.S. from Colonial Times to the Present
(Washington, D.C.: G.P.O., 1957); p. 421. Figures used for each data are the average of the value of production of office and store mechinery and
equipment (1913 prices) for the 3 years around the turn of each decade.
        Growth rates for NNP are computed from the indexes for decade averages presented by Robert Gallman in Lance Davis, et al, American
Economic Growth (New York: Harper and Row, 1972), p. 34.
        Clerical and non-agricultural labor force from Table 4.1.

downward sloping demand curve for clerical output, technological advance will result in a fall in the price of clerical output. The effect of the technological advance on the market for clerical labor is illustrated in panel III. The value of marginal product ($VMP_{CL} = MPP_{CL} \cdot P_{co}$) of clerical labor increases, indicating that at every possible wage rate, a greater amount of such labor will be demanded.

If there is more than one variable input, the situation is more complicated and the outcome for hiring is problematical. Two effects are possible: (1) a substitution effect whereby the cheaper capital would be substituted for labor reducing the amount of labor hired (so long as the elasticity of substitution is greater than zero some such input substitution will take place), and (2) an output effect whereby the reduction in the price of one factor leads to a movement to a higher isoquant and the increased hiring of both factors.[28] If the substitution effect dominates, the demand curve for clerical labor would shift leftward in response to a fall in the price of capital (technological advance). If the output effect dominates, the demand curve will shift rightward. In theory it is possible for either effect to dominate.

The issue is basically an empirical one in this case of whether technological advances led to the hiring of more or less clerical labor. Some conclusions on this issue can be drawn from figure 4.2 which presents evidence on the relationship between the hiring of clerical labor and the use of clerical capital from 1870 to 1930. The solid line shows the ratio of the average annual growth rate of clerical labor to the average annual growth rate of the non-agricultural labor force. The dashed line is the ratio of the growth rates of office equipment production to Net National Product. That the two series move generally together suggests that capital and labor were co-operating factors in the production of clerical output and that the output effect of technological advances dominated to shift the demand curve for clerical labor to the right over time.

The two decades of most rapid growth in office equipment production coincided with the decades of greatest clerical labor force growth, i.e., 1880–1890 and 1910–1920. It is likely that the growth in the 1880s largely reflects the changes associated with the adoption and spread of the typewriter, which was first produced commercially in 1873 and was widely adopted in the 1880s. The later part of the decade 1910–1920 saw a wave of new inventions in the office that was associated with the spread of Taylorism.

The Demand for Clerical Output as an Input Used in the Production of Goods for Final Demand. The other major shift variable for the demand

curve for clerical labor is the demand for clerical output. The demand
function for clerical output may be written as:

$$D_{co_i} \quad = \quad f\,[\,P_{co},\ P_{I_i},\ D_{F_i},\ (co/co + I)_i\,].$$

where

D_{co_i}	=	the demand for clerical output by industry i.
P_{co}	=	the price of clerical output which is determined by the prices and productivities of the inputs used to produce clerical output.
P_{I_i}	=	the prices of all other inputs used in producing the finished output of industry i.
D_{F_i}	=	the demand for the finished product of industry i.
$(co/co + I)_i$	=	the share of clerical output in the total amount of inputs used in production by industry i. This will depend on technological considerations and institutional factors which govern the amount of clerical output used in the production processes of industry i. Firm size, government requirements for record keeping, and use of scientific management principles would tend to influence the amount of clerical output used by an industry.

The demand curve for clerical output is expected to be negatively sloped
with more clerical goods demanded at lower prices. The price of clerical
output is related to the prices and productivities of inputs used. A
reduction in the price of clerical output due to technological advance
leads to more clerical output being demanded because of movement
down the demand curve. The elasticity of demand is related to the
technical substitution possibilities in the production of the final good, the
elasticity of demand for the final good, and the share of clerical costs in
the total costs of the industry. Therefore, the demand for clerical output
will be less elastic in industries in which technological or institutional
factors limit the substitution possibilities, in industries which use a small
amount of clerical output in the production of the final good, and in
industries in which the demand for the final good is inelastic.

The major shift variables for the demand curve for clerical output
are D_{F_i}, the demand for the final good, and $(co/co + I)_i$, the share of
clerical output in the total inputs used in the industry, which is
determined by technological and institutional factors. It is possible to
make some determination of the strengths of these two shift variables by
examining the changing industrial distribution of the clerical labor force
over time. Some portion of the increased demand for clerical output can

TABLE 4.5

INDUSTRIAL DISTRIBUTION OF GAINFUL WORKERS, 1870–1930

	1870	1880	1890	1900	1910	1920	1930
Agriculture/Forestry/Fishing	50.2	50.1	42.8	37.6	31.6	27.4	22.0
Mining	1.5	1.8	2.0	2.6	2.9	3.0	2.4
Manufacturing	17.4	18.2	20.0	21.8	22.4	26.1	22.5
Construction	5.8	4.8	6.1	5.7	6.3	5.2	6.2
Transportation/Public Utilities	5.0	4.9	6.4	7.2	8.7	10.1	9.9
Trade	6.1	6.7	7.7	8.5	9.2	9.8	12.3
Finance/Real Estate/Insurance	0.3	0.4	0.7	1.0	1.4	1.9	2.9
Professional (includes education)	2.6	3.0	3.6	4.0	4.5	5.4	7.0
Domestic/Personal Service	9.2	8.3	9.1	9.3	10.0	8.0	9.9
Government (includes military)	0.8	0.8	0.8	1.0	1.5	2.2	2.1
Not allocated	1.1	1.1	0.7	1.3	1.6	0.9	2.7
TOTAL	100.0	100.0	100.0	100.0	100.0	100.0	100.0
Commodity Producing	75.0	74.8	70.9	67.7	63.1	61.7	53.0
Service Producing	23.9	24.0	28.3	31.0	35.3	37.4	44.2
Not allocated	1.1	1.1	0.7	1.3	1.6	0.9	2.7
TOTAL	100.0	100.0	100.0	100.0	100.0	100.0	100.0

Source: Derived from Solomon Fabricant, "The Changing Industrial Distribution of Gainful
Workers: Comments on the Decennial Statistics, 1800–1940," in Universities
National Bureau of Economic Research, Conference on Research in Income and Wealth,
XI (New York: NBER, 1949) p. 42. NOTE: Distribution between trade and financial
sectors derived from p. 47.

be related to increased production in the various industries; the remainder would be due to the increased use of clerical output within industries. It would be preferable to have information on the industrial distribution of output and the value of clerical output used in the production of each industry. Such information is not available, and we will be forced to make inferences from data on the industrial distribution of the labor force. This implicitly ignores the effects of other inputs and different productivity changes among inputs and industries, but since we are interested mainly in the demand for labor, the exercise should have significant value.

The Industrial Distribution of the Labor Force. Table 4.5 shows the proportion of all gainful workers in each industry at each census date. Over the 60-year period the total labor force grew at an average annual rate of 3.0%. Since all industries except agriculture/forestry/fishing grew faster than the total labor force, their shares of total employment increased. Employment in five of the six service-producing industries grew faster than did employment in the non-agricultural labor force. The fastest growth in employment came in the finance/real estate/insurance industry which was small throughout the period but grew at a long term annual rate of 6% so that it contained 3% of total gainful workers by 1930. Government and professional service also experienced spectacular growth but remained comparatively small. Trade and transportation/public utilities are the other two industrial sectors which exceeded the long term growth rate for the non-agricultural labor force. Over the 60-year period both industries approximately doubled their share of the total labor force. The decline of the agricultural sector can be clearly seen in its fall from 50% of the labor force in 1870 to 22% in 1930. The manufacturing sector increased its share of the total labor force; but since it grew slower than the total non-agricultural labor force, its share of non-agricultural employment declined.

Although detailed breakdowns of output by industry are not available to parallel the labor force figures, enough information about changes in the industrial breakdown of output is available to determine that there are important differences between movements in output and employment by industry. Therefore we may be aware of some of the biases resulting from using labor force data to make inferences about output.

Robert Gallman and Edward Howle provided distributions of value added in agriculture and industry and distributions of national income originating in commodity production and all other sectors for this period.[29] Gallman and Howle found little trend in the distribution of output between commodity and service production, though the share of service-producing industries in the labor force grew considerably.

Because the service sectors' share of labor recources grew faster than did their share of output, it may be concluded that labor productivity was increasing at a slower rate in the service-producing sectors than in the economy as a whole. This finding parallels findings by Kuznets for a larger number of countries.[30] Within the commodity-producing sector Kuznets found that agriculture's share of output declined at about the same rate as did its share in the labor force. This implies that the productivity of labor employed in agriculture grew at about the same rate as the productivity of labor in the economy as a whole, while the productivity of labor employed in industry grew at greater than the economy-wide rate.[31]

Gallman and Howle estimated sectoral levels of labor income per worker for commodity and service production before 1900. They found that income was higher in service production but that there was convergence over time in sectoral income levels.[32] The implication of this is that the productivity of labor employed in services was higher, but increased slower than, labor employed in commodity production. As we shall see, clerical workers were largely employed in service-producing industries.

The growth in clerical employment is closely tied to the demand for service output because most clerical workers were employed in service-producing industries though a growing proportion were employed in the manufacturing sector as time went on. The findings of Gallman and Howle, and Kuznets suggest that the productivity of clerical labor was probably not growing as fast as productivity in the economy as a whole and that therefore clerical output did not grow at as fast a rate as did the clerical labor force.

The Industrial Distribution of Clerical Employment. This section uses information in the industrial distribution of clerical employment to divide the total growth in the clerical labor force into three component parts:

(1) the number of clerical workers who would have been employed at time $(t+n)$ if all industries had grown at the same rate as did the total labor force and if there had been no change in the percentage clerical in the work force of each industry since time (t). This change will be referred to as Type I or change due to *labor force growth.*

(2) the additional number of clerical workers who would have been employed at time $(t+n)$ if industries had grown at their actual rate but there had been no change in the percentage clerical in each industry's

TABLE 4.6

CLERICAL EMPLOYMENT BY INDUSTRY, 1870, 1880, 1910, 1930

	1870	1880	1910	1930
Agriculture/Forestry/Fishing	0	0	2801	7396
Mining	0	0	11563	24003
Manufacturing	5861	10114	407151	945562
Construction	0	0	14682	50343
Transportation/Public Utilities	8332	14187	246444	498933
Trade	31177	59790	424487	670091
Finance/Real Estate/Insurance	8671	13087	200754	584276
Professional (includes education)	6292	25467	63415	247867
Domestic/Personal Service	5243	10916	59474	106258
Government (includes military)	8672	16849	123937	284708
Unallocated	0	0	0	282841
TOTAL	74248	150410	1553708	3702278

Sources: Figures compiled from:

1870 - U. S. Bureau of the Census, 1870 Census Compendium pp. 604-615.

1880 - U. S. Bureau of the Census, 1880 Census Compendium p. 1368-1377.

1910 - U. S. Bureau of the Census, 1910 Census of Population, IV, Occupations, pp. 302-433.

1930 - U. S. Bureau of the Census, 1930 Census of Population, V, General Report on Occupations, pp. 412- 587.

work force since time (t). This will be referred to as Type II or change due to *differential industrial growth.*

(3) the additional number of clerical workers who were hired because of changes within industries in the percentage clerical of the industry's work force. This will be referred to as Type III or *intra-industry clerical growth.*

This division explicitly recognizes that changes in the employment of clerical labor were related to changes in the amounts and kinds of goods produced for final demand and to changes in the methods used to produce these goods.

Breakdowns of occupational data by industry were not routinely provided in the U.S. census during the period before 1940. However, the 1910 and 1930 censuses published tables of industrial employment by occupation which allow for computation of clerical employment in each industry for those dates. In addition, the 1870 and 1880 censuses presented data on clerical employment in such a way that it was possible to assign clerical employment to various industries in those years. The results of the collection of these industry-occupation breakdowns for 1870, 1880, 1910, and 1930 are presented as table 4.6. The numbers are total clerical workers employed in each industry. The totals for 1910 and 1930 are not precisely equal to the totals of clerical employment for those dates as presented in table 4.1. The figures in table 4.1 are based on those developed by Alba Edwards, and they embody a number of correction factors.[33] Those in table 4.6 were developed by counting up entries in the occupation-by-industry tables in the various censuses. No attempt was made to correct the totals to conform with Edwards's data. The numbers are quite similar to Edwards's, and there is no reason to believe that the industrial distribution of clerical workers as it appeared in the censuses is seriously biased. The figures for 1870 and 1880 are computed on the basis of similar data and are therefore comparable; the same may be said for 1910 and 1930. The comparability of the two sets of data is probably less reliable.

Table 4.7 shows how the share of clerical labor in the industries' work forces changed over time, and table 4.8 shows how total clerical employment was distributed over industries. Examination of these two tables reveals those industries which were responsible for the largest shares of clerical employment. Table 4.7 shows that the finance/real estate/insurance industry had the highest proportion of its labor force in clerical occupations at all dates. Over 20% of all workers in that industry were employed in clerical jobs in 1870, when only 1% of the total labor force was in clerical work. By 1930 over 40% of all workers in the finance industry were classified as clerical. Government service was the

TABLE 4.7

CLERICAL WORKERS AS A PROPORTION OF THE LABOR FORCE,
BY INDUSTRY, 1870, 1880, 1910, 1930

	1870	1880	1910	1930	Ratio of Compound Growth Rates $\frac{\dot{LF}\text{ (industry)}}{\dot{LF}\text{ (total)}}$ 1870-1930
Agriculture/Forestry/Fishing	----	----	0.02	0.07	0.36
Mining	----	----	1.10	2.09	1.36
Manufacturing	0.26	0.32	4.95	8.60	1.23
Construction	----	----	0.64	1.16	1.09
Transportation/Public Utilities	1.30	1.65	7.74	10.29	1.55
Trade	3.96	5.17	12.60	11.11	1.59
Finance/Real Estate/Insurance	20.17	20.77	38.61	41.15	2.73
Professional (includes education)	1.91	4.90	3.80	7.27	1.82
Domestic/Personal Service	0.44	0.96	1.62	2.20	1.09
Government (includes military)	8.67	12.04	22.95	27.12	1.82
TOTAL	0.57	0.86	4.23	7.58	
Non-Agricultural Labor Force	1.14	1.71	6.17	9.64	1.37

Sources: See Table 4.6

TABLE 4.8

INDUSTRIAL DISTRIBUTION OF CLERICAL EMPLOYMENT,
1870, 1880, 1910, 1930

	1870	1880	1910	1930
Agriculture/Forestry/Fishing	0.00	0.00	0.18	0.20
Mining	0.00	0.00	0.74	0.65
Manufacturing	7.90	6.72	26.21	25.54
Construction	0.00	0.00	0.94	1.36
Transportation/Public Utilities	11.22	9.43	11.86	13.48
Trade	41.99	39.75	27.32	18.10
Finance/Real Estate/Insurance	11.68	8.70	12.92	15.78
Professional (includes education)	8.49	16.93	4.08	6.70
Domestic/Personal Service	7.06	7.26	3.83	2.87
Government (includes military)	11.68	11.20	7.93	7.69
Unallocated	0.00	0.00	0.00	7.64
	100.0	100.0	100.0	100.0

Sources: See Table 4.6

second most clerical intensive industry at each date. Both of these industries employed small though rapidly growing shares of the total work force.

The final column of table 4.7 presents information on the relative rapidity of growth of total employment in each industry over the entire period. The number is the average annual compound growth rate of employment in the industry divided by the growth rate of total employment in the economy. These figures reveal that the financial sector, which was the industry most likely to hire clerical labor, was also the fastest growing in terms of employment. The result of this rapid growth is that in 1870 11.68% of all clerical workers were in the financial industry, and by 1930 nearly 16% of all clerical workers were in that same industry (see table 4.8). Total employment in government service grew somewhat slower and the propensity to hire clerical workers grew faster in some of the larger industries so that by 1930, 7.69% of all clerical workers were employed by the government, and 27.12% of all government employees were clerical workers.

Table 4.7 shows that although there were increases in the proportion clerical in all industries, there was little change in the ranking of industries by their propensity to hire clerical workers from 1870 to 1930. In general the industries that were most likely to hire clerical help in 1870 are the same that were most likely to do so in 1930. The most notable change was in the manufacturing industry which hired over one-quarter of all clerical workers in 1930 and which experienced growth in the clerical share of its labor force from 0.26% to 8.6%.

By comparing the growth rates of total employment in the final column of table 4.7 with the clerical shares of industrial employment in the other columns, we can note the tendency of those industries with the greatest propensity to hire clerical labor also to be the industries which experienced the fastest growth in overall employment. A statistical test of the strength of this association can be performed by computing the Spearman rank order correlation coefficient for percentage clerical with overall growth rates. Such a test was performed using the ranking of percentage clerical in each industry's total employment in 1930 and the ranking of relative growth for each industry's total labor force over the period 1870–1930. The resulting Spearman rank-order correlation coefficient is .88 which is significant at the 1% level, indicating a very high correspondence between an industry's propensity to hire clerical workers and its long term rate of growth in total employment.

As described earlier, it is possible to break down the total change in the clerical labor force over a given period into three measurable parts by using a simple components of difference technique.

(1) Type I or *labor force growth* equals the portion of the actual change in clerical employment that would have resulted if employment in all industries had grown at the same rate and there had been no change in the percentage of each industry's work force in clerical occupations. For any change from period (t) to period (t+n), type I change within an industry is computed as:

$$\left[\Delta E \cdot \left(\frac{E_i}{E} \right)_t \cdot \left(\frac{C_i}{E_i} \right)_t \right] / \Delta C$$

where   E = employment (all industries)
        E_i = employment in industry i
        C = clerical employment (all industries)
        C_i = clerical employment in industry i.

If there were no differential growth in labor productivity among industries, Type I change would merely reflect the increased scale of the economy, holding constant the industrial distribution of output and the production functions for final products.

(2) Type II change is equal to the proportion of the actual change in clerical employment that is associated with *differential industrial growth.* It has already been noted that the most rapidly growing industries (in terms of employment) were those which had relatively high proportions of their labor forces in clerical jobs. In general employment will grow fastest in industries which produce goods with high income elasticities, low price elasticities, and low productivity growth. Type II growth reflects the effects of these differing elasticities of demand and the relative labor intensities of production processes in the various industries.

Type II change for any industry is calculated as:

$$\left[E_{t-n} \cdot \Delta \left(\frac{E_i}{E} \right) \cdot \left(\frac{C_i}{E_i} \right)_t \right] / \Delta C$$

This is the proportion of the growth of clerical employment, additional to that attributable to Type I growth, which would have taken place in an industry if the labor force in the industry had grown at its actual historical rate but there had been no changes in the propensity to hire clerical workers. This calculation, because it uses the industry employment level at time (t+n), includes clerical employment growth attributable to the interaction between overall labor force growth and differential growth of industries.[34]

(3) Type III change (*intra-industry clerical growth*) is equal to the actual change in clerical employment within an industry over a given period exclusive of the changes due to labor force growth and differential

TABLE 4.9

APPORTIONING OF PERIOD CHANGES IN CLERICAL EMPLOYMENT TO CAUSE, BY INDUSTRY

	1870-1880				1880-1910				1910-1930				1870-1930			
	Type I	Type II	Type III	TOTAL	Type I	Type II	Type III	TOTAL	Type I	Type II	Type III	TOTAL	Type I	Type II	Type III	TOTAL
AGRICULTURE FORESTRY FISHING	0.0	0.0	0.0	0.0	0.0	0.0	0.2	0.2	0.0	-0.0	0.2	0.2	0.0	0.0	0.2	0.2
MINING	0.0	0.0	0.0	0.0	0.0	0.0	0.8	0.8	0.2	-0.1	0.5	0.6	0.0	0.0	0.6	0.6
MANUFACTURING	2.7	0.5	2.4	5.6	0.8	0.3	27.1	28.2	6.2	0.1	18.7	25.1	0.4	0.2	25.3	25.9
CONSTRUCTION	0.0	0.0	0.0	0.0	0.0	0.0	1.0	1.0	0.2	0.0	1.4	1.6	0.0	0.0	1.4	1.4
TRANSPORTATION COMMUNICATION PUBLIC UTILITIES	3.8	0.0	3.9	7.7	1.1	1.6	13.8	16.6	3.8	2.2	5.8	11.8	0.6	0.9	12.0	13.5
TRADE	14.2	5.1	18.3	37.6	4.7	3.4	17.8	25.9	6.5	9.1	-4.2	11.4	2.4	3.3	11.9	17.6
FINANCE INSURANCE REAL ESTATE	3.9	1.4	0.5	5.8	1.0	5.7	6.6	13.4	3.1	13.1	1.7	17.9	0.7	7.0	8.2	15.9

TABLE 4.9 (Continued)

	1870-1880				1880-1910				1910-1930				1870-1930			
	Type I	Type II	Type III	TOTAL	Type I	Type II	Type III	TOTAL	Type I	Type II	Type III	TOTAL	Type I	Type II	Type III	TOTAL
PROFESSIONAL SERVICE (INCLUDES EDUCATION)	2.9	1.9	20.4	25.2	2.0	2.0	-1.3	2.7	1.0	2.1	5.5	8.6	0.5	1.1	5.0	6.6
DOMESTIC AND PERSONAL SERVICE	2.4	-0.9	6.0	7.4	0.9	0.3	2.3	3.5	0.9	0.0	1.3	2.2	0.4	0.0	2.3	2.8
GOVERNMENT SERVICE (INCLUDES MILITARY)	3.9	0.6	6.2	10.7	1.3	2.1	4.2	7.6	1.9	3.5	2.0	7.4	0.7	1.6	5.3	7.6
UNALLOCATED TO INDUSTRY	0.0	0.0	0.0	0.0	0.0	0.0	0.0	0.0	4.4	3.0	5.8	13.2	0.0	0.0	7.8	7.8
TOTAL	33.8	8.5	57.8	100.0	11.9	15.5	72.5	100.0	28.2	33.0	38.7	100.0	5.7	14.2	80.1	100.0

Type I = % of period change in clerical employment due to overall labor force growth

Type II = % of period change in clerical employment due to differential growth of industries.

Type III = % of period change in clerical employment due to change in % clerical within industries.

Sources: See Table 4.6.

industrial growth. It includes all the additional clerical employment associated with changes within industries in the propensity to use clerical labor in the production of final output, i.e., production function changes.

Type III change for an industry is calculated as:

$$\left[E_{t+n} \cdot \left(\frac{E_i}{E} \right)_{t+n} \cdot \Delta \left(\frac{C_i}{E_i} \right) \right] / \Delta C$$

This takes as given the growth of the labor force and the change in industries' share of employment from (t) to (t+n). Therefore Type III growth includes all interactions of Type I and Type II growth with changes in clerical share of employment.[35]

Both Type I and Type II changes reflect the effects on clerical employment of changes in the level and structure of final demand which accompanied economic development from 1870 to 1930. Type III, on the other hand, reflects changes on the supply side of the various industries, i.e., changes in the amounts of clerical inputs used in production processes.

The industrial breakdowns of clerical employment as presented in table 4.6 have been used to compute the shares of change in total clerical gainful workers associated with Type I, Type II, and Type III changes in each industry for various periods. The results of this computation are presented as table 4.9. The cell entries are the percentage of the period change in total clerical employment due to each type of change for each industry. For example, for the period 1870-1880 we see that 5.6% of the total change in clerical employment was due to the growth of clerical employment in the manufacturing industry. The 5.6% change can be broken down into 2.7% due to simple growth of employment in the industry, an additional 0.5% due to the fact that manufacturing employment grew faster than overall employment, and 2.4% due to the increased propensity of manufacturing establishments to hire clerical labor. Overall, for this decade, 33.8% of total clerical employment growth was due to simple labor force growth, 8.5% was due to the fact that industries with a greater propensity to hire clerical workers grew faster than the overall rate, and 57.8% was due to increased propensities to hire clerical workers within industries. The industries which contributed most to clerical employment growth were professional services where the overwhelming cause of change was the greater clerical share of employment within the industry in 1880, and trade, where both Type I and Type III growth were important.

The results for the period 1880–1910 present a number of difficulties. The first is that the industrial breakdowns of clerical employment are not strictly comparable for the two dates, and the second is that for a 30-year period production function changes are more important than they would be over a shorter period. We therefore expect to find Type III change to be more important when the analysis takes place over such a long period, especially a period such as 1880–1910, which saw massive changes in the structure of the economy and the technology of clerical work. As expected, the analysis finds that the overwhelming portion (72.5%) of the total growth was due to Type III change.

Much can be learned, though, by examining the distribution of growth over industries. Over 28% of the 30-year increase in clerical employment was located in the manufacturing industry; virtually all of this was due to the increase in the propensity of manufacturing firms to use clerical labor as an input in the manufacturing production process. Trade, transportation, and financial services all contributed significantly to the growth in clerical employment. The largest share of the growth in clerical employment in these industries was due to increases in the proportion of clerical workers in the industries' total employment. However, nearly 6% of the 30-year clerical growth was due to the extremely rapid growth of the financial industry which had a high propensity to hire clerical workers as early as 1880.

The most reliable data for analyzing clerical employment change by industry is available for the period 1910–1930. Over these 20 years one-quarter of the growth in clerical employment was in the manufacturing sector, with most of it being due to production function (Type III) changes. The second most important industry was finance/insurance/real estate, which showed little change in the propensity to hire clerical workers but which contributed 13% of total clerical increase due to the disproportionate growth of the sector.

The transportation industry contributed 11.8% of total clerical growth, 3.8% due to labor force growth, 2.2% due to differential industrial growth, and 5.8% due to intra-industry clerical growth. Trade contributed 11.4% of total clerical growth, even though the proportion of total employment in trade represented by clerical workers declined over the 20 years. Both government and professional service contributed significantly to the growth of employment of clerical labor from 1910 to 1930; in professional service, the major cause was production function changes, whereas, in government the growth of the sector itself was the major cause of clerical increase.

Overall, for the 20 years from 1910 to 1930, 28.2% of total clerical employment growth was due to overall labor force growth, 33% was due to differential industrial growth and 38.7% was due to intra-industry clerical growth.

For the long period, 1870 to 1930, the picture is, as expected, dominated by structural change in the way that goods were produced,

FIGURE 4.3

ILLUSTRATION OF INCREASED USE OF CLERICAL OUTPUT

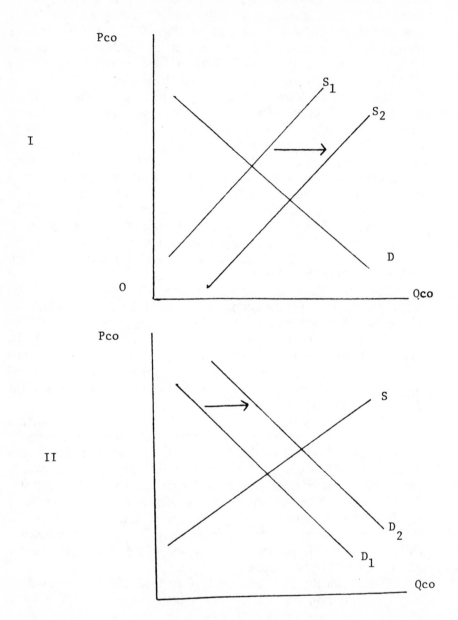

Pco = price of clerical output

Qco = quantity of clerical output

i.e., Type III changes. Within all industries there was a significant increase in the propensity to use clerical services in the production of final goods. The biggest contributor to growth was the manufacturing sector, where virtually all of the change was due to Type III changes. In one case there is a significant contribution to the long term growth of clerical employment made by the disproportionately rapid growth of a clerical intensive industry. Seven percent of the 60-year increase in clerical employment was due to the growth of the financial services industry.

Causes and Effects of Demand Changes. This section uses the results of the components of difference analysis as reported in table 4.9 to draw inferences about the importance of various factors which increased demand for clerical labor. The emphasis will be on mechanisms which led to shifts in the demand curve for clerical labor; supply factors are largely ignored. Consequently, the results presented in this section are maximum estimates of total clerical employment growth attributable to various demand related causes.

As was discussed earlier, the demand for clerical labor is derived from the demand for clerical output, which is in turn derived from the demand for goods and services produced using clerical output. Increases in the quantity of clerical output demanded will lead to greater demand for clerical labor. Factors which affect the amount of clerical output demanded can be divided into two broad catogories:

(1) Volume and industrial distribution of final goods and services produced by the economy. Increased levels of output will shift the demand curve for clerical output to the right, which will induce a similar shift in the demand curve for clerical labor. The proportion of clerical employment change due to such factors is measured as Type I and Type II changes.

(2) Propensities to use clerical output as an input in the production of final goods and services; i.e., the nature of production functions. Type III change estimates the portion of clerical employment growth attributable to these production function changes. An increase in the amount of clerical output used in production processes within industries can be accomplished through two mechanisms. They are illustrated in figure 4.3. In Panel I, the amount of clerical output demanded by an industry could increase as a result of a rightward shift in the supply curve of clerical output which would reduce the price, causing more to be purchased for any given demand schedule. A likely cause of this situation in the clerical output market is technological advance which reduced the unit price of clerical output and increased the value of

TABLE 4.10

SUMMARY OF CAUSES OF CHANGE IN THE DEMAND FOR CLERICAL LABOR

<u>DEMAND FOR GOODS CHANGES</u>

CASE A -- measured as Type I change

• increased scale of economy (population growth) (and income growth) → increased demand for all final goods → shifts demand curve for final goods to right → shifts demand curve for clerical output to right → shifts demand curve for clerical labor to right

CASE B -- measured as Type II change

• increased income per capita with
• differing income elasticities of demand
• more complex, urbanized society

→ change in structure of final demand → shifts demand curve for final goods to right → shifts demand curve for clerical output to right → shifts demand curve for clerical labor to right

<u>PRODUCTION FUNCTION CHANGES</u>

CASE C -- measured as part of Type III change

• technological advance in the production of clerical output (mechanical and organizational) → shift supply curve for clerical output to right → reduces price of clerical output by movement downward along demand curve → increases producti-vity of clerical labor → shifts demand curve for clerical labor to right

CASE D -- measured as part of Type III change

• increased firm size
• concentrated industries
• scientific management
• government regulation
• tax laws

→ increases demand for clerical output within industries → shifts demand curve for clerical output to right → shifts demand curve for clerical labor to right

marginal product of clerical labor. An exogenous increase in the supply of labor to the clerical market would have the same effect by lowering the cost of producing a unit of clerical output and causing the supply curve to shift to the right.

Panel II of figure 4.3 illustrates the other major demand related cause of increased use of clerical output within industries. An exogenous shift in the demand curve for clerical output will increase the amount of clerical output purchased for any given supply schedule. Reasons for shifts in industries' demand curves for clerical labor include: larger, multi-plant, vertically integrated firms whose complex organizational structures depended on collection, transmission, and analysis of unprecedented amounts of information;[36] increased interregional and international trade which stimulated more long distance communication; spread of scientific management techniques which required more measuring and record keeping; increased role of government, which demanded more record keeping of businesses because of regulation and tax laws, and which used greater numbers of clerical workers within its own growing bureaucracy.

The mechanisms which led to shifts in the demand curve for clerical labor are summarized in table 4.10. The second column lists underlying historical changes in the structure of the economy which contributed to changes in the demand for clerical labor.

The first case is straightforward. Increased scale of the economy (greater population and income) led to increases in the demand for all final goods and services and therefore resulted in the hiring of more clerical labor. Such simple growth was responsible for 34% of all clerical labor force growth from 1870 to 1880, 12% from 1880 to 1910, and 28% from 1920 to 1930.

Case B, change in the structure of final demand, is due partly to the effect of differing income elasticities of demand for the output of various industries. As per capita income grew over time the proportion spent on various goods changed. The classic example of this was pointed out by Engle in the nineteenth century: as income increases, the proportion spent on food declines. As income increased in the U.S. and as the economy became more complex, larger portions of the labor force were in manufacturing and service industries as the agriculture sector shrank in relative terms. Service employment grew much faster than manufacturing employment (see table 4.5). We know that manufacturing's share of total demand increased faster than its share of the labor force and that for the service sector, labor input increased faster than output relative to the entire economy.

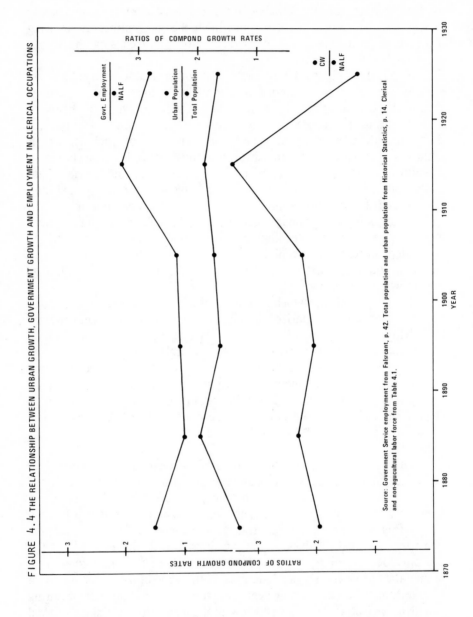

FIGURE 4. 4 THE RELATIONSHIP BETWEEN URBAN GROWTH, GOVERNMENT GROWTH AND EMPLOYMENT IN CLERICAL OCCUPATIONS

RATIOS OF COMPOND GROWTH RATES

Govt. Employment / NALF

Urban Population / Total Population

CW / NALF

Source: Government Service employment from Falscrant, p. 42. Total population and urban population from Historical Statistics, p. 14. Clerical and non-agucultural labor force from Table 4.1.

Kuznets, and Gallman and Howle found no trend in the value of output of the service sector relative to total output in the economy.[37] However, the production of service output tends to be labor intensive; even with no trend in output share, there was an observed increase in the proportion of the labor force employed in services. Kuznets offers a number of possible reasons for the increase in service production, all of them related to increased complexity and concentration of the modernizing economy and to varying income elasticities of demand. He argues that the rise in demand for labor intensive service output is related to the greater complexity of the expanding economy with larger production units, more concentrated commodity production necessitating more complex distribution networks, more intermediaries between producers and consumers, concentrated urban populatons demanding government services, and rising consumers' incomes leading to greater demand for health care, recreation, education and other such services which have high income elasticities of demand.[38]

Many of the explanations offered above are related to the expanded need for services that accompany greater population concentrations. We would therefore expect to see an association between clerical employment growth and urbanization. The two lower curves on the graph in figure 4.4 show the correspondence between the growth of the clerical labor force relative to the total non-agricultural labor force and the rapidity of urban growth relative to total population growth. The data points are ratios of average annual compound growth rates for decades graphed at the mid-point of the decade. We see some tendency for decades of most rapid urban growth to be decades of most rapid growth in clerical employment. This suggests that the structure of demand associated with urban growth does indeed work in favor of increasing the clerical component of the labor force.

The industries which contributed most to clerical employment through their very rapid growth were trade, finance/insurance/real estate, and government. Some of the largest users of clerical labor in the trade sector were the mail order houses for retail selling, such as Montgomery Ward and Sears, Roebuck and Company. These began in the 1870s and '80s and grew rapidly around the turn of the century. Chain stores such as A & P, which opened in the 1870s, were also big users of clerical labor.[39] Information on the expansion of the role of government in the economy can be seen in the top curve in figure 4.4. This shows movement over time in the ratio of the growth rate of government employment (minus military) relative to the growth of the non-agricultural labor force. After 1890 the pattern of growth of government employment was similar to the pattern of total clerical growth. The finance/insurance/real estate industry was the fastest growing industry and employed the greatest proportion of clerical labor. Growth of this sector was extremely rapid throughout the period. Thomas Cochran suggests that part of the growth of the sector in the later decades was due to the automobile, which led to suburbanization and a real estate boom, and to World War I, in which "government military life and endowment policies . . . made people more familiar with insurance."[40]

The portion of total clerical employment growth due to the differential growth of industries with high propensities to use clerical labor was 8.5% in 1870–80, 15.5% in 1880–1910, and 33% in 1910–30.

As described in Case C (table 4.10) increases in the supply of clerical output would lower the equilibrium price of such output and increase the quantity demanded. Among the major forces acting to lower the price of clerical output were technological advances in office production of the sort discussed earlier in this chapter. This mechanization and routinization of office production increased the productivity of labor employed in producing clerical output, thereby shifting the demand curve for such labor to the right. In general these technological changes were economy-wide so that all industries experienced similar possibilities for reduction in the price of clerical output. However, not all industries had the same elasticity of demand for clerical output so not all would expand hiring in the same way in response to a given technological advance.

The effect on clerical employment growth of technologically-induced changes in the productivity of clerical labor is included in Type III change in table 4.9. Type III change accounted for 58% of total clerical employment growth from 1870 to 1880; 72.5% from 1880 to 1910; and 39% from 1910 to 1930. Also included in Type III change are the effects of exogenous changes in the demand for clerical output and exogenous changes in the supply of clerical labor. These effects will be discussed below. Unfortunately, the data available do not allow Type III change to be separated into portions contributed by each of these three effects.

Exogenous increases in the demand for clerical labor within industries (Case D) resulted from various changes in the organization of productive activity and in the relations between government and business. Increased size of business firms and greater use of the corporate form of organization worked in favor of greater use of clerical output. Larger firms tended to have proportionally larger and more structured managerial bureaucracies that increased the amount of paperwork. Corporations needed to prepare financial statements and other records to submit to stockholders. Pressure by the New York Stock Exchange and the passage of laws requiring financial disclosure by corporations in most states forced greater data collection and dissemination of information on the conditions of corporations. This also stimulated the growth of the accounting profession.[41]

Larger, vertically integrated businesses resulting from mergers and from the growth of multi-plant firms and multi-divisional plants increased the demand for communication and detailed record keeping. These large, complex businesses were more likely to adopt principles of scientific management that required detailed monitoring of operations and data collection in order to make appropriate decisions.[42]

The government, through its expanding roles as regulator of business and tax collector, was responsible for increasing the demand for clerical output. The first corporate income tax law was passed in 1909 and the Sixteenth Amendment was ratified in 1913 allowing for personal income taxes. The financing of World War I led to the first substantial income tax levy.[43] Government regulatory agencies, which increased in number at the beginning of the century, required that businesses maintain records in standardized ways and submit regular reports. The Federal Reserve Board (begun in 1913) not only required data submission from banks under its aegis but also set standards for the kinds of data that banks had to collect from loan applicants. Not all such agencies were successful in actually regulating business practices, but they tended to be effective as demanders of paperwork. In the case of one such agency it was said, "the useful functions of the FTC became the compiling of a mass of data helpful to economists."[44] The effects of government actions on business practices which stimulated clerical demand were greatest in the decades after 1910.

One possible cause of increased demand for clerical output that was often suggested by contemporary observers has to do with the effect of the invention and spread of office machinery on the standards of business communication and record keeping. The argument was that the availability of the means of producing typed letters, telephone messages, regularly-audited accounts, multiple copies of everything, etc. changed habits in the office and altered preferences for the ways that business was conducted. Not everyone thought that this was a beneficial outcome. An early writer complained "The invention of the typewriter has given impetus to the dictating habit . . . . This means not only greater diffuseness, inevitable with any lessening of the tax on words which the labor of writing imposes, but it also brings forward the point of view of the one who speaks."[45] It is difficult for us to tell how much of these new habits and preferences were manifestations of the effect of lowered prices for clerical output and how much was due to fascination with the machines.

FIGURE 4.5

THE EFFECT OF A SHIFT IN THE SUPPLY CURVE OF CLERICAL LABOR

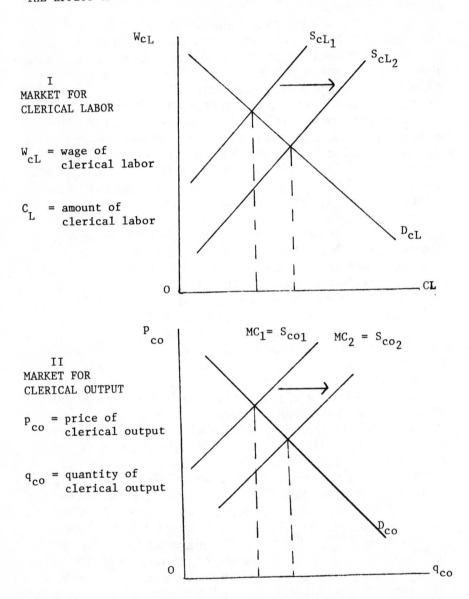

I
MARKET FOR
CLERICAL LABOR

W_{cL} = wage of
clerical labor

C_L = amount of
clerical labor

II
MARKET FOR
CLERICAL OUTPUT

P_{co} = price of
clerical output

q_{co} = quantity of
clerical output

Increased Supply of Clerical Labor

The growth in clerical employment was influenced by supply factors as well as by the demand conditions discussed in the previous section. Figure 4.5 illustrates the effect of an exogenous shift in the supply curve of clerical labor on the amount of clerical labor hired and on the amount of clerical output used. Panel I shows that a shift to the right in the supply curve of clerical labor leads to an increase in the amount of clerical labor hired given a fixed demand curve. This also results in a decrease in the wage which, so long as clerical labor is a normal factor, causes a rightward shift in the marginal cost (supply) curve for clerical output (see panel II of figure 4.5).

Certainly the supply of clerical labor did increase during the period from 1870 to 1930. The clerical labor force absorbed a large portion of the expanded number of female gainful workers over this period. Chapters 2 and 3 examined the increase in the supply of women to the overall labor force. The analysis in chapter 3 tied the increase in the labor supply of young unmarried women to the decline in the family economy. These were the same women who made up the overwhelming majority of female clerical workers. The increase in their supply to the labor market would have had the effect of stimulating the growth of employment in the clerical sector even without a shift in the demand curve. Chapters 5, 6, and 7 will be devoted to a more detailed examination of the growth of female employment in clerical work.

In addition to the separate demand and supply shifts, there is a possible interaction between supply and demand that may be important for explaining the expansion of the clerical sector. It is likely that the supply of young women to this market was highly elastic — more elastic than the supply of men who had previously made up the bulk of the clerical work force. If this was so, then this group would exhibit greater supply responsiveness to any shift in the demand curve so that the clerical sector would grow more rapidly in response to demand shifts as it became more feminized.

This expectation is supported by empirical studies of labor supply which have uniformly found that women exhibit a greater positive response to changes in their own wages than do men of all ages.[45] In chapter 3 of this study a positive response of women to own wages was found for 1890 and 1930. This evidence suggests that women may be expected to exhibit a more elastic supply response and lends credence to the suggestion that the supply of clerical labor became more elastic as the occupation was feminized.

This study is unable to answer in any definite way the question of whether the expansion of the clerical sector in this period was caused mostly by supply or demand shifts. However, the timing of the growth of the clerical sector suggests an explanation. As was noted in chapter 2 female participation in the paid labor force expanded at a fairly steady rate throughout the period, with the most rapid increases coming in the 1880s and 1900–1910 decade. The clerical labor force grew more rapidly and in a much more erratic fashion; the 1880s and 1910s saw extremely dramatic increases in clerical employment. If the growth in the clerical sector were being driven largely by the increased supply of women workers, the two series should move more closely together over time. Probably the most plausible explanation is that the trend in the growth of the clerical force is closely related to the long term increase in female participation, but the timing of clerical employment growth is related mostly to short run variations in demand—most particularly to the changes in clerical technology which took place in the 1880s and 1910.

Summary

This chapter has detailed the rapid growth of clerical employment in the United States over the period 1870–1930 and has examined reasons for the increased demand for such labor.

The demand for clerical labor was discussed as a derived demand with the demand for clerical output (an intermediate good) and the demand for final goods being important determining factors. Major causes of the growth in the demand for clerical services were seen to be the growth and structure of production of final goods, the decline in the cost of producing clerical output (due to technological advance), and alterations in the organization of production and institutional changes which led to greater demand for clerical output. The industrial breakdown of the growth in clerical employment for three periods allowed the identification of industries and forces which were most important for expanding clerical employment. Change in the clerical proportion of the industries' work forces was the most important cause of growth in each period; manufacturing was the industry that increased its hiring of clerical labor most. The very rapid growth of industries with high propensities to hire clerical labor was also an important cause with finance/insurance/real estate and the government sector being responsible for substantial growth.

The increased supply of labor to the clerical market was related to increased labor force participation by women. It was argued that the feminization of the clerical labor force caused the supply of labor to this occupation to become more elastic over time.

The timing of the growth of clerical employment was compared with the growth of female labor force participation. The clerical labor force was found to display more rapid and more irregular growth. This timing suggests that while the long term trend in clerical labor force growth may be related to supply factors, the timing of short run variations was more related to specific demand factors. Two decades were distinguished by particularly rapid growth of clerical employment relative to non-agricultural labor force growth. The 1880s saw rapid growth in clerical employment associated with the adoption of the newly invented typewriter. The decade 1910-1920 was characterized by a vastly expanding role of government through regulation and tax laws and by changes in business organization associated with the spread of Taylorism. Both decades were characterized by above average growth in the urban share of population.

5

The Growth of Women's Employment in Clerical Occupations

This chapter focuses on the dramatic growth of women's participation in the expanding clerical sector. We will review the pace and pattern of this employment growth and will describe the female clerical labor force in terms of demographic characteristics. Information on the distribution of women clerical workers across industries and sub-occupations will be used to detail changes in the use of women to perform clerical jobs and to assess the importance of changes in the industrial structure of the economy for female clerical employment.

Overview of the Change in Women's Employment in Clerical Occupations

The six decades covered by this study are distinguished not only by the rapid growth of total employment in clerical occupations but by the even more rapid increase in the numbers of female clerical workers so that women's share of total clerical employment increased from 2.5% in 1870 to 52.5% in 1930 (see table 4.1). This takeover of clerical jobs by women continued after 1930. By 1979, women were 80% of all U.S. clerical workers; and 35% of all employed women were working in clerical jobs.[1]

Chapter 2 discussed the strong tendencies for the occupational structure to be segregated by sex and for women to be concentrated in a small number of occupations. Because of the concentrated and segregated nature of women's employment, the great bulk of the growth in women's labor force participation is attributable to the growth of employment in occupations which were dominated by women as early as 1870. Clerical occupations are a notable exception. Nearly one-quarter of the increase

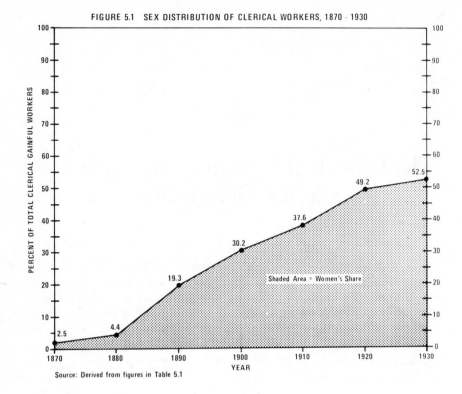

FIGURE 5.1   SEX DISTRIBUTION OF CLERICAL WORKERS, 1870 - 1930

Source: Derived from figures in Table 5.1

TABLE 5.1

PARTICIPATION RATES OF FEMALES IN THE NON-AGRICULTURAL LABOR FORCE
AND THE CLERICAL LABOR FORCE, 1870-1930

	1870	1880	1890	1900	1910	1920	1930
I Percent of population, ages 10+, employed in non-agricultural labor force:							
Total	20.85	23.96	28.21	31.33	36.01	37.44	38.85
Females	10.13	11.21	13.91	15.26	18.14	18.45	20.17
Males	31.38	36.21	41.76	46.62	52.69	55.61	57.08
II Percent of population, ages 10+, employed in clerical occupations:							
Total	.255	.409	.803	1.222	2.129	3.430	3.787
Females	.013	.037	.318	.758	1.659	3.451	4.028
Males	.492	.767	1.262	1.663	2.568	3.409	3.552
III Percent of non-agricultural labor force, age 10+, employed in clerical occupations:							
Total	1.22	1.70	2.84	3.89	5.91	9.15	9.74
Females	.12	.33	2.38	4.96	9.14	18.69	19.95
Males	1.73	2.11	3.02	3.56	4.87	6.13	6.22

Source: All data used to compute above figures except clerical employment for 1900 from Alba
Edwards, Comparative Occupation Statistics for the United States, 1870-1940, United States
Bureau of the Census (United States Printing Office, 1943), pp. 91, 100.

Clerical employment for 1900 corrected for inclusion of clerks in stores by estimation
of equation: log (Clerks) = a+b (time) on Edwards data for 1880, 1890, 1910, 1920.
Estimation done separately for females and males.

in the size of the female non-agricultural labor force from 1870 to 1930 was due to increased employment of women in clerical jobs.

Figure 5.1 pictures the change in the sex distribution of clerical employment from 1870 to 1930. The shaded portion of the figure represents women's share of total clerical employment. The proportion of clerical workers who were female increased during every decade with the fastest growth taking place from 1880 to 1890. In order for women to increase their share in the clerical sector so dramatically, their participation in clerical work had to increase much faster than men's particiption in the same sector. Table 5.1 shows levels of participation by sex in the non-agricultural labor force and in clerical employment. In 1870 only about one out of every 1000 gainfully employed women was working at a clerical job. In the same year 17 of every 1000 working males were in clerical jobs. By 1890 2.38% of female gainful workers and 3.02% of male gainful workers were clerical workers. In 1900, for the first time, the rate at which women non-agricultural workers participated in clerical occupations exceeded the rate for males. In every year after that the differential grew. By 1930 nearly 20% of all women gainful workers and 4% of all women over the age of 10 were employed in clerical occupations. The comparable figures for men were 6% and 3.5%.

Table 5.2 shows the annual rates at which the clerical labor force grew and compares the experience of females and males with each other and with the total non-agricultural labor force. Panel II shows that the number of women clerical workers grew faster than did the number of male clerical workers in every decade. Panel V compares the growth rates of female clerical workers to males in the same occupations. In the 1880s the number of women in clerical employment grew almost 3.5 times as fast as did males. The 1890s and the 1910s are also typified by particularly rapid increase in the number of female clerical workers. Panel III of table 5.2 compares the growth of the clerical labor force to the growth of the total non-agricultural labor force for each sex and for both sexes together. Both males and females increased their numbers of clerical workers more rapidly than their numbers in the non-agricultural labor force generally, but women's numbers increased much more rapidly than did men's. In two decades, 1880–1890 and 1910–1920, female clerical employment grew at over five times the rate of the female non-agricultural labor force. These were also the two decades of most rapid growth in total clerical employment relative to all non-farm employment.

Table 5.3 demonstrates the importance of the movement of women into clerical employment for explaining the growth of the total female labor force. Over the 60-year period clerical work accounted for 23.43% of all additional female non-agricultural workers. The pattern over time

TABLE 5.2

AVERAGE ANNUAL GROWTH RATES: NON-AGRICULTURAL LABOR
FORCE AND CLERICAL LABOR FORCE, BY SEX, 1870-1930

		1870-1880	1880-1890	1890-1900	1900-1910	1910-1920	1920-1930	1870-1930
I	Growth rates of Non-agricultural labor force = NALF							
	Total	3.78	4.27	3.10	3.56	1.85	2.16	3.12
	Females	3.28	4.37	3.04	3.77	1.77	2.80	3.23
	Males	3.94	4.13	3.14	3.49	1.89	1.95	3.08
II	Growth rates of Clerical labor force = CẄ							
	Total	7.31	9.73	6.40	7.96	6.41	2.80	6.75
	Females	13.74	27.20	11.31	10.34	9.31	3.47	12.34
	Males	7.10	7.89	4.85	6.77	4.25	2.10	5.48
III	Ratios of growth rates: $\frac{CẄ}{NALF}$							
	Total	1.93	2.28	2.06	2.24	3.46	1.30	2.16
	Females	4.19	5.75	3.72	2.74	5.26	1.24	3.82
	Males	1.80	1.91	1.55	1.94	2.25	1.08	1.78
IV	Ratios of growth rates $\frac{Female\ CẄ}{All\ CẄ}$	1.88	2.80	1.77	1.30	1.52	1.24	1.83
V	Ratios of growth rates $\frac{Female\ CẄ}{Male\ CẄ}$	1.94	3.45	2.33	1.53	2.19	1.65	2.25

Source: Computed from figures in Table 4.1.

TABLE 5.3

PERCENT OF DECADAL INCREASE IN NON-AGRICULTURAL
LABOR FORCE DUE TO INCREASE IN NUMBER OF
CLERICAL WORKERS, 1870-1930

		1870-1880	1880-1890	1890-1900	1900-1910	1910-1920	1920-1930	1870-1930
I	Change in clerical workers / Change in non-agricultural labor force	2.79	5.04	6.85	10.71	25.24	12.22	11.35
II	Change in female clerical workers / Change in female non-agricultural labor force	.86	5.62	12.78	18.33	68.73	23.92	23.43
III	Change in female clerical workers / Change in total clerical workers	6.29	28.98	43.00	44.01	62.63	63.08	53.56

Source: For computation see Table 4.2.

TABLE 5.4

AGE DISTRIBUTION OF FEMALE NON-AGRICULTURAL WORKERS
AND FEMALE CLERICAL WORKERS 1890-1930

	1890	1900	1910	1920	1930
PERCENT DISTRIBUTIONS					
I Percent of Female Non-agricultural Labor Force Ages:					
10-15	7.12	6.33	3.62	2.12	.81
16-24	47.23	43.28	81.00	39.34	36.08
25-44	33.09	36.98		41.26	43.54
Over 45	12.08	13.11	15.22	17.08	19.44
	100.00	100.00	100.00	100.00	100.00
II Percent of Female Clerical Workers Ages:					
10-15	n.a.	2.32	1.26	1.15	.17
16-24	n.a.	58.84	95.88	58.28	50.07
25-44	n.a.	36.33		36.48	43.01
Over 45	n.a.	2.38	2.84	3.97	6.70
		100.00	100.00	100.00	100.00

Sources: Computed from: U. S. Bureau of the Census:

1900 Census, Special Report on Occupations, pp. cxix and 16-17.

1910 Census of Population, Vol. 4, pp. 302-303, 343.

1920 Census of Population, Vol. 4, pp. 376.

1930 Census of Population, Vol. 4, pp. 40, 62-63.

TABLE 5.5

PARTICIPATION RATES FOR WOMEN IN THE NON-AGRICULTURAL
LABOR FORCE AND THE CLERICAL WORK FORCE,
BY AGE, 1890-1930

	1890	1900	1910	1920	1930
PARTICIPATION RATES					
I Percent of female population ages 10+ in non-agricultural labor force:					
All females ages 10+	13.91	15.26	18.14	18.45	20.17
10-15	5.57	5.78	4.23	2.56	1.13
16-24	27.04	27.76	24.29	34.26	35.15
25-44	11.86	15.79	24.29	20.20	23.92
45+	7.64	8.81	11.61	12.30	14.12
II Percent of female non-agricultural labor force in clerical occupations: All females ages 10+	2.29	4.94	9.15	18.75	19.96
10-15	n.a.	1.78	1.86	10.16	4.23
16-24	n.a.	6.72	12.32	27.70*	27.70*
25-44	n.a.	4.85	12.32	16.53	19.72
45+	n.a.	.90	10.13	4.35	6.91
*16-19				26,73*	24,52*
20-24				28.43	29.58

Sources: Same as for Table 5.4.

in clerical work's share of additional workers was similar for women and for the total labor force with steady growth up to 1910, then a spectacular rise in the clerical sector from 1910 to 1920. Over that decade 25% of all added non-farm labor was in clerical employment, and nearly 69% of all added women non-farm workers entered clerical jobs. By comparison with the 1910s, the contribution of clerical labor to the growth of the work force in the twenties was moderate, but it exceeded the experience of every decade prior to 1910. Almost 25% of the increase in female non-farm employment from 1920 to 1930 was accounted for by additional female clerical workers.

Panel III of table 5.3 shows women's share of the change in clerical employment for each decade and for the entire period. Women made up over half of the 60-year change in clerical employment. In the eighties almost 30% of all new clerical workers were women. From 1890 to 1910, over 40%, and from 1910 to 1930, over 60% of the change in the number of clerical workers is attributable to increased participation by women in these jobs.

Demographic Characteristics of Female Clerical Workers

Age. From the age distributions of female non-agricultural workers and female clerical workers in table 5.4 we can conclude that women in clerical jobs were on average younger than other women workers. At every date for which information is available, a larger proportion of women in clerical work were under age 25 than were women non-agricultural workers generally, and at least half were between the ages of 16 and 24. At all dates, smaller percentages of women clerical workers were under age 16, undoubtedly reflecting the need for higher levels of education in clerical work. As time went on the average age of women workers increased. Of all women in the non-farm labor force 54.35% were under 25 in 1890; by 1930 this had fallen to 36.89%. The decline in the proportion under 25 in the overall labor force was fairly steady over the entire period. Among clerical workers there was little change in the age distribution until the twenties when there was a large increase in the proportion over age 25. This implies that the difference between the average age of women clerical workers and other women workers increased over time.

Participation rates by age (table 5.5) show the increases in women's labor force attachment. Women ages 16–24 had higher levels of participation throughout, but older women's participation increased faster. Panel II of table 5.5 shows the proportion of women workers of various ages who were working in clerical occupations. At every date

TABLE 5.6

RACE-NATIVITY DISTRIBUTION OF FEMALE NON-AGRICULTURAL
WORKERS AND FEMALE CLERICAL WORKERS 1890-1930

	1890	1900	1910	1920	1930

PERCENT DISTRIBUTIONS

I Percent of Female Non-agricultural Labor Force
   (ages 10+)

	1890	1900	1910	1920	1930
Native white of native parentage	35.71	36.99	39.61	44.95	74.11
Native white of foreign or mixed parentage	24.45	26.54	26.37	27.59	(74.11)
Foreign-born white	22.92	19.28	18.61	14.45	11.47
Black and others	16.90	17.17	15.38	12.99	14.40
	100.00	100.00	100.00	100.00	100.00

II Percent of Female Clerical
   Workers, (ages 10+):

	1890	1900	1910	1920	1930
Native white of native parentage	52.67	50.82	51.68	54.80	93.54
Native white of foreign or mixed parentage	38.06	40.66	40.98	38.29	(93.54)
Foreign-born white	8.87	8.15	6.84	6.36	5.74
Black and others	0.40	0.34	0.48	0.52	0.70
	100.00	100.00	100.00	100.00	100.00

Sources: Computed from: U. S. Bureau of the Census,
          1890 Census of Population, part 2, pp. cxvii-cxix.
          1900 Census, Special Report on Occupations, pp. 10-11.
          1910 Census of Population, Vol. 4, pp. 11, 67, 302-303.
          1920 Census of Population, Vol. 4, pp. 341, 358-359.
          1930 Census of Population, Vol. 4, pp. 24, 34.

working women 16-24 were more likely to be in clerical jobs than were women of other ages. In both 1920 and 1930 nearly 28% of all female non-farm gainful workers in this age group were in clerical jobs. Within the age group there was a decline over the decade in clerical participation by women ages 16–19 and an increase by those 20–24. Clerical participation by women in the two older age groups also increased.

To sum up the evidence on age structure of clerical employment: women clerical workers were younger than were women workers in general throughout the period with the differential increasing at least until 1920. In the decade of the twenties there was an increase in clerical participation by women over 25 and a large decline in the proportion of women clerical workers under age 25. There are a number of possible explanations for the tendency for clerical workers to be younger than other women workers. Clerical work required relatively high levels of education. The average educational attainment of the population increased over time so that it was younger women who were most likely to have the level of education necessary to qualify for clerical employment. This was true particularly after education in clerical skills began to be routinely offered in public high schools. Throughout much of this period working in an office was an unconventional way for women to earn money. Younger women may have been more likely to have the daring to flaunt convention by taking clerical jobs. A third possible explanation may be found in the preferences of of employers. Many employers saw the addition of a women to their office staff as being partly decorative and preferred to hire young attractive women. A writer for the *Typewriter Trade Journal* in 1904 found that "firms in the financial district . . . prefer a pretty girl of liberal education and refinement who would grace their offices."[2]

Race and Nativity. Literacy in the English language was required of most who performed clerical functions. Therefore it is not surprising that in every census decade, over 90% of female clerical workers were native-born whites although such women made up a much smaller proportion of all non-farm gainful workers (see table 5.6). In every year for which breakdowns of workers by parentage are available, more than half of all women clerical workers were of native parentage. Blacks and members of other races made no appreciable gains in clerical employment during this time period; indeed, it was not until the 1960s that black women were hired in significant numbers as clerical workers.[3] Foreign-born women made up smaller proportions of the population, the labor force, and the clerical work force as time went on. As immigration slowed, the foreign-born population aged, and their work force participation declined.

TABLE 5.7

PARTICIPATION RATES FOR WOMEN IN THE NON-AGRICULTURAL LABOR FORCE AND THE CLERICAL WORK FORCE, BY RACE AND NATIVITY 1890-1930

	1890	1900	1910	1920	1930
PARTICIPATION RATES					
I Percentage of female population (ages 10+) in non-agricultural labor force:					
All women (ages 10+)	13.91	15.26	18.14	18.45	20.17
native white of native parentage	9.26	10.83	13.66	15.45	19.56
native white of foreign or mixed parentage	20.43	21.07	23.59	24.25	
foreign-born white	18.51	18.21	20.72	17.74	18.40
black and others	20.91	22.53	26.16	23.99	26.52
II Percentage of female non-agricultural labor force in clerical occupations:					
All women (ages 10+)	2.29	4.94	9.15	18.75	19.96
native white of native parentage	3.34	6.76	11.93	22.80	25.20
native white of foreign, or mixed parentage	3.53	7.54	14.22	25.95	
foreign-born white	0.88	2.08	3.66	8.24	10.0
black and others	0.05	1.00	0.29	0.75	0.98

Sources: Same as for Table 5.6.

TABLE 5.8

MARITAL STATUS DISTRIBUTION OF FEMALE NON-AGRICULTURAL
WORKERS AND FEMALE CLERICAL WORKERS, 1890-1930

	1890	1900	1910	1920	1930
PERCENT DISTRIBUTION					
I Percentage of female non-agricultural labor force (ages 15+):					
married	12.10	13.43	19.43	20.90	28.42
single, widowed, divorced, unknown	87.90	86.57	80.57	79.10	71.58
	100.00	100.00	100.00	100.00	100.00
II Percentage of female clerical workers (ages 15+):					
married	4.07	3.96	5.34	8.93	18.23
single, widowed, divorced, unknown	95.93	96.39	94.64	91.07	81.77
	100.00	100.00	100.00	100.00	100.00

Sources: Joseph A. Hill, Women In Gainful Occupations, 1870-1920,
U. S. Census Monographs, IX, (Washington, D. C.,
G. P. O. 1929), pp. 76, 77.

U. S. Bureau of the Census, 1930 Census of Population,
Vol. 4, p. 68.

TABLE 5.9

PARTICIPATION RATES FOR WOMEN IN THE NON-AGRICULTURAL
LABOR FORCE AND THE CLERICAL WORK FORCE, BY
MARITAL STATUS, 1890-1930

	1890	1900	1910	1920	1930
PARTICIPATION RATES					
I Percentage of female population (ages 15+) in non-agricultural labor force:					
all women (ages 15+)	15.32	16.79	20.52	21.07	22.92
married	3.30	3.96	6.77	7.26	10.66
single, widowed, divorced, unknown	31.20	36.42	40.19	42.31	42.17
II Percentage of female non-agricultural labor force in clerical occupations:					
all women (ages 15+)	2.44	5.23	9.27	18.80	20.00
married	0.81	1.41	2.55	8.03	12.83
single, widowed, divorced, unknown	2.67	5.82	10.85	21.64	22.85

Sources: Same as for Table 5.8.

Nevertheless, there was an increase in the participation by foreign-born women in clerical work so that by 1930, 10 out of every 100 employed foreign-born women held clerical jobs (table 5.7). There was also a dramatic increase in participation by native women of foreign parentage. However, because of the even greater increase in over-all participation by native women of native parentage, the share of women with foreign-born parents in the clerical labor force did not increase.

Marital Status. Table 5.8 presents distributions of the female non-agricultural labor force and the female clerical labor force by marital status. At every date clerical workers were more likely to be unmarried than were women workers generally. Single women made up over 90% of female clerical workers through 1920. From 1920 to 1930 there was a large increase in the number of married clerical workers. Despite this impressive increase, nearly 82% of all women in clerical employment in 1930 were unmarried. The movements in participation rates tell much the same story (table 5.9). In 1890 fewer than 1% of all married working women were clerical workers. By 1930 this had risen to almost 13%. In the same year almost 23% of all unmarried women non-farm gainful workers were in clerical jobs. Table 5.10 allows better understanding of these trends by presenting growth rates, by marital status, for the female clerical labor force relative to the female non-agricultural labor force and distributions of labor force growth by marital status. Panel I shows that single women's participation in the clerical labor force increased far more rapidly than did married women's during the first two decades. From 1910 to 1920 the rates of growth were very high for all women, and in the twenties the growth rate was higher for married women. Panel III presents impressive evidence of the importance of the actions of single women for clerical labor force growth up to 1920. Almost 97% of the growth in the size of the female clerical labor force from 1890 to 1900 was due to increased numbers of unmarried women in clerical jobs. As late as the 1920s unmarried women accounted for over 88% of the decade's change. Spectacular increases in the number of married women clerical workers in the twenties changed the figures abruptly. Between 1920 and 1930, 41% of all new female clerical workers were married women.

There are a number of possible explanations for the dominance of clerical work by single women and the increase in the numbers of married clerical workers in the later years of the period. A major explanation for the preponderance of single women was undoubtedly the age factor; single women were younger than married women and more likely to have the education and other attributes which employers

TABLE 5.10

GROWTH RATES OF FEMALE CLERICAL LABOR FORCE BY MARITAL STATUS
AND DISTRIBUTION OF CHANGES IN FEMALE NON-AGRICULTURAL
LABOR FORCE AND FEMALE CLERICAL WORK FORCE OVER
MARITAL STATUS CATEGORIES, 1890-1930

	1890–1900	1900–1910	1910–1920	1920–1930	1890–1930
I Ratio of average annual growth rates $\frac{\text{female C}\overset{.}{\text{W}}}{\text{female N}\overset{.}{\text{A}}\text{LF}}$					
married	2.44	1.85	5.80	1.84	2.44
single, widowed, divorced, unknown	3.85	2.91	5.33	1.31	3.29
II Percent of change in female non-agricultural labor force due to increased employment of:					
married	16.80	31.08	28.17	51.58	35.55
single, widowed, divorced, unknown	83.20	68.92	71.83	48.42	64.35
	100.00	100.00	100.00	100.00	100.00
III Percent of change in female clerical workers due to increased employment of:					
married	3.37	6.37	11.43	40.93	18.77
single, widowed, divorced, unknown	96.63	93.63	88.57	59.07	81.22
	100.00	100.00	100.00	100.00	100.00

Sources: Same as for Table 5.8.

preferred in clerical workers. As time went on levels of educational attainment rose and the average age at first marriage fell so that a larger proportion of married women also had the educational qualifications for clerical employment.

Reasons for the rapid increase in the participation of married women in clerical employment may be found either in preferences of employers or in preferences of the women themselves. There is clear evidence that employers had strong preferences for employing unmarried women in clerical occupations. Many firms had policies against hiring married women for office work, and it was common to fire women clerical workers when they married.[4] Some employers argued that married women were "clock watchers" and less reliable.

That these policies were not merely reflections of the preferences of the women themselves is evidenced by the frequent complaints by women office workers of discrimination based on marital status and age. In a 1925 study of women clerical workers in Minneapolis, policies against employing married women were noted as problems for some of the women surveyed.[5] In a later study of working women in a large number of business and professional occupations, teachers and clerical workers complained of discrimination against married women, and clerical workers most frequently reported discrimination because of age.[6]

Employers may have been most able to exercise this preference for unmarried clerical employees when the number of women so employed was small relative to the number of qualified single women desiring clerical employment. The large increase in demand for clerical workers in the 1910s coupled with the decline in the median age at first marriage (see table 2.8) may have put pressure on employers to reexamine their employment policies. Faced with the possibility of an insufficiency of their preferred work force, some employers may have been willing to relax their proscriptions against married employees rather than raise wages to attract more single women or men. In the 1920s it seems likely that this force was at work. In addition, many of the women who had been hired when they were single were too valuable to firms because of their experience to be blithely fired when they married.

In 1931 the Women's Bureau made a study of women clerical workers in seven large cities. Data were collected from places of employment. Many of the firms in the study had policies against employing married women; large firms had the most drastic policies. The author of the report felt that these policies were routinely circumvented by employees who did not report changes in their marital status.[7] The original data collection sheets for this study are available in the National Archives. By reading through answers to questions on policies toward

TABLE 5.11

DISTRIBUTION OF CLERICAL EMPLOYMENT OVER SUB-OCCUPATIONS, BY SEX, 1870-1930

	1870	1880	1890	1900	1910	1920	1930
PERCENTAGE DISTRIBUTIONS							
Panel I							
Percent of TOTAL CLERICAL WORKERS:							
Bookkeepers, cashiers, accountants	42.40	52.18	41.85	36.08	31.93	25.88	24.89
Clerks (except in stores)	57.38	47.81	49.36	48.03	47.28	52.43	53.41
Stenographers, typists	0.20	n.a.	8.77	15.88	20.78	21.67	21.69
	100.00	100.00	100.00	100.00	100.00	100.00	100.00
Panel II							
Percent of FEMALE CLERICAL WORKERS:							
Bookkeepers, cashiers, accountants	24.20	38.62	37.84	34.64	32.65	25.72	24.57
Clerks (except in stores)	76.50	61.37	33.09	25.12	21.40	33.82	35.96
Stenographers, typists	0.38	n.a.	28.98	40.23	45.94	40.45	39.45
	100.00	100.00	100.00	100.00	100.00	100.00	100.00
Panel III							
Percent of MALE CLERICAL WORKERS:							
Bookkeepers, cashiers, accountants	58.25	52.50	42.80	36.70	31.50	26.04	25.24
Clerks (except in stores)	41.54	47.19	53.24	57.96	62.87	70.45	72.72
Stenographers, typists	0.20	n.a.	3.95	5.32	5.61	3.49	2.03
	100.0	100.0	100.0	100.0	100.0	100.0	100.0

Source: See Table 5.1.

married employees, one is able to learn much about the preferences of the companies and the pressures that they felt. Over half the companies had policies against either hiring or retaining married female clerical employees. Virtually all had had such policies in the past and some were re-instituting them because of the Depression. Some firms did not hire married women but kept those who married while in their employ. Of the firms that had dropped their discriminatory policies, most offered as explanation the difficulties attendant with firing valuable experienced personnel. Some said that they found married women to be more solid and dependable employees. Most, however, apologized for not discriminating against married women and implied that the morally correct policy was to employ only unmarried women.[8]

The small proportion of married women in clerical work may also reflect the desired employment patterns of those women. There is a well-established negative relationship between husband's earnings and wife's labor force participation. Female clerical workers were drawn from higher socio-economic groups than were women in most other occupations. Such women would be more likely to marry high-earning men and therefore be employed after marriage. The increase in participation by married women in the 1920s may then be due to the fact that the big increase in the number of women clerical workers from 1910 to 1920 drew into office employment women of lower socio-economic classes who had lesser prospects for marrying high-earning men. This, together with the overall growth in labor force participation of married women associated with secular changes in attitudes, higher earnings for women, and reduction of household duties because of smaller family size and technological advance in home production, contributed to the greater increase in the number of married women clerical workers in the final decade of this period.

Occupational Distribution of Female Clerical Employment

As was discussed in the preceding chapter, the census allows the breakdown of total clerical employment into three suboccupations for each date covered by this period. The sub-occupations are: (1) book-keepers, cashiers, and accountants, (2) clerks (except clerks in stores), and (3) stenographers and typists. Clerks made up the largest category of clerical employment at every date. Gainful workers in all three sub-occupations increased over time, and women's share of each also grew.

Table 5.11 shows the distribution of total clerical employment over sub-occupations for females, males, and both sexes together. In 1870 there were fewer than 2000 female clerical workers, over 3/4 of whom were classified as clerks. In fact most of these clerks (943) were working in government offices where women had first been hired because of the shortage of qualified male workers during the Civil War. The government was generally pleased with the results of its experiment of using female clerks, and the women were kept on after the war ended.[9] There were 422 women working as bookkeepers, cashiers and accountants and seven women professional shorthand writers. By 1880 there were 6,618 women in clerical jobs; about 60% of these were classified as clerks and the rest were enumerated as bookkeepers, cashiers, and accountants. This division into the two sub-occupations is quite arbitrary since the actual census category for some industries was "bookkeepers, copyists and clerks," and in these cases employment figures were divided equally between the two sub-occupational categories.

The 1880 Census did not report stenographers and typists as a separate category although there were clearly women working at this occupation in 1880. Persons working as stenographers and typists in 1880 may be in either of the two other sub-occupational categories listed. Probably much of the growth shown in the tables in the bookkeeping and clerk categories was actually accounted for by the first typists. Alba Edwards estimated that there were perhaps 5,000 stenographers and typists in 1880, and 60% of these were females;[10] but his estimate can be little more than a guess. What is certain is that women began working typewriters as soon as they were invented and that women moved into office employment in a substantial way in conjunction with the adoption of the typewriter. The earliest producers saw the typewriter as similar to the sewing machine and considered it appropriate for women. C. Latham Sholes, the inventor of the typewriter, used his daughter to demonstrate the machine. This was duplicated in many cities as the most common way to advertise the typewriter, setting up demonstrations in hotel lobbies and pubic expositions. Pretty young women were invariably used as the demonstrators. The typewriter companies trained young women to work the machine and sent them along when a typewriter was purchased.[11] As early as 1875 advertisements for the typewriter touted it as leading to good employment for women: "And the benevolent can, by the gift of a 'Type-Writer' to a poor, deserving, young woman, put her at once in the way of earning a good living as a copyist or corresponding clerk. No invention has opened for women so broad and easy an avenue to profitable and suitable employment as the 'Type-Writer', and it merits the careful consideration of all thoughtful and charitable persons interested in the subject of employment for women."[12] It is likely that many of the over 6,000 female clerical workers in 1880 were actually working as typists (or typewriters as they were then called) even though they were not enumerated as such. In 1890, when stenographers and typists were first counted by the census, 30% of all female clerical workers were so employed.

Over the entire period it was stenography and typewriting which accounted for the greatest difference in the occupational distributions of female and male clerical workers. This occupation was always a minor livelihood for males. At its highest in 1910, stenography and typewriting accounted for only 5.6% of total male clerical employment, and after that date the absolute number of males in the sub-occupation declined. By contrast, at every date from 1900 on, more women were employed operating the writing machine than in any other clerical job.

After 1890 the proportion of both females and males working as bookkeepers, cashiers, and accountants declined. This reflects both the relative increase in the other two clerical sub-occupations and the relative decline in the number of bookkeepers that occurred as bookkeeping was mechanized and standardized. It is probable that the number of women working as bookkeepers was overstated throughout the period, though it would be difficult to estimate the degree of overstatement. In its 1914 study of clerical workers in Boston, the Women's Educational and Industrial Union found that the number of women who reported themselves as bookkeepers was much larger than the number of bookkeepers reported by firms. The study described the division of labor and the mechanization which had recently revolutionized bookkeeping and noted that bookkeepers had been replaced by "many clerks who each do a small part of the bookkeeping and are called ledger clerks, billing clerks, billing machine operators, pay roll clerks and others according to the nature of the business of the employer. The results of the work of these many clerks are collected and combined by one bookkeeper, usually a man."[13]

Women's share of clerical employment by sub-occupation is examined in table 5.12. Women's share of all employed as bookkeepers, cashiers, and accountants grew from about 1% in 1870 to nearly 52% in 1930 with the greatest percentage increase in women's share coming in the 1880s and declining thereafter. In 1890, the first year that stenographers and typists were enumerated, women already made up 64% of those so employed. Women's dominance in the typewriting trade expanded so that by 1930 over 95% of all workers classified as typists or stenographers were women. Women expanded their role in the clerk category much more slowly. By 1910 only 17% of all clerks were women. After 1910 women's share of this category expanded very rapidly. We know that the decade 1910–1920 was particularly important in the growth of the female clerical labor force. During this decade the number of

TABLE 5.12

WOMEN'S SHARE OF EMPLOYMENT IN CLERICAL
SUB-OCCUPATIONS, 1870-1930

	1870	1880	1890	1900	1910	1920	1930
female clerical workers / all clerical workers							
Bookkeepers, Cashiers, Accountants	1.34	3.25	17.42	29.03	38.45	48.88	51.86
Clerks (except in stores)	3.27	5.64	13.02	15.81	17.02	31.73	35.38
Stenographers, and Typist	4.54		63.64	76.60	83.14	91.80	95.55
TOTAL	2.45	4.39	19.37	30.24	37.60	49.19	52.54

Source: See Table 5.1.

TABLE 5.13

EMPLOYED WORKERS, CLERICAL WORKERS AND WOMEN CLERICAL WORKERS
IN ALL INDUSTRIES, OHIO 1914-1932 WITH CLERICAL SHARE OF
TOTAL EMPLOYMENT AND WOMEN'S SHARE OF
TOTAL CLERICAL EMPLOYMENT

	Total Employed Workers	Total Clerical Workers	Gainful Workers % Clerical	Female Clerical Workers	Clerical Workers % Female
1914	641737	58889	9.18	23838	40.5
1915	734472	66574	9.06	27523	41.3
1916	923935	79360	8.58	33008	41.6
1917	101633	91247	8.96	39688	43.5
1918	1041993	104264	10.01	50269	48.2
1919	1039150	116185	11.18	57337	49.3
1920	1123955	130857	11.64	64312	49.1
1921	812646	110481	13.60	54678	49.5
1922	912160	112283	12.31	n.a.	n.a.
1923	1070998	126470	11.80	62472	49.4
1924	1055721	133235	12.62	65779	49.5
1925	1121840	138800	12.37	68945	49.7
1926	1175950	146255	12.45	73008	49.9
1927	1171268	150848	12.88	75842	50.3
1928	1197885	154287	12.88	76946	49.9
1929	1278992	168127	13.15	84870	50.5
1930	1133846	174099	15.35	n.a.	n.a.
1931	963791	153136	15.89	n.a.	n.a.
1932	817862	134296	16.42	n.a.	n.a.

Sources: Amy Maher, "Bookkeepers, Stenographers and Office Clerks
in Ohio, 1914-1929," U. S. Department of Labor, Women's
Bureau, Bulletin no. 95 (Washington, D. C.:
G. P. O., 1932), p. 11.

and Fred C. Croxton, Frederick E. Croxton and Frank
C. Croxton, "Average Annual Wage and Salary
Payments in Ohio, 1916-1930. U. S. Bureau of
Labor Statistics, Bulletin No. 613,
(Washington, D. C.: G. P. O,, 1935).

women in clerical jobs grew more than five times as fast as the overall female non-agricultural labor force and more than twice as fast as the male clerical labor force (see table 5.2). It can now be seen that the bulk of this spectacular growth was related to the expansion of women's share of employment in the clerk category.

Women's share of clerical employment in the period after 1914 can be examined more closely by looking at time series data from the state of Ohio. The Ohio Division of Labor Statistics collected employment and earnings data annually and classified the data by sex and by broad occupational categories, one of which is clerical. Table 5.13 presents this data on clerical employment and women's share of such employment. The figures do not refer to all gainful workers but to employed gainful workers only. From 1914 to 1920 the clerical share of total employed workers increased from 9.18% to 11.64%. Over the same period women's share of clerical employment increased from 40.5% to 49.1%. The most striking phenomenon, however, is the pattern of change in women's share. Virtually the entire increase took place during the years of American involvement in World War I with a 7.7 percentage point growth in women's share from 1916 to 1919. The war both increased the role of clerical labor in total employment and increased women's role in the clerical labor force. The national figures suggest that this was mainly due to the hiring of women in clerk positions previously held by men. We can also see that women did not lose their gains in the clerical sector when the war ended. This differs from the situation in some other occupations such as streetcar conducting, which women entered during the war but in which they were quickly replaced by men when the war ended.[14]

The data in table 5.13 also allow some inferences to be drawn about the effect of business cycle movements on clerical employment and on women's share of such employment. During the depressions of the early 1920s and the 1930s, the share of clerical workers in the total labor force rose, indicating that clerical employment fell less drastically during business downturns. Clearly, clerical employment was less volatile than employment in other sectors. Women's share of clerical employment did not fall in 1921 when the economy underwent a sharp downturn. This seems to indicate that women clerical workers were not more likely to be let go during slack conditions than were men clerical workers. Indeed, many early writers who emphasized the virtues of clerical employment for women mentioned that clerical workers were less likely to suffer unemployment than were workers in other occupations.[15]

TABLE 5.14

WOMEN'S SHARE OF CLERICAL EMPLOYMENT, BY INDUSTRY 1870, 1880, 1910, 1930

female clerical workers all clerical workers	1870	1880	1910	1930
Agriculture/forestry/fishing	----	----	25.67	54.41
Mining	----	----	12.51	26.80
Manufacturing	3.75	1.91	36.47	45.50
Construction	----	----	31.67	48.28
Transportation/public utilities	0.13	0.46	15.14	35.40
Trade	0.94	3.96	53.71	60.45
Finance/insurance/real estate	0.32	0.97	29.65	57.75
Professional service (includes education)	4.04	6.47	72.04	78.22
Domestic/personal service	1.47	2.26	30.25	53.06
Government service (includes military)	10.88	11.73	21.93	37.89
Unallocated to industry	----	----	46.85*	66.46
TOTAL	2.46	4.40	36.75	52.13

*estimated

Sources: 1870 – U.S. Bureau of the Census, 1870 Census Compendium, pp. 604-605
1880 – U.S. Bureau of the Census, 1880 Census Compendium, pp. 1368-1377
1910 – U.S. Bureau of the Census, 1910 Census of Population, IV, Occupations, pp. 302-433
1930 – U.S. Bureau of the Census, 1930 Census of Population, V, General Report on
Occupations, pp. 412-587

Industrial Distribution of Female Clerical Employment

The U.S. Census provides information which allows breakdowns of female clerical employment by industry for 1870, 1880, 1910, and 1930. Table 5.14 shows women's share of clerical employment in each industry. No clerical employment was reported for the agriculture, mining, and construction industries for the first two dates. Women's share of clerical employment increased over time in all industries, but there was considerable variation among industries in the importance of the role played by women. In 1870 women constituted nearly 11% of clerical employment in government service when women's share of total clerical employment was only 2.46%. Professional service and manufacturing were the other industries in which women made up over 2% of clerical workers. By 1910 professional service had the most female dominated clerical labor force with 72% of all clerical workers in professional service being women. In the trade sector over 50% of all clerical workers were women by 1910. Clerical employment in mining and transportation had the smallest representation of women. By 1930, over 52% of all clerical workers were women. Professional service still had the clerical work force with greatest female representation; and mining and transportation still were least likely to hire women in clerical jobs, but both of these industries had impressive growth in women's share in 20 years. Very notable increase in women's share was also experienced in the financial sector, which was the industry with the greatest proportion of its total work force in clerical employment.

Table 5.15 shows how female clerical workers were distributed among industries in 1870, 1880, 1910, and 1930. In 1870 over half of all female clerical workers were employed by the government. By 1880 trade had become the largest employer of women clerical workers with professional service and government service also employing significant numbers. This is probably indicative of the rather early acceptance of the typewriter in sales operations and among professionals. In 1910 trade was still the largest employer of women office workers, but manufacturing had become the second largest. In 1930 women clerical workers were much more evenly distributed over industries with manufacturing, trade, and finance being the major employers.

The change in female clerical employment can be divided into three component parts in a manner similar to that used in chapter 4 to analyze overall clerical growth. The analysis described below takes as given the change in the proportion of industries' employment in clerical work. The focus is on the determinants of the employment of women in these jobs.

TABLE 5.15

PERCENT OF FEMALE CLERICAL WORKERS IN EACH INDUSTRY, 1870, 1880, 1910, 1930

PERCENT DISTRIBUTION:	1870	1880	1910	1930
Agriculture/forestry/fishing	0.00	0.00	0.13	0.21
Mining	0.00	0.00	0.25	0.33
Manufacturing	12.04	2.92	26.00	22.34
Construction	0.00	0.00	0.81	1.26
Transportation/public utilities	0.60	0.98	6.53	9.17
Trade	16.03	35.74	39.93	21.03
Finance/insurance/real estate	1.53	1.92	10.43	17.52
Professional service (includes education)	13.89	24.89	8.00	10.07
Domestic/personal service	4.20	3.72	3.15	2.93
Government service (includes military)	51.59	29.86	4.76	5.60
Unallocated industry	----	----	----	9.76
TOTAL	100.00	100.00	100.00	100.00

Source: Same as for Table 5.14.

(1) Type I change measures the effect on female clerical employment of overall labor force growth and of change in the clerical share of industries' work forces. It is the portion of the actual change in the number of female clerical workers that would have resulted if employment in all industries had grown at the same rate and if all industries had experienced their actual changes in the clerical share in their work forces but there had been no change in women's share of clerical employment.

For any industry, Type I change in female clerical employment from period (t) to period (t+n) is computed as:

$$\left\{ \left[\Delta E \cdot \left(\frac{E_i}{E}\right)_t \cdot \left(\frac{C_i}{E_i}\right)_t \cdot \left(\frac{FC_i}{C_i}\right)_t \right] \right.$$
$$\left. + \left[E_{t+n} \cdot \left(\frac{E_i}{E}\right)_t \cdot \Delta\left(\frac{C_i}{E_i}\right) \cdot \left(\frac{FC_i}{C_i}\right)_t \right] \right\} / \Delta FC$$

where E = employment (all industries)
E_i = employment in industry i
C = clerical employment (all industries)
C_i = clerical employment in industry i
FC = female clerical employment (all industries)
FC_i = female clerical employment in industry i.

The first term in the numerator measures the simple effect of increased labor force size. The second term in the numerator measures the effect of changes in the proportion of the industry's work force in clerical occupations plus the effect of interaction between this and labor force growth.

(2) Type II change measures the portion of the actual change in female clerical employment that is attributable to differential industrial growth. It therefore captures the effect of the possibility that industries with higher propensities to employ women in clerical jobs might also be the fastest growing industries in terms of total employment. Type II change is computed as:

$$\left[E_{t+n} \cdot \Delta\left(\frac{E_i}{E}\right) \cdot \left(\frac{C_i}{E_i}\right)_{t+n} \cdot \left(\frac{FC_i}{C_i}\right)_t \right] / \Delta FC$$

In addition to the pure effect on female clerical employment of differential industrial growth, Type II change includes all interactions among labor force size (E), clerical share of industry employment

$\left(\dfrac{C_i}{E_i}\right)$, and industry differentials $\left(\dfrac{E_i}{E}\right)$.

(3) Type III change measures the portion of actual change in female clerical employment attributable to changes within industries in the propensity toward hiring females in clerical jobs. It is computed as:

$$\left[E_{t+n} \cdot \left(\frac{E_i}{E}\right)_{t+n} \cdot \left(\frac{C_i}{E_i}\right)_{t+n} \cdot \Delta\left(\frac{FC_i}{C_i}\right) \right] / \Delta FC$$

Type III change includes the pure effect of changes in women's share of clerical employment within industries

$$\left(\frac{FC_i}{C_i}\right)$$

plus the effects of interactions between this and all other terms in the formula.

Table 5.16 divides changes in female clerical employment over the periods 1870–1880, 1880–1910, 1910–1930, and 1870–1930 into the three types of change by industry. The cell entries are the proportion of total female clerical employment growth attributable to each type of change in each industry. For the period 1870–1880 trade contributed 43.2% of total growth in female clerical employment; the bulk of this change was due to the increased share of women in the clerical labor force in trade. Professional service and government service also contributed significant proportions of the overall growth of women's clerical employment. Thirteen percent of all additional women hired in clerical jobs over this decade were attributable to Type I growth of professional service, and another 13% were due to the increased share of women in clerical employment in professional service. Most of the growth in female clerical employment contributed by the government sector was due to growth of overall employment in that sector with very little change in the propensity to hire women. In manufacturing the number of women reported in office employment actually declined. The very small total contribution of Type II change from 1870 to 1880 indicates that it was not the industries with the highest propensities to hire female clerical workers in 1870 which experienced the fastest 10-year growth in overall employment.

Over the long period from 1880 to 1910 the great bulk (92.7%) of total female clerical employment growth was due to Type III changes. This is to be expected because we know that over this period there was tremendous structural change in the way that clerical work was

TABLE 5.16

APPORTIONING OF PERIOD CHANGES IN FEMALE CLERICAL EMPLOYMENT TO CAUSES, BY INDUSTRY

	1870-1880				1880-1910				1910-1930				1870-1930			
	Type I	Type II	Type III	TOTAL	Type I	Type II	Type III	TOTAL	Type I	Type II	Type III	TOTAL	Type I	Type II	Type III	TOTAL
AGRICULTURE FORESTRY FISHING	0.0	0.0	0.0	0.0	0.0	0.0	0.1	0.2	0.1	-0.1	0.2	0.2	0.0	0.0	0.2	0.2
MINING	0.0	0.0	0.0	0.0	0.0	0.0	0.2	0.2	0.2	0.0	0.2	0.4	0.0	0.0	0.3	0.3
MANUFACTURING	3.0	0.4	-3.9	1.1	1.1	0.3	24.9	26.2	14.3	0.1	6.3	20.7	1.4	0.4	20.5	22.3
CONSTRUCTION	0.0	0.0	0.0	0.0	0.0	0.0	0.8	0.8	0.8	0.0	0.6	1.4	0.0	0.0	0.2	0.2
TRANSPORTATION COMMUNICATION PUBLIC UTILITIES	0.2	0.0	1.0	1.1	0.1	0.1	6.4	6.6	2.1	0.7	7.4	10.2	0.0	0.0	9.1	9.1
TRADE	4.6	1.0	37.6	43.2	1.7	0.8	37.4	40.0	2.9	6.8	3.3	13.0	0.1	0.2	20.7	21.0
FINANCE INSURANCE REAL ESTATE	0.2	0.1	1.8	2.1	0.1	0.3	10.2	10.5	1.8	6.5	12.1	20.4	0.0	0.1	17.4	17.5
PROFESSIONAL SERVICE (INCLUDES EDUCATION)	13.0	3.1	12.9	29.1	0.2	0.2	7.4	7.8	5.2	4.6	1.1	10.9	0.2	0.3	9.5	10.0

TABLE 5.16 (Continued)

	1870-1880				1880-1910				1910-1930				1870-1930			
	Type I	Type II	Type III	TOTAL	Type I	Type II	Type III	TOTAL	Type I	Type II	Type III	TOTAL	Type I	Type II	Type III	TOTAL
DOMESTIC AND PERSONAL SERVICE	2.1	-0.4	1.8	3.5	0.2	0.0	3.0	3.1	1.1	0.0	1.8	2.8	0.1	0.0	2.8	2.9
GOVERNMENT SERVICE (INCLUDES MILITARY)	17.1	1.5	3.0	21.6	1.1	1.2	2.2	4.5	1.1	1.5	3.3	5.9	0.5	1.0	4.0	5.5
UNALLOCATED TO INDUSTRY	0.0	0.0	0.0	0.0	0.0	0.0	0.0	0.0	5.8	3.9	4.1	13.8	0.0	0.0	9.7	9.7
TOTAL	40.2	5.3	54.2	100.0	4.4	2.9	92.7	100.0	35.5	24.0	40.5	100.0	2.4	2.0	95.6	100.0

Type I = % of period change in female clerical employment due to overall labor force growth and change in clerical share of employment within industries

Type II = % of period change in female clerical employment due to differential growth of industries.

Type III = % of period of change in female clerical employment due to change in women's share of clerical employment within industries.

Source: Same as for Table 5.14.

performed, with women's share of clerical employment increasing greatly in all industries. The industries which contributed most to the increased role of women in clerical work were manufacturing and trade, the two industries which contributed most to overall clerical growth (see table 4.9). The transportation and finance industries, which also contributed significantly to overall clerical growth, were less important in the hiring of women in this period. Women's share of clerical employment increased less in these two important industries than it did overall.

From 1910 to 1930 the three types of change all contributed significantly to overall change in the number of women in clerical jobs. Of all women clerical workers added over that period, 35.5% were hired because of normal labor force growth and actual change in the clerical share of industries' work forces with no change in the propensity to hire women for clerical jobs (Type I). An additional 24% were employed because the industries with greater propensities to hire women clerical workers grew faster than others (Type II). The remainder of the change (40.5%) was due to the increase in women's share of clerical employment within industries. The most important industries for increasing women's clerical employment from 1910 to 1930 were manufacturing and finance. In manufacturing most of the increase in the number of women clerical workers was due to Type I change. In finance, however, the bulk of the growth was due to a change in the propensity to hire women for clerical jobs within the industry. This change in hiring practices was extremely important because the financial sector had a higher proportion of its labor force in clerical occupations than did any other industry. However, as late as 1910, this industry showed a relatively low propensity to hire women for clerical jobs. Therefore, even though the finance sector was small in terms of total employment, the change in women's share of clerical employment in this sector contributed 12% of the total increase over these 20 years.

During the entire period (1870–1930) growth in the number of women clerical workers was dominated by Type III change, and the most important industries were manufacturing, trade, and finance. The professional service sector contributed only 10% of the overall growth even though it had the highest propensity to hire women in the later years (72% female in 1910 and 78% in 1930). This is because of the relatively small size of the sector and the small percentage clerical of total employment in the sector. Government service contributed only 5.5% of the 60-year increase in female clerical employment even though it started out as the biggest employer of women clerical workers. The reason for this is that the female share of clerical employment in government failed to grow as fast as the female share in other industries did.

TABLE 5.17

PERCENT OF CLERICAL WORKERS IN EACH SUB-OCCUPATION, BY INDUSTRY, 1910

	Bookkeepers Cashiers Accountants	Clerks	Shipping Clerks	Stenographers Typists	Total Clerical
Agriculture/forestry/fishing	57.3	31.4 ⎤ 31.4	----	11.3	100.0
Mining	48.1	40.3 ⎤ 40.3	----	11.5	100.0
Manufacturing	30.4	39.5 ⎤ 50.9	11.4	18.7	100.0
Construction	45.3	37.3 ⎤ 37.3	---	17.5	100.0
Transportation/public utilities	20.0	67.8 ⎤ 69.4	1.6	10.7	100.0
Trade	50.8	14.0 ⎤ 20.9	6.9	28.3	100.0
Finance/insurance real estate	37.4	35.6 ⎤ 35.6	----	18.0	100.0
Professional service (includes education)	12.0	26.9 ⎤ 26.9	----	61.1	100.0
Domestic/personal service	28.4	67.3 ⎤ 67.5	0.2	4.1	100.0
Government service (includes military)	6.1	85.0 ⎤ 85.0	---	8.9	100.0
TOTAL	33.3	41.1 ⎤ 46.2	5.1	20.5	100.0

Source: Compiled from U. S. Bureau of the Census, 1910 Census of Population, IV, Occupations, pp. 302-433.

TABLE 5.18

PERCENT OF CLERICAL WORKERS IN EACH SUB-OCCUPATION BY INDUSTRY, 1930

	Accountants	Book-keepers Cashiers	}	Clerks	Office Appliance Operators	Shipping Clerks	}	Steno-graphers Typists	Total Clerical
Agriculture/ forestry/fishing	4.4	37.5	41.9	33.9	0	0.2	34.1	22.1	100.0
Mining	10.2	23.5	33.7	47.9	0.6	1.6	50.1	16.2	100.0
Manufacturing	4.9	17.9	22.8	47.5	1.3	10.1	58.9	18.4	100.0
Construction	5.4	36.5	41.9	36.5	0.4	0.6	37.5	20.6	100.0
Transportation/ public utilities	5.7	14.2	19.9	64.7	1.2	1.2	67.1	13.0	100.0
Trade	6.3	35.4	41.7	29.7	1.2	6.0	36.9	21.3	100.0
Finance/insurance real estate	3.9	18.3	22.2	50.8	0.6	0.1	51.5	26.3	100.0

TABLE 5.18 (Continued)

	Accountants	Book-keepers Cashiers	Clerks	Office Appliance Operators	Shipping Clerks	Steno-graphers Typists	Total Clerical
Professional services (includes education)	6.4	13.4	40.7	0.3	0.2	39.0	100.0
		{19.8}		{41.2}			
Domestic/personal service	3.1	33.2	56.7	0.1	0.6	6.2	100.0
		{36.3}		{57.4}			
Government service (includes military)	3.3	4.8	76.2	0.4	0.1	15.2	100.0
		{8.1}		{76.7}			
Unallocated	5.8	16.6	41.6	2.3	1.5	32.1	100.0
		{22.4}		{45.4}			
TOTAL	5.1	20.0	48.7	1.0	4.0	21.3	100.0
		{25.1}		{53.7}		21.3	100.0

Sources: U. S. Bureau of the Census, 1930 Census of Population, VI, General Report on Occupations, pp. 412–587.

TABLE 5.19

WOMEN'S SHARE OF EMPLOYMENT IN CLERICAL SUB-OCCUPATION, BY INDUSTRY, 1910

	Bookkeepers Cashiers Accountants	Clerks	Shipping Clerks	Stenographers Typist	Total Clerical
Agriculture/forestry/fishing	21.4	15.3	---	76.3	25.7
Mining	7.5	4.2	---	62.4	12.5
Manufacturing	32.6	26.4 ⎱21.2⎰	3.2	84.3	36.5
Construction	31.1	9.7	---	80.0	31.7
Transportation/public utilities	18.7	7.7 ⎱7.5⎰	1.5	58.0	15.1
Trade	48.6	32.3 ⎱22.3⎰	2.0	86.7	53.8
Finance/insurance/real estate	16.1	14.3	---	88.3	29.6
Professional service (includes education)	59.9	39.4	---	88.8	72.0
Domestic/personal service	59.0	14.6 ⎱14.7⎰	3.2	88.1	30.3
Government service (includes military)	25.0	17.4	---	62.9	21.9
TOTAL	36.1	18.4 ⎱16.6⎰	2.7	83.2	36.7

Source: Same as for Table 5.17.

What accounts for the differing rates at which women increased their share of clerical employment in the various industries? It might be expected that those industries which experienced the fastest growth in their clerical labor forces would have the fastest increases in the number of women clerical workers as well. To test this supposition, correlation coefficients were computed for the relationship between the growth rates of total clerical employment and female clerical employment by industry for the periods 1870–1880, 1880–1910, and 1910–1930. For the two later periods there was significant positive correlation (1880–1910, r = .84; 1910–1930, r = .66) between these growth rates. There was no significant relationship found for 1870–1880.

The differences among industries in women's share of clerical employment will be, in part, related to the kinds of clerical functions performed in the various industries. We know, for example, that women made up a very large proportion of stenographers and typists and a much smaller proportion of clerks. Therefore, industries which employed many typists would tend to have a much higher female share of clerical employment. For 1910 and 1930 the U.S. census provides information which allows for the examination of the occupational distribution of clerical workers by sex within each industry. Tables 5.17 and 5.18 present distributions of clerical employment among sub-occupations by industry. For 1910 clerical employment is broken into the three standard sub-occupations with information provided separately on shipping clerks for those industries which employed a significant number of shipping clerks. For 1930 (table 5.18) a more detailed occupational breakdown is available with six categories: accountants, bookkeepers, and cashiers; clerks; office appliance operators, shipping clerks; stenographers and typists. The figures underneath the brackets re-aggregate the distribution into the three standard sub-occupations to allow easy comparison with 1910. Overall, there was a decline from 1910 to 1930 in the proportion of clerical workers who were bookkeepers, cashiers, and accountants, a small increase in the proportion who were stenographers and typists, and a large increase in the proportion who were clerks. Since most stenographers and typists were women and most clerks were men, we would expect industries that used proportionately more stenographers and typists to have greater female shares of their labor forces.

Tables 5.19 and 5.20 show women's share of employment in each sub-occupation, by industry, for 1910 and 1930. There was considerable variation among industries in the propensity to hire women even within occupations. In 1910, 36% of all bookkeepers, cashiers, and accountants were female, but women's share of the sub-occupation varied from 7.5% in mining to nearly 60% in professional service. In 1910 the mining

TABLE 5.20

WOMEN'S SHARE OF EMPLOYMENT IN CLERICAL SUB-OCCUPATIONS BY INDUSTRY, 1930

	Accountants	Book-keepers Cashiers	Clerks	Office Appliance Operators	Shipping Clerks	Steno-graphers Typists	Total Clerical
Agriculture/ forestry/fishing	9.2 46.18	50.5	41.0	---- 39.23	9.5	94.6	54.4
Mining	3.2 17.75	24.1	12.7	79.4 13.27	1.6	87.4	26.8
Manufacturing	7.6 46.88	57.6	33.9	80.6 29.63	3.1	94.4	45.5
Construction	6.5 43.74	49.2	28.0	64.8 27.92	1.2	94.7	48.3
Transportation/ public utilities	19.4 38.45	50.1	23.2	91.2 24.04	1.6	89.3	35.4
Trade	10.6 61.93	70.9	43.5	92.8 38.35	2.0	96.5	60.5
Finance/insurance real estate	10.0 31.64	57.0	40.8	84.8 41.23	5.6	97.8	57.7

TABLE 5.20 (continued)

	Accountants	Book-keepers Cashiers	Clerks	Office Appliance Operators	Shipping Clerks	Steno-graphers Typists	Total Clerical
Professional services (includes education)	7.7	81.9	69.9	67.3	2.6	97.8	78.2
		57.84		69.50			
Domestic/personal service	18.8	78.2	35.6	85.7	29.0	96.9	53.1
		73.12		36.05			
Government services (includes military)	12.6	50.5	27.6	71.2	4.7	90.3	37.9
		35.21		27.77			
Unallocated	7.4	67.5	52.5	87.8	3.6	96.1	66.5
		51.68		52.67			
TOTAL	8.9	63.1	36.8	85.9	2.9	95.4	52.1
		52.0		35.24			52.1

Sources: Same as for Table 5.18.

industry was least likely to hire women for clerical jobs in all occupations and professional service was most likely to hire women. It is not always true that an industry with a low propensity to hire women in one occupation would have a similarly low propensity in others. For example, in finance/insurance/real estate women made up a smaller proportion of bookkeepers and accountants but a larger proportion of stenographers and typists than they did nationally. An overwhelming majority of shipping clerks were males in all industries, probably because this occupation had a large manual component.

By 1930 women's share had risen in every industry and in virtually every sub-occupation within each industry. The finer occupational breakdown reveals that the 5% of all clerical workers who worked as accountants were mostly males. There was almost no change in the female share of shipping clerks over the 20 years. The category of office machine operator, which first appeared in the 1930 census, is very interesting even though only 1% of all clerical workers were enumerated in that occupation. We know that the use of office appliances was much more widespread than this figure would indicate and that many of those counted as bookkeepers and clerks regularly used office machines other than typewriters in their work.[16] What is so significant about the office appliance category here is the overwhelming dominance of females in the occupation. Eighty-six percent of those enumerated as office appliance operators were women, which hints at the importance of mechanization of clerical tasks for women's employment in the office.

Changes in the number of female clerical workers can be related to the distribution of employment across clerical sub-occupations. Increased employment of women clerical workers in an industry can be seen as stemming from:

(1) growth of employment within sub-occupations holding female share of sub-occupational employment constant. An industry which has a high percentage of its clerical work force in relatively female-dominated sub-occupations will contribute disproportionately to the growth in the number of women clerical workers. A change in the composition of clerical employment in favor of female-dominated sub-occupations will increase women's share of the clerical work force even without a change in the propensity to hire women within sub-occupations. The proportion of the total period increase in the number of female clerical workers related to changing employment within a sub-occupation (E-change in table 5.21) for an industry is measured as:

$$\left[S_i \cdot \left(\frac{FS_i}{S_i} \right)_t \right] / \Delta FC$$

where S_i =   total employment in a sub-occupation in industry i

FS$_i$ =   female employment in a sub-occupation in industry i

ΔFC =   period change in total female clerical employment (all industries, all sub-occupations).

(2) change in the female share of employment within sub-occupations. The proportion of total period change in female clerical employment related to the effect of change in the sex composition of employment within a sub-occupation (SC-change in table 5.21) for an industry is measured as:

$$\left[S_{t-n} \cdot \Delta\left(\frac{FS_i}{S_i}\right) \right] / \Delta FC$$

This term includes a pure effect of changes in sex composition

$$\left[S_{i_t} \cdot \Delta\left(\frac{FS_i}{S_i}\right) \right] / FC$$

plus the effect of interaction between sex composition and employment changes

$$\left[\Delta S_i \cdot \Delta\left(\frac{FS_i}{S_i}\right) \right] / \Delta FC$$

Table 5.21 divides the increase from 1910 to 1930 in the number of female clerical workers into these two component parts. The cell entries are the proportion of total female clerical employment growth over the two decades attributable to E-change and SC-change in sub-occupations and industries. For example, 5.44% of added female office workers were related to increased hiring of clerks in manufacturing, and an additional 3.44% were due to the greater propensity of manufacturing firms to hire women to be clerks. Overall, 55.76% of the two-decade increase in female clerical workers can be attributed simply to expanded clerical employment, independent of any change in the propensity to hire women within sub-occupations. The largest contributors to this growth were the manufacturing, financial, and professional service industries because of more hiring of clerks, stenographers, and typists. Included in total E-change is any increase in female clerical employment due to changes in the composition of clerical employment in favor of female dominated sub-occupations. This effect was calculated, but the results are not reported in the table because the effect is very small and slightly negative overall. This indicates that the increase in women's share of clerical employment cannot be explained by more rapid employment growth in

TABLE 5.21

DIVISION OF INDUSTRIAL CHANGE IN FEMALE CLERICAL EMPLOYMENT INTO COMPONENT
PARTS DUE TO CHANGING SUB-OCCUPATIONAL DISTRIBUTION AND CHANGING
PROPENSITY TO HIRE WOMEN WITHIN SUB-OCCUPATIONS 1910–1930

	Bookkeepers, Cashiers, Accountants		Clerks (except in Stores)		Typist & Stenographers		Total	
	E-change	SC-change	E-change	SC-change	E-change	SC-change	E-change	SC-change
Agriculture/ forestry/ fishing	0.02	0.06	0.02	0.05	0.07	0.02	0.11	0.13
Mining	0.01	0.06	0.02	0.08	0.18	0.07	0.21	0.21
Manufacturing	2.21	2.26	5.44	3.44	6.08	1.30	13.73	7.00
Construction	0.33	0.19	0.10	0.25	0.46	0.11	0.89	0.55
Transportation	0.69	1.44	0.91	4.07	1.65	1.50	3.25	7.01
Trade	2.31	2.68	2.60	2.93	1.47	1.04	6.38	6.65
Finance/ insurance/ real estate	1.56	3.12	2.34	5.96	7.40	1.07	10.30	10.12

TABLE 5.21 (Continued)

	Bookkeepers, Cashiers, Accountants		Clerks (except in Stores)		Typist & Stenographers		Total	
	E-change	SC-change	E-change	SC-change	E-change	SC-change	E-change	SC-change
Professional service	1.83	-0.07	2.47	2.26	3.78	0.64	8.08	2.83
Domestic/personal/service	0.94	0.41	0.23	0.94	0.27	0.05	1.44	1.40
Government service	0.29	.18	1.45	1.66	1.49	0.87	3.23	2.71
Unallocated	1.13	1.28	2.08	2.88	4.93	1.43	8.14	5.59
TOTAL	10.32	11.61	17.66	24.52	27.78	8.10	55.76	44.23
							100.00	

E-change = % of total change in female clerical employment due to increased hiring within sub-occupations without change in proportion female.

SC-change = % of total change in female clerical employment related to increase in % female within sub-occupations.

Sources: Same as for Table 5.17.

the sub-occupations that were relatively more female intensive at the beginning of the period. However, because the analysis is based on such highly aggregated categories, this cannot be regarded as a strong result.

SC-change measures the effect on female clerical employment of increases in women's share of employment within sub-occupations. Overall, this accounted for 44.23% of the two-decade change in the number of female clerical workers and all of the change in women's share of total clerical employment. The industries which contributed most to SC-change were manufacturing, transportation, trade, and most importantly the finance/real estate/insurance sector which showed a notable increase in the propensity to hire women as bookkeepers and clerks. From table 5.21 it can be concluded that over this 20-year period the most important causes of female clerical labor force growth were the greater propensity to hire women to be clerks in all industries (SC-change) and the rapid increase in the number of typists and stenographers. (E-change).

Summary

This chapter has examined the growth of women's employment in clerical occupations that took place from 1870 to 1930 and has described the female clerical labor force in terms of demographic characteristics, occupational and industrial distributions. At the beginning of the period only about .1% of all female non-agricultural gainful workers were in clerical jobs, and 2.5% of all U.S. clerical workers were women. By 1930, office work provided employment for nearly 20% of all employed women, and women held over half of all clerical positions. Female participation in office production increased in every decade, but the most notable changes came in 1880–90 and 1910–20.

Women in clerical jobs were more likely to be unmarried, young, native-born, and white than were women workers generally. This was due in part to the greater educational attainment of young women and to the preferences of employers for young, unmarried clerical workers. Despite increased participation by older and married women in the field, as late as 1930 82% of women clerical workers were unmarried and over half were under age 25.

In the early years of the period, government and professional service were the biggest employers of female clerical labor. By 1930, trade, manufacturing, and finance hired the largest numbers of female office employees. All industries experienced substantial changes in their propensities to hire women for office work.

Female clerical workers were generally found in the most routine and mechanical jobs. A viable typewriter was produced in 1874, and its use spread quickly. Women operated the writing machine almost from the beginning, and a large proportion of the growth of female clerical employment, particularly in the early years, was related to the rapid growth of employment in the stenographer-typist category. Later on, women were increasingly employed in clerking and bookkeeping positions. In the 1910–20 decade, many women were hired to fill clerk positions during the First World War.

6

What Caused the Change in the Sex Composition of the Clerical Labor Force?

This chapter considers explanations for the dramatic increase in women's share of clerical employment. The analysis in chapter 2 showed that most of the increase in women's participation in the non-agricultural labor force from 1870 to 1930 was associated with growth of employment in occupational categories already dominated by women at the beginning of the period. The one major exception is the clerical sector, where women substantially "took over" the occupational category. The female share of clerical employment increased from 2.5% in 1870 to 52.5% in 1930. This expanded employment of women in clerical jobs accounted for nearly one-quarter of the 60-year growth in the size of the female non-agricultural labor force (see tables 2.13 and 2.14). An understanding of the forces which contributed to the female "takeover" of clerical occupations is therefore vital to any examination of the change in women's role in the American labor force. This change is all the more interesting because of the continuing extreme sexual segregation of the work force. The feminization of the clerical sector presents a rare instance of substantial change in the sexual division of labor.

Few histories of the American labor force have devoted serious attention to the causes of increased employment of women in clerical occupations. Even studies focused specifically on women workers have dealt mainly with women in blue collar jobs or in the professions, though the past few years have seen more scholarly research devoted to white collar non-professionals. Despite this comparative neglect, many have noted the extremely rapid expansion of women's role in the clerical sector and have offered suggestions as to likely causes. This chapter will discuss and evaluate a series of possible explanations for the feminization of the clerical work force, many of them derived from the literature that has touched on this issue. These explanations can be divided into two categories: those which emphasize supply side considerations and others which stress demand factors.

Supply Related Explanations

Overall Increase in Women's Labor Force Participation. As was described in chapter 2, women's overall participation in the non-agricultural labor force increased during every decade covered by this study. The analysis in chapter 3 suggested that this was related to changes within the family economy such that daughters' labor force decisions became less closely associated with economic conditions within their parents' families. Many of the young women who increasingly made independent decisions about participation in the work force found jobs in the expanded clerical sector. It is therefore plausible to argue that the actions of employers in hiring women for office jobs represented an adjustment to this exogenous increase in the supply of labor. If this is correct, then the fundamental changes are those that occurred in the family economy and that led more women to allocate more productive time to market pursuits. The employment of women in clerical jobs would merely represent a reaction on the part of the labor market to this supply shift.

This explanation predicts that the timing of increased female participation in clerical employment should parallel the timing of overall female labor force participation growth. An examination of table 5.2 reveals that female participation in the total non-agricultural labor force increased at a comparatively steady rate with the most rapid growth coming in the 1880s and the 1900–1910 decade. The female clerical labor force grew more rapidly and in a much more erratic fashion, with the greatest increases in the 1880s and in the first decade of the twentieth century. This lack of correspondence in timing of the two series suggests that, although the increase in the supply of female labor was undoubtedly a stimulus to the hiring of women for clerical jobs, it is not the whole story.

Increased Educational Levels of Women. Women who obtained clerical jobs were required to have achieved comparatively high levels of education.[1] Most who entered office work, particularly before World War I, were native white daughters of the respectable middle class.[2] Few opportunities for acceptable gainful employment were available to these women. "The respectable woman, if forced to earn a living might properly make and sell preserves or pies, illustrate seashells or teach

TABLE 6.1

WOMEN'S SHARE OF PUBLIC HIGH SCHOOL ENROLLMENT, 1890-1930
AND TOTAL HIGH SCHOOL GRADUATES 1870-1930

	1870	1880	1890	1900	1910	1920	1930
Women high school graduates as percent of all high school graduates	55.85	55.13	57.58	59.87	59.29	60.26	54.96
Women enrolled in public high schools as percent of all persons enrolled			42.10	41.64	43.55	47.54	48.03

Sources: Graduation figures from: U. S. Office of Education,
Biennial Surveys of Education, 1950-1952, United States
Department of Health, Education, and Welfare (United
States Government Printing Office, 1955), p. 22.

Enrollment figures from: U. S. Bureau of Education,
Bulletin, no. 20, part 2 (United States Government
Printing Office, 1931), p. 607.

TABLE 6.2

NUMBER OF STUDENTS AND WOMEN'S SHARE OF ENROLLMENT IN PRIVATE COMMERCIAL AND BUSINESS
SCHOOLS 1871-1929 AND IN COMMERCIAL COURSES IN PUBLIC HIGH SCHOOLS, 1914-1925

	Private Commercial and Business Schools			Enrollment in Commercial Courses in Public High Schools		
	total students	female students	percent female	total students	female students	percent female
1871	6,460	281	4.34			
1875	26,109	2,332	8.93			
1880	27,146	2,770	10.20			
1885	47,176	7,167	15.19			
1890	81,898	23,059	28.15			
1895	80,662	25,489	31.60			
1900	91,549	33,465	36.21			
1905	146,086	61,464	42.07			
1910	134,778	61,891	45.92			
1914	168,063	82,631	49.17	161,250	92,650	57.46
1915	183,286	88,416	48.24	208,605	116,379	55.79
1916	192,388	93,254	48.47	243,185	138,043	56.76
1918	289,519	193,130	66.69	278,275	173,857	62.48

TABLE 6.2 (Continued)

	Private Commercial and Business Schools			Enrollment in Commercial Courses in Public High Schools		
	total students	female students	percent female	total students	female students	percent female
1920	336,032	196,551	58.49	430,975	286,984	66.59
1925	188,363	120,116	63.77			
1929	179,759	121,215	67.43			

Sources: Private Schools:

1871–1895   Edwin G. Knepper, History of Business Education in the United States (Bowling Green: Ohio, 1941) p. 92.

1900–1918   U. S. Bureau of Education, Bulletin, no. 47, 1919, p. 5.
1920   U. S. Bureau of Education, Bulletin, no. 4, 1922, p. 1.
1925   U. S. Bureau of Education, Bulletin, no. 14, 1926, p. 3.
1929   U. S. Bureau of Education, Bulletin, no. 25, 1930, p. 3.

Public Schools: U. S. Bureau of Education, Bulletin, no. 25, 1928.

school, but that was about all till clerical positions began to open up."[3] Because of increased rates of school attendance there was rapid expansion of the group of young women who had the levels of educational attainment required of clerical workers. Female enrollment in public high schools increased relative to male's, and women were more likely to stay in high school through graduation (see table 6.1).

Many historians have seen this expanded pool of young educated women who faced limited employment opportunities as the crucial supply side cause of the feminization of the clerical labor force. For example, Margery Davies says, "there were literally thousands of women with training that qualified them for jobs that demanded literacy, but who could not find them. Excluded from most professions, these women were readily available for clerical jobs."[4]

Not only was general education important to persons seeking clerical employment, but specific training in stenography, typing, bookkeeping and other office skills was vital to success in the office. Separate schools taught business skills as early as 1852, offering instruction in business arithmetic, penmanship, and shorthand. After 1880 most schools added typewriting to their curricula and admitted women students. The number of private business colleges increased substantially.[5] Female enrollment in these schools grew quickly resulting in an increase in the supply of women trained to be clerical workers. Table 6.2 presents enrollment figures for private and public business education. In every year women made up a larger percentage of persons enrolled in private commercial education than they did of the clerical labor force, suggesting that the supply of trained women expanded even faster than employment. Also, women made up an even larger percentage of commercial students in public high schools. Public high schools began offering commercial instruction in the 1890s which effectively lowered the cost of such training and increased the supply of clerical labor. As early as 1912–1913, 63.4% of all girls in Boston public high schools were enrolled in one or more commercial subjects.[6]

The secular increase in general educational attainment certainly contributed to expanding the supply of young women who could satisy the educational requirements for clerical jobs. However, men also participated in this educational revolution, and had higher enrollment rates than women throughout the period. The increase in women's educational level is not, therefore, sufficient to explain why it was educated young women more than educated young men who filled clerical positions.

The impressive increase in women's enrollment in formal commercial education testifies to the willingness of young women to acquire the necessary training to compete for clerical jobs, and in the case of private business colleges, to bear the direct costs of such training. The figures in table 6.2 suggest that women were eager to join the clerical labor force and invested heavily in acquiring the necessary skills. It is likely, though, that the enrollment of women in commercial education courses was more a reaction to expanded employment opportunities than a cause.

Non-Pecuniary Attractions of Clerical Employment.

> For several decades office work has been look upon by large numbers of girls as the most desirable field in which to seek employment. It has been considered more desirable than the domestic, industrial and commercial job opportunities because of less physical effort involved, shorter hours, income that normally is more regular and tenure that is more secure, combined with more specious advantages such as better working conditions, generally more central and desirable working conditions and the prestige of being in the white collar group.[7]

There is no doubt that clerical work was widely regarded as attractive employment for women. Working conditions were much better than those experienced by women in manufacturing, domestic service, and retail sales. The workplace was usually clean, and office workers were not subjected to the sorts of discomforts and health hazards that were common in manufacturing work.[8] Clerical workers enjoyed much higher status than did women in other occupations, with the exception of teachers and the few other women professionals. However, there was still significant cultural disapproval of women who worked outside their homes, and young women with middle or upper-class aspirations generally hoped to avoid the necessity of entering office service. The office girl heroines of the twenties (e.g., Alice Adams and Kitty Foyle) were tragically driven to seek clerical employment by the death or business failure of a father.[9]

For daughters of the working class, clerical employment was regarded as the best work to which women could aspire and an avenue of upward mobility. Of course, for women upward mobility meant marrying a mate with good economic prospects, and many believed that white collar employment would enhance a woman's chances of marrying well. Certainly stories of clerks marrying professional men were common in the popular press.

The non-pecuniary advantages of office work help to explain the willingness of young women to offer their services to the clerical sector. The superiority of clerical work in terms of prestige and working conditions was substantial. There is, however, no evidence that the differential between clerical and other occupations in terms of these advantages changed over time in such a way as to explain the continuing increase in the participation of women in clerical jobs. And, of course, the attractiveness of the work to women does not explain why employers increasingly hired women for office jobs.

Occupational Differentials in Women's Earnings. Throughout the period 1870–1930 earnings of most women in clerical jobs were considerably higher than those of women in any of the other non-professional jobs commonly held by women. In the early part of the period female clerical workers earned even more than most teachers. These comparatively high earnings made clerical employment attractive to women workers who had few other good earnings possibilities. Studies of women's wages in this period showed that most women earned less than subsistence wages for full time work.[10]

Continuous series on occupational earnings by sex are not available so it is impossible to trace, in a systematic fashion, changes over time in occupational wage differentials. Paul Douglas found that clerical wages fell relative to manufacturing wages for the period 1890–1926, but his figures do not refer specifically to women. He concluded that "the day seems not far off when all differences in remuneration between the upper group of hard-handed and the soft-handed groups will disappear, and only compensating differences will exist."[11] Despite the lack of continuously comparable data, information from a variety of sources allows some conclusions to be drawn about changes over time in the earnings of women in clerical occupations relative to earnings of women in other occupations.

In 1876, when the first women clerks were being hired in federal offices at an average annual salary of $900, public school teachers in the District of Columbia earned between $400 and $700, with a few making as much as $800.[12] "In 1886, when a saleswoman in a dry goods store earned only $6 a week, a proficient woman typist in a business office earned $15."[13] Smuts gives the following figures on weekly wages for women in northeastern cities in 1890: domestic service, $2–$5 plus room and board; sales workers in stores, $1.50–$8; factory workers, $4–$8, stenographers and typists, $6–15.[14] In that same year, data collected by the Rhode Island Bureau of Industrial Statistics revealed that many women clerical workers still earned more than teachers.[15] In order to carry out the regression analyses in chapters 3 and 7, information from the U. S. census and the U. S. Personnel Classification Board was used to estimate wages paid to women in clerical occupations in 56 cities in 1890, and 89 cities in 1930. Detailed descriptions of this data and average wages for all cities are presented in appendix B. Based on this information, women's clerical wages in 1890 were, on average, 1.8 times women's wages in manufacturing jobs in the same city. By 1930 the ratio had fallen to 1.3. In a series collected by the Ohio Bureau of Labor Statistics for the period 1914-1926, women's clerical wages fell from 1.45 to 1.37 times women's wages in manufacturing.[16] The earnings advantage which clerical workers enjoyed over teachers seems to have disappeared by the early twentieth century. In a 1927 study of earnings of members of the National Federation of Business and Professional Women's Clubs, clerical workers with less than five years experience received annual salaries equal to 85% of salaries of similarly experienced teachers, and Club members were among the most ambitious and skilled of all women clerical workers.[17]

Based on the above information we must conclude that earnings of female clerical workers fell relative to earnings of women in other occupations throughout the 1870–1930 period. By the twentieth century, clerical workers earned less than teachers though they had previously enjoyed an advantage. In 1930 women office workers still earned more on average than women who worked in manufacturing, sales, and service jobs, but the differential had declined markedly. It is therefore unlikely that the feminization of the clerical work force can be explained by widening wage differentials which "pulled" increasing numbers of women into clerical work from other occupations.

It is possible that the decline in the relative economic rewards received by clerical workers was not as great as the figures presented here imply. Earnings simply measure the benefits associated with employment in an occupation. Also of interest are the costs which must be incurred by someone wishing to enter the occupation, i.e., the investment in human capital. If the level of skill of clerical workers fell, and/or if the costs of acquiring the necessary skills fell, it may be that the return received on human capital investment by clerical workers remained high despite the decline in relative wages.

In the early part of the period the level of education required of clerical workers was similar to that required of teachers. However, by 1930 the educational requirements for teaching had risen considerably as most states demanded at least a normal school diploma. At the same time there was an expansion of employment in lower level clerical jobs as office production became more mechanized and routine. In addition the private investment needed to acquire clerical skills declined as public schools expanded their offerings in commercial subjects. By the end of the period the human capital investment required of clerical workers was closer to that required of women in manufacturing and service employment than it was to that required of teachers. It is therefore likely that returns received by clerical workers on human capital investments did not decline as precipitously as did their relative earnings.

Demand Related Explanations

Increased Demand for Clerical Output. The demand related factor most commonly mentioned as contributing to the expansion of women's role in the clerical labor force is the rapid increase in demand for clerical output that was stimulated by the development of a larger, more complex economy, i.e., the greater need for communication and recordkeeping in bureaucratically organized business firms and government agencies. In a 1929 study of women's expanding role in clerical occupations, Grace L. Coyle gave central place to growth in the extent and kind of clerical work that "arose with the need by business and industry for accurate record-keeping and the development of large scale business practices, and with modern methods used in distributing the output of a vastly expanded economy."[18]

Robert Smuts also emphasized the importance of increased demand for clerical output: "In industry, in commerce, in government, and in every other sector of the economy, the expanding scope and complexity of operations has brought a vast increase in the need for record-keeping and communicating—a need which has been met mainly by women. . . ."[19] In a recent article which focused on explanations for the feminization of the clerical labor force, Margery Davies says "The expansion and consolidation of enterprises in the 1880s and 1890s created a large demand for clerical labor," and notes that, "in order to fill the need for clerical workers, employers turn to the large pool of educated female labor."[20]

The analysis in the previous chapter focused on this shifting demand for clerical output and its effect on the employment of clerical labor. Certainly the six decades covered by this study were characterized by major changes in the structure of organizations and of the economy which stimulated demand for clerical labor. However, by itself this shift in demand can be only a partial explanation for the increased employment of women in clerical jobs. We must discover why it was women more than men who were hired to fill the new clerical positions.

Female Comparative Advantage in Clerical Work. Both scholars and contemporary commentators have suggested that women had a comparative advantage in the performance of certain clerical tasks and that there was a disproportionate increase in the demand for workers to perform these specific tasks. This argument is usually linked with the effects of greater mechanization and routinization of tasks in office production that took place beginning with the adoption of the typewriter and continuing throughout the period. Elizabeth F. Baker discussed the relationship between technology and women's work and the development of almost assembly line division of labor in the office.[21] Nathan Rosenberg observed that: "Those inventions which lowered the cost of office work—the typewriter, telephone and other new office equipment—increased employment opportunities of a kind which were readily undertaken by females."[22] This suggests that technological change led to a change in the composition of demand for clerical labor in favor of workers with different characteristics from those who had performed clerical jobs before. After mechanization of office production, it was common to see the replacement of men's jobs by a combination of women, machines, and new techniques. In a classic office text written in 1919 the recorder of a sugar company is quoted: "all the bookkeeping of this company . . . is done by three girls and three bookkeeping machines. . . . With the aid of the six adders on the three machines the work is always in balance and one operator takes the place of three men."[23]

Many writers suggested that women had particular characteristics which gave them a comparative advantage in the mechanized office. A widely-held belief was that "women seemed to be especially suited as typists and switchboard operators because they were tolerant of routine, careful, and manually dexterous."[24] And nearly everyone seemed to believe that women were born to be file clerks:

> File clerks must be rapid and accurate at detail work, attentive to operations which are continually repeated but slightly varied, and must have automatic carefulness in replacing papers. The nature of the activity calls for intelligent and trained women rather than men or boys. Women can handle detail work with more persistent accuracy and patience and with swift, automatic expertness. The head of a centralized filing department, however, occupying a position coordinate with that of the other department heads should preferably be a man.[25]

In addition of their flying fingers and tolerance for boredom, women were thought by some observers to be particularly suited to work in the transformed office because they were docile and lacked ambition. In 1904 a correspondent for the *Typewriter Trade Journal* interviewed typewriter concerns about the desires of the employers who came to them looking for trained stenographers to hire. He found that "of course, the principle reason why women are more preferable is that they lack ambition that men usually possess and are therefore content to remain in a stenographer position . . . while the men are more restless . . . ."[26]

Margery Davies has suggested that mechanization may have contributed to the feminization of the office work force by changing the nature of the work process enough to circumvent stereotyped ideas of the appropriate sexual division of labor, thereby allowing the growth of demand for women to perform clerical jobs. She contends that the typewriter was "sex-neutral" and therefore" [s]ince typing had not been identified as a masculine job, women who were employed as typists did not encounter the criticism that they were taking over 'men's work".[27]

There is certainly a striking coincidence of feminization of the clerical work force with mechanization and routinization of office production.   It is less clear that this coincidence is related to a fundamental female comparative advantage in the performance of clerical tasks.   Judith Smith, in a study of attitudes toward women as clerical workers as reflected in the popular press, has found that dramatic changes in the perception of the suitability of women to perform clerical tasks accompanied employment changes.[28]   It is quite possible that the perceived comparative advantage of women in clerical work was merely a rationalization for changes in employment practices which were due to other causes.   At the end of this chapter we will discuss an economic model which ties feminization of clerical work to technological change without depending on argument of female comparative advantage in office tasks.

Female-Male Earnings Differential in Clerical Occupations. The character-istic of female clerical workers which most endeared them to employers was, of course, their low wages. Most studies have held that the employment of women in offices was related to the relative cheapness of female labor. Although data on wages of clerical workers is sketchy, it is certain that women received lower wages than men in clerical occupations throughout the period. The first women clerks hired by the Treasury Department to clip currency during the Civil War were paid half of what men were paid for the same work.[29] Most comparisons of women's wages with men's in clerical work are questionable because women and men often did not perform the same clerical tasks. The 1890 Census of Manufactures published data on wages paid in 1889 to "officers, firm members and clerks" in manufacturing establishments (see appendix B). The female-male earnings ratio based on these figures is .48; but this certainly overstates the sex differential because there were many more high-salaried male officers included in the data.

The longest continuous series on clerical wages in this period was collected by the Ohio Bureau of Labor Statistics for 1914–1926. Based on median weekly wage rates, we find that the female-male ratio of clerical wage rates was .602 in 1914 and .587 in 1926 with little variation in between.[30] For 1929–30 there are two studies which allow comparisons of the average wages received by females and males in similar clerical jobs. Based on the data collected by the U.S. Personnel Classification Board on 193,000 employees in private industry jobs equivalent to government classifications CAF-1 and CAF-2 (the lowest clerical levels), the female-male ratio was .84 in CAF-1 and .80 in CAF-2.[31] The differentials were smaller when wages of employees in the same industry were compared. The Life Office Management Association studied wages of all clerical workers employed by U.S. life insurance companies in 1930. Overall, women earned on average 65% of men's wages. However, when comparisons were made of employees in the same job class, the average female-male ratio was .83.[32]

The data on clerical wages is not reliable or consistent enough to draw firm conclusions about movement over time in the female-male earnings gap. It is clear that women in office work usually earned less than did men throughout the period. This would provide a continued incentive for employers to hire women for clerical jobs. However, in order for the wage differential to explain the increase in women's share of clerical employment, it would be necessary for women's wages to have fallen relative to men's, holding relative productivities constant. None of the available evidence suggests that this was the case. It appears more likely that the sex differential in clerical wages narrowed or remained constant. Alternatively, an increase in women's productivity relative to men's (at a constant wage differential) would lead to increased feminization of the work force. The next section will present the argument that technological change produced just such a differential effect on productivities.

A Human Capital Explanation for Change in the Sex Composition of the Clerical Labor Force

We have considered and evaluated a number of possible explanations for the observed change in the sex composition of clerical employment. This was a complex phenomenon involving factors on both the demand and supply sides of the market; no one factor should be expected to explain all, or even most, of the employment shift. The explanations discussed above should not be viewed as competing hypotheses. They are more properly seen as pieces of the puzzle; all contribute in some degree to an understanding of this remarkable change in the sexual division of labor. However, despite this plethora of explanations, problems remain, and the story is incomplete.

On the supply side, secular growth in educational attainment and changes in the family economy contributed to an increase in the number of young, native white women desiring remunerative and respectable employment. This supply increase was necessary to the feminization of the clerical labor force, but it is not a sufficient explanation. Variations over time in women's share of clerical employment do not coincide well with variations in women's labor force participation. We must ask why so large a portion of this increased supply found employment in this particular sector.

On the demand side, growth in the size and complexity of organizations stimulated the development of administrative systems that required more clerical output; and women's low wages were an incentive to hire them. There are, however, many other instances in which demand increases have not stimulated such changes in the composition of the work force, and women's wages are lower than men's in all occupations. We must look for factors which were peculiar to the clerical sector in this period and which led to the massive change in the employment of women.

Some have suggested that changes in clerical work processes in this period led to an increase in the demand for skills that were particularly feminine. During these 60 years, clerical production was transformed by the adoption of new office machines and procedures. Work was subdivided and routinized, and office production came to resemble industrial production with specialized labor and continuous work processes. Different skills were required of workers in the new office, but it is questionable that these were feminine in any essential way. Training in skills suitable to clerical employment was not included in conventional female socialization in the same way as was training in housekeeping, sewing, and child nurturing. Attitudes about the relationship between stereotypically female personality traits and the suitability of women for office employment were changing during this period; and as is common, people showed a strong tendency to believe that whatever many women do it is "natural" for them to do.[33] The observed changes in attitudes were probably a response to, rather than a cause, of employment change.

A close correspondence exists between the timing of changes in women's share of clerical employment and changes in clerical technology. In particular, the 1880s and the 1910s, the decades of greatest change in office production techniques, saw the most spectacular increases in women's role in the clerical labor force. (See discussion in chapter 4 on changes in clerical technology.) A complete explanation for the change in the sex composition of clerical employment requires that a mechanism be specified which convincingly connects technologically related transformations in clerical work processes to the employment of women.

The following human capital model makes such a connection and thereby fills a crucial hole in the story of the feminization of the clerical work force.

The movement of women into clerical employment took place in two ways. First, some women simply took over, with no substantial change in job content or responsibility, work which had previously been done by men. This was the case when women were first hired to clip bills at the Treasury in the 1860s. The U.S. Treasurer, Elias Spinner, was pleased with the results of this experiment saying that "Some females are doing more and better work for $900 per annum than many male clerks who were paid double that amount."[34] In such cases it is to be expected that women's ability to do the same work for less remuneration would lead to complete female domination of the occupation as soon as employers learned of women's productivity. Females would accept lower wages when their alternatives were limited either by discrimination, by their own preferences for job characteristics, or by factors which lowered their productivity in other pursuits. There would be a tendency for the occupation to become segregated, though imperfect information about women's productivity, discriminatory preferences, or other entry barriers might produce time lags and variations among employers in the hiring of women. Recent work by Cindy Aron using federal personnel records from 1862 to 1890 has uncovered instances in which women and men were employed in the same clerical jobs in government offices for prolonged periods of time. She has also found considerable variation among individual offices in their propensities to hire women for certain posts; this variation seems to be due to discriminatory preferences on the part of supervisors who made personnel decisions.[35]

The second way that feminization of the clerical labor force took place was much more common. Here women found employment in clerical positions that were significantly different from those held by men. The outputs may have been substantially the same, but the production methods differed. In her classic study of women's occupations, Janet Hooks commented, "In taking on the functions of clerical workers, women did not replace men. Rather they found entirely new opportunities."[36] The usual situation in clerical work was the transformation of the work process so that women produced clerical output in an environment where tasks were routine and divided over a number of workers, office machines were used, and decision-making responsibility rested in the hands of managers who were separate from the clerical work force.

The discussion of the pre-modern office in chapter 4 emphasized the following qualities of clerical jobs prior to the development of the mechanized office: (1) Clerical jobs involved more skills that would now be considered managerial, and clerical workers were expected to assume some responsibility for business decision making. (2) Clerical jobs were the accepted entry point into managerial careers and therefore included training which developed managerial skills. (3) A substantial portion of the skills of clerical workers were specific to individual firms and therefore could only be acquired on the job.

Human capital theory suggests a model which embodies a mechanism that can be used to tie changes in the kinds of skills required of clerical workers to changes in the sex composition of the clerical labor force. The model uses Becker's distinction between firm-specific skills and firm-general skills. Specific skills are those that increase a worker's productivity more in the firm providing the training. General skills are those that increase productivity in all firms. The theory predicts that whenever skills are firm-specific, the individual firm will be willing to absorb at least part of the investment in training and will pay a premium over the wage that the employee could command in other firms. However, the willingness of the firm to offer specific training and absorb the costs is inversely related to the expected turnover rate of the employee.[37] Since women were expected to have shorter tenure with an employer because they usually left the labor force when they married, the theory predicts that women would most likely be hired for occupations in which the required skills were general rather than specific and that women would be expected to move into jobs whenever the required skills became more general.[38]

The changes which took place in clerical work during this period fit the model very well. Mechanization and routinization reduced the specific skill component of most clerical jobs. Training in the new general skills could take place in schools where costs would be borne by the students (and by the public in the case of commercial education in public schools). Employers would be willing to hire women, despite their high expected turnover, for jobs in which the on-the-job training requirement was low. Since women's wages were lower than men's, women would be expected to completely dominate in jobs with the lowest firm-specific skill component. This appears to be the case in the most mechanical and routine jobs such as typing and filing which were rapidly taken over by women. When men were observed to be working in these jobs, they were often serving as entry points to high level positions. In 1914 the Women's Industrial and Educational Union of Boston commented that:

> While stenography and typewriting is almost exclusively a women's occupation, less than 1/5 being men, many railroad offices, some government and occasional

business offices demand or prefer men stenographers, who may learn the business of the office and later be in line for promotion to more responsible places. Several offices visited in this investigation gave this reason for their preference for men as stenographers.[39]

And in 1926 the National Industrial Conference Board observed that when men were found in the lower levels of clerical jobs, it was usually the beginning of on-the-job training for a position leading to further advancement.[40]

Employers clearly expected women to have short tenure in the office, and this kept them from investing in the training of women. In a standard business text of the day, J. W. Schultze gave the following advice: "The office manager may as well make up his mind at once that the hiring of female clerks with a view toward development for executive positions is an uncertain problem because so many girls marry just as they have become most efficient. Occasionally this possibility may be foreseen. More often it cannot."[41]

In addition, men were preferred for supervisory positions because women were expected to have lower productivity as supervisors because of discrimination by fellow employees. After noting that most chief clerks were men, the National Industrial Conference Board explained: "It is generally recognized that employers are reluctant to place women in positions involving supervision of a large number of male employees. It is also true, as a general rule, that women employees work more willingly and contentedly under the supervision of a man than under that of a woman."[42]

In 1927 a survey was taken of the preferences of office managers for the sex of persons filling various office jobs. The survey found that managers had strong preferences about the sex of persons to fill most jobs and produced the following list:[43]

Women's trades	*Men's trades*	*Mixed trades*
file clerk	correspondent	ledger clerks
secretarial stenographer	receiving clerk	statistical clerk
stenographer	shipping clerk	cost clerk
dictating machine operator	timekeeper	payroll clerk
bookkeeping machine operator	stock clerk	mail clerk
calculating machine operator		bookkeeper
typist		

Women's trades (cont.)
billing clerk
multigraph operator

The women's jobs on this list were the most routine and mechanical. The men's jobs were supervisory (timekeeper), had a high proportion of firm-specific skills (correspondent), and required physical strength (shipping, receiving and stock clerks). In addition, when men were found in the mixed trades, they were more commonly in higher paid supervisory positions or were in training for more advanced positions in the company.

The human capital model presented here contributes a crucial element to the explanation of change in the sex distribution of the clerical labor force because it specifies a mechanism that connects technological changes with the employment of women. Over time, mechanization and routinization of clerical procedures led to reductions in the firm-specific components of many office jobs and consequently to greater willingness to employ women who had higher expected turnover. Moreover, the analysis in chapter 5 shows that jobs listed above as "women's trades," i.e., the general skills occupations, were among the fastest growing in the clerical cateogory.

Summary and Conclusion

This chapter has reviewed and evaluated a series of explanations for changes in the sex composition of clerical employment that took place from 1870 to 1930. Substantial changes on both the supply and demand sides of this market contributed to the overall increase in clerical employment and to the dramatic "takeover" of clerical work by women.

The pattern of increase over time in women's share of clerical employment corresponds closely to the timing of advances in clerical technology. Two decades, 1880–1890 and 1910–1920, witnessed the greatest changes in the sex distribution of clerical employment. The experience of the 1880s was related to the adoption of the typewriter and the revolution in office production that accompanied it. The 1910–1920 decade was notable for relative shortages of male labor because of the war and for rapid increases in mechanization and routinization of office production associated with widespread application of scientific management techniques. The human capital model presented in this chapter ties the feminization of the clerical work force to changes in office technology by focusing on the relationship between changing general/specific skill components of clerical jobs and the propensity of employers to hire workers with high expected turnover.

Few women were hired for clerical jobs when the skills required of office workers were mostly firm-specific. Both workers and employers shared the expectation that women in clerical occupations, the great majority of whom were under age 25 and unmarried, would exhibit high turnover. Employers were unwilling to invest large amounts of specific training in workers with short term attachments to the labor force. As time went on, however, the nature of clerical work was transformed by the mechanization and routinization of production processes and by the increased separation of managerial functions from clerical ones. The result was that the skills required of clerical workers became more firm-general and less firm-specific, and increasingly women were hired as these technological innovations were adopted.

This analysis suggests that the crucial changes which determined the pace of feminization of the clerical work force took place on the demand side of the market, specifically the relative increase in the demand for workers with firm-general skills. It appears that the available supply of young women willing to work in clerical jobs at prevailing wage rates outstripped the demand for such workers during most of this period. The steady increase in women's labor force participation, together with the monetary and non-monetary advantages of clerical jobs over available alternatives, insured that employers faced a highly elastic supply of female clerical labor. Under these conditions employers would be expected to react by adjusting the conditions of office employment so as to favor the hiring of women. Thus, the availability of an abundant supply of cheap female labor provided an incentive to adopt the mechanized and routine production techniques that used workers with firm-general skills. In this way, supply conditions interacted with demand forces to stimulate innovation and diffusion of just those productive techniques that increased employment of women in clerical jobs.

7

Analysis of Women's Participation in Clerical Occupations in U. S. Cities in 1890 and 1930

Previous chapters have described the importance of clerical employment for the growth of women's labor force participation. In this chapter the analysis turns to the determinants of the proportion of working women in clerical employment. The model used is developed on the basis of occupational choice considerations and structural variables. Data from samples of U. S. cities in 1890 and 1930 will be used to estimate equations which predict participation by employed women in clerical occupations as a function of earnings in clerical work, earnings in other occupations, education, demographic structure of cities, and industrial-occupational structures of cities.

Women's Role in Clerical Work in Urban Areas

Chapters 5 and 6 discussed the increase in women's participation in clerical employment and the increase in women's share of clerical employment and suggested reasons for these changes. Since much of the production that used clerical labor took place in urban areas, patterns observed in urban areas should be similar to the national patterns. In table 7.1 the average figures for large urban areas are compared with national figures on the proportion of female clerical workers in the non-agricultural labor force and women's share of total clerical employment. It can be observed that the experience of urban areas did indeed parallel the national experience with women's participation and women's share being higher in urban areas at every date.

TABLE 7.1

EMPLOYED WOMEN'S PARTICIPATION IN CLERICAL EMPLOYMENT AND WOMEN'S SHARE OF CLERICAL EMPLOYMENT FOR U.S. AND MEANS FOR URBAN SAMPLE

	1870	1880	1890	1900	1910	1920	1930	
PERCENT OF EMPLOYED WOMEN WORKING IN CLERICAL OCCUPATIONS								
Urban Sample (mean values)	0.24	0.49	3.70	7.15	11.98	21.33	22.69	(1)
η=	30	50	57	95	99	103	103	
National	0.12	0.33	2.38	4.96	9.14	18.69	19.95	(2)
WOMEN'S SHARE OF CLERICAL EMPLOYMENT								
Urban Sample (mean values)	3.10	5.26	22.15	31.78	38.03	49.47	53.44	(3)
η=	30	50	57	95	99	103	103	
National	2.45	4.39	19.27	30.24	37.60	49.19	52.54	(4)

Sources: National figures: Alba M. Edwards, Comparative Occupation Statistics for the United States, 1870-1940. U. S. Bureau of the Census (Washington, D. C.: G. P. O. 1948) pp. 112, 121, 129. Clerical employment for 1900 estimated. (See Table 4.1).

Urban sample: from U. S. Census of Population, 1870-1930. See Appendix B.

At any point in time there was considerable variation among cities in women's participation in clerical employment. The remaining portion of this chapter will analyze this cross-sectional variation for 1890 and 1930.

The Theory of the Supply of Labor to Occupations

Economic theories of occupational choice and human capital investment are based on the premise that people will seek to realize a return on their investment in human capital much as they would for any other investment. Returns to human capital investments are realized largely as increased future earnings.[1] It is expected that people will choose occupations with an eye toward maximizing the return on their human capital investment, and that over time there will be net movements of workers into occupations in which the return to human capital is high. While economists emphasize the relationships between earnings, training costs, and occupational choice, it is clear that non-pecuniary factors also play an important part in decisions about occupations. In many cases these non-pecuniary factors may be the dominant condition in decision making.[2] Of course, the number of persons found in an occupation is a function of both supply and demand factors so that the availability of jobs will also be a determinant of the level of employment in any occupation.

Most of the work done on occupational supply has been concerned with markets for highly trained personnel, particularly engineers. Much of this work has been done by Glen Cain, Richard B. Freeman, and W. Lee Hansen and has been summarized by them in a volume entitled *Labor Market Analysis of Engineers and Technical Workers.* Using various approaches and individual data, they found significant responsiveness to earnings in this market.[3] In another study of engineers by John F. O'Connell, similar results were obtained using employment and earnings data by states from the 1960 census.[4] Thus, analyses of occupational supply have tended to confirm the expectation of a positive response to occupational earnings. City level data from the 1890 and 1930 censuses will be used to determine if this positive response to earnings can be observed in the market for women's services in clerical work.

The Model

A simple estimatable model of the supply of women to clerical occupations may be specified as:

$$CW/L = \beta_0 + \beta_1 WF_c + \beta_2 WF_m + \beta_3 E + \beta_4 D + \beta_5 I$$

where

CW/L	=	percent of women gainful workers in clerical occupations
WF_c	=	average annual earnings of women in clerical occupations
WF_m	=	average annual earnings of women in alternative occupations
E	=	educational attainment of women
D	=	controls for differing demographic structures of cities
I	=	demand for female workers in various occupations as reflected in the occupational-industrial structure.

Equations of this type will be estimated for two cross-sections of American cities. Fifty-six cities are included in the sample for 1890; 89 cities are included in 1930.

Independent Variables

Earnings of Females in Clerical Occupations. Since the theory of occupational choice leads us to expect that more people will enter an occupation that produces relatively high returns to human capital, a positive relationship is predicted between occupational earnings and occupational participation in a cross section. If training costs do not vary significantly among cities, then cities with high earnings for an occupation would be cities with high returns to human capital for persons in that occupation.

Earnings of Women in Alternative Occupations. The predicted relationship between the proportion employed in one occupation and earnings in another occupation is negative, controlling for the earnings of the first occupation. The relationship should be stonger if the occupations used similar amounts and kinds of human capital so that workers might easily change occupations in response to earnings differentials. The alternative earnings measure used here is annual earnings of employed women in manufacturing. It is likely that the educational attainment of manufacturing workers was closer to that of clerical workers in 1930 than it was in 1890. At the earlier date, levels of education were generally lower, the manufacturing labor force contained more foreign-born women, and clerical work was less standardized than it was later.

Educational Attainment of Women. Since clerical work required more education than did most other jobs in which women were commonly employed, female participation in clerical occupations should be positively related to educational levels. The variable used as a proxy for educational attainment in the regressions is the proportion of females in a given age group who were enrolled in school. The age group is 15–19 in 1890 and 16–17 in 1930. While these variables measure school enrollment rather than educational attainment, it is expected that cities which had a high percentage of women currently enrolled in school would also have high average educational attainment on the part of the female population. One factor which might cause a difference between these two distributions is the proportion of immigrants in the cities' populations. This is partially dealt with by including a control for nativity among the demographic variables.

Demographic Variables. Variables will be employed to control for differences among cities in age structure, nativity structure, proportion of the female population who were married, and city size.

In chapter 5 it was learned that the demographic structure of the female clerical labor force differed significantly from the demographic structure of the total female labor force. Clerical workers were more likely to be young, unmarried, native-born, and white than were other women workers. Women in these demographic groups were more likely to have the level of educational attainment required of clerical workers, and they were preferred by employers to fill clerical posts. Therefore it is expected that cities with high proportions of young, unmarried native-born white women would have a larger proportion of women employed as clerical workers.

City size is used as a control variable because employers in large cities may have been more innovative and therefore more likely to adopt the most modern clerical technologies and hire female clerical workers. Also, the scale of enterprise may have been larger in big cities, allowing for more specialization and routinization of clerical production. In most cases the dependent variable will refer only to the white population so that a control for race will not normally be employed. The study focuses on the white population because the participation by black women in clerical work was negligible throughout the period.

Demand for Female Workers as Reflected in the Industrial-Occupational Mix. The industrial-occupational structure of cities determined the availability of various kinds of jobs. Two dummy variables are employed to control for occupational mix. One (DUM1) equals 1 when the percent of the total labor force employed in clerical work is one standard deviation or more above the mean. Thus, there is some control for cities which had particularly high availability of clerical employment. A second

TABLE 7.2

DEFINITIONS OF VARIABLES USED IN CLERICAL PARTICIPATION EQUATIONS

Dependent Variables

	Used in table:
WFCW = $\dfrac{\text{white female clerical workers ages 10+}}{\text{white female gainful workers ages 10+}}$	7.4
FSINGCW = $\dfrac{\text{female single clerical workers ages 15+}}{\text{female single gainful workers ages 15+}}$	7.5
FMARCW = $\dfrac{\text{female married clerical workers ages 15+}}{\text{female married gainful workers ages 15+}}$	7.6
WFSINGCW for age groups 10-19, 20-24, 25-34 (1930)	7.7
WFMARCW for age groups 15-19, 20-24, 25-34 (1930)	7.7

Independent Variables

FWAGE-CW = average annual earnings of women in clerical occupations	7.4 7.5 7.6 7.7

TABLE 7.2 (continued)

Independent Variables

	Used in table:			
FWAGE-MFG = average annual earnings of women in manufacturing occupations	7.4	7.5	7.6	7.7
FSC1617 = $\dfrac{\text{females attending school ages 16–17 (1930)}}{\text{females ages 16–17}}$	7.4	7.5	7.6	7.7
FSC1519 = $\dfrac{\text{females attending school ages 15–19 (1890)}}{\text{females ages 15–19}}$	7.4	7.5	7.6	
WPFNW = $\dfrac{\text{native-born white women ages 10+}}{\text{all white women ages 10+}}$	7.4	7.5	7.6	7.7
PMAR = $\dfrac{\text{married women ages 15+}}{\text{all women ages 15+}}$	7.4			7.7
PF25 = $\dfrac{\text{Women ages 10–25}}{\text{all women ages 10+}}$	7.4	7.5	7.6	
PWHITE = $\dfrac{\text{white women ages 10+}}{\text{all women ages 10+}}$		7.5	7.6	
POP = total population	7.4	7.5	7.6	7.7
DUM1 = 1 if the proportion of the total labor in clerical occupations is more than one standard deviation above the mean	7.4	7.5	7.6	7.7
DUM2 = if the proportion of the female labor force in manufacturing occupation is more than the one standard deviation above the mean	7.4	7.5	7.6	7.7

dummy variable (DUM2) equals 1 when the percent of the female labor force employed in manufacturing is one standard deviation or more above the mean. This controls for the presence in the sample of such cities as Fall River and Lowell, Massachusetts, textile centers with very high demand for women manufacturing workers but small clerical labor forces. One dummy (DUM1) is constructed on the basis of all clerical employment. The other (DUM2) is based on only female manufacturing employment. This is because of the greater substitutability of women for men in clerical production.

Data

The data employed to estimate the model are the same two cross-sections of American cities used in chapter 3. However, the 1930 sample used here includes 89 cities. A detailed description of the data can be found in appendix B. Demographic data are taken from the published schedules of the U. S. *Census of Population.* Earnings data is derived from the U. S. *Census of Manufactures* in 1890 and 1930 and from the U. S. Personnel Classification Board study of clerical salaries in 1929.

Findings

Results are presented in this section for regression equations (OLS) which estimate the proportion of female workers employed in clerical jobs in U. S. cities for 1890 and 1930. Table 7.2 defines the variables used in estimating the occupational participation equations and indicates the tables in which they appear in regression results. Table 7.3 provides mean values of variables used in the regressions. All variables (except dummies) are entered in logarithmic form so that coefficients may be interpreted as elasticities.

In table 7.4 results are presented that show the relationship between the proportion of the total female labor force employed in clerical jobs and the various explanatory variables. The most startling results are the signs on the wage variables. For both 1890 and 1930, working women's participation in the clerical labor force was negatively related to clerical earnings and positively related to manufacturing earnings. For 1890 these variables are not significant, but for 1930 they are.

The other variables all have the expected signs except PMAR in 1890. At both dates the education variable is positive and highly significant, indicating that cities with high female enrollment at later ages had high proportions of working women employed in clerical occupations. For 1890 and 1930 cities with younger populations and

TABLE 7.3

MEAN VALUES OF VARIABLES USED IN REGRESSIONS

	$\eta =$	89 1930	56 1890	
Dependent Variables				
WFCW		23.00	4.33	
FSINGCW		26.07	3.97	
WFSINGCW (10-19)		29.38		
WFSINGCW (20-24)		40.82		
WFSINGCW (25-34)		37.15		
FMARCW		15.39	1.49	
WFMARCW (15-19)		20.10		
WFMARCW (20-24)		30.79		
WFMARCW (25-34)		25.97		
Independent Variables				
FWAGE-CW		$1105	$463	
FWAGE-MFG		$ 868	$263	
FFSC1617		75.71	20.85	FSC1519
WPFNW		82.14	68.74	

TABLE 7.3 (continued)

	$\eta =$ 89	56
	1930	1890

Independent Variables

PMAR	52.30	45.30
PF25	32.48	40.12
PWHITE	90.82	92.30
POP	396465	207163

% total labor
force in clerical occupations
(used for DUM1)   13.31   4.20

% female labor
force in manufacturing occupations
(used for DUM2)   20.12   37.41

higher percentages of the white population who were native-born had greater clerical participation, though these variables are significant only in 1930. In both years the size of the city was positively and significantly related to clerical participation.

The dummy variables for job availability have the predicted signs for both years but are significant only in 1930. PMAR, the proportion of the female population who were married, is not significant in 1930. In 1890 it is positive and highly significant. The result is somewhat surprising since we know that married women were very unlikely to be employed as clerical workers. A possible explanation for the positive sign on this variable in 1890 is that a larger proportion of women were married in cities with high male earnings so that PMAR may be measuring the general prosperity of the city. It was the more prosperous cities which tended to have larger commercial sectors. In an earlier specification of this equation the level of male wages was included as an independent variable. Male wages were highly correlated with the education variable and with the proportion of total gainful workers in clerical employment as well as with PMAR. When male wages were dropped from the equation the other variables gained in significance with very little change in R^2.

The general conclusion that can be drawn from the results reported in table 7.4 is that the standard predictions of the occupational choice model are not borne out by the experience of female clerical workers in 1890 or 1930. The most important explanatory variables seem to be education and job availability once controls are provided for demographic factors.

Tables 7.5 and 7.6 present results for similar equations with marital status included in the dependent variable. An additional control for racial structure of the population is added because the dependent variable refers to the total population. For single women we see similar results to those observed for the total white population, with education and industrial-occupational structure being important explanatory variables. The demographic controls all have the expected signs, and most are significant for both dates. For married women (table 7.6) the coefficients on education and the dummies are larger and the controls for demographic structure are generally less important than they were for single women.

The most detailed breakdown available is presented in table 7.7 where we can analyze clerical participation by age-marital status group in 1930. For unmarried women, education had a positive and significant effect for all but the oldest age group. Location in a commercial city rather than in a manufacturing city is important in explaining clerical

TABLE 7.4

MULTIPLE REGRESSION ANALYSIS OF INTERCITY DIFFERENCES
THE PARTICIPATION OF EMPLOYED WOMEN IN CLERICAL WORK,
1890 AND 1930

DEPENDENT VARIABLE = WFCW = $\dfrac{\text{WHITE FEMALE CLERICAL WORKERS AGES 10+}}{\text{WHITE FEMALE GAINFUL WORKERS AGES 10+}}$

	1930	1890	
FWAGE-CW	-0.582** (0.280)	-0.504 (0.318)	
FWAGE-MFG	0.378** (0.152)	0.273 (0.250)	
FSC1617	0.471*** (0.188)	0.937*** (0.196)	FSC1519
PF25	0.432* (0.229)	0.561 (0.616)	
WPFNW	0.453*** (0.141)	0.359 (0.275)	
PMAR	-0.495 (0.886)	0.122*** (0.543)	
POP	0.215*** (0.570)	0.157** (0.073)	
DUM1 (Clerical)	0.245** (0.050)	0.044 (0.064)	
DUM2 (mfg)	-0.364*** (0.629)	-0.098 (0.085)	
Constant	-0.394 (2.548)	0.152 (0.898)	
R^2	.694	.706	
n	89	56	

*** = significant at .01
 ** = significant at .05
  * = significant at .10

All variables (except dummys) in log form
Standard errors in parentheses

TABLE 7.5

MULTIPLE REGRESSION ANALYSIS OF INTERCITY DIFFERENCES IN THE
PARTICIPATION OF EMPLOYED SINGLE WOMEN IN CLERICAL
WORK, 1890 AND 1930

DEPENDENT VARIABLE = FSINGCW = FEMALE SINGLE CLERICAL WORKERS AGES 15+ / FEMALE SINGLE GAINFUL WORKERS AGES 15+

	1930	1890
FWAGE–CW	−0.578**	−0.759*
	(0.281)	(0.352)
FWAGE–MFG	0.439***	0.414
	(0.165)	(0.251)
FSC1617	0.400*	0.970*** FSC1519
	(0.210)	(0.200)
WPFNW	0.427***	0.676**
	(0.153)	(0.313)
PF25	0.008	1.175*
	(0.259)	(0.061)
POP	0.224***	0.127*
	(0.063)	(0.086)
PWHITE	1.343***	3.156***
	(0.248)	(0.379)
DUM1 (clerical)	0.267***	0.157**
	(0.060)	(0.046)
DUM2 (mfg)	−0.266***	−0.146*
	(0.070)	(0.087)
Constant	−1.158	0.305
	(2.359)	(0.943)
R^2	.659	.776
η	89	56

*** = significant at .01
 ** = significant at .05
  * = significant at .10

All variables (except dummys) in log form
Standard errors in parentheses

TABLE 7.6

MULTIPLE REGRESSION ANALYSIS OF INTERCITY DIFFERENCES IN THE
PARTICIPATION OF EMPLOYED MARRIED WOMEN IN CLERICAL
WORK, 1890 AND 1930

DEPENDENT VARIABLE = FMARCW = FEMALE MARRIED CLERICAL WORKERS AGES 15+ / FEMALE MARRIED GAINFUL WORKERS AGES 15+

	1930	1890
FWAGE-CW	0.207 (0.383)	-0.745 (0.508)
FWAGE-MFG	0.725*** (0.225)	0.218 (0.365)
FSC1617	1.200*** (0.286)	1.418*** FSC1519 (0.291)
WPFNW	0.151 (0.216)	-0.205 (0.502)
PF25	0.766** (0.353)	0.662 (0.883)
POP	0.008 (0.086)	0.103* (0.106)
PWHITE	0.763** (0.339)	4.516*** (0.558)
DUM1 (clerical)	0.179** (0.082)	0.251** (0.140)
DUM2 (mfg)	-0.527*** (0.095)	-0.132 (0.130)
Constant	-6.974*** (3.221)	0.374 (0.136)
R^2	.663	.781
n	89	55

*** = significant at .01
** = significant at .05
* = significant at .10

All variables (except dummys) in log form
Standard errors in parentheses

TABLE 7.7

MULTIPLE REGRESSION ANALYSIS OF INTERCITY DIFFERENCES IN THE PARTICIPATION OF EMPLOYED WOMEN IN CLERICAL WORK, BY AGE-MARITAL STATUS GROUPS, 1930
DEPENDENT VARIABLES = WFCW (AGE-MARITAL STATUS GROUPS)

	Unmarried			Married		
	10-19	20-24	25-34	15-19	20-24	25-34
FWAGE-CW	0.023 (0.171)	-0.020 (0.118)	-0.090 (0.102)	0.024 (0.266)	0.173 (0.193)	0.204 (0.190)
FWAGE-MFG	0.101 (0.097)	0.037 (0.067)	0.080 (0.059)	-0.065 (0.152)	0.096 (0.110)	-0.016 (0.108)
PFSC1617	0.241** (0.116)	0.153** (0.080)	0.071 (0.069)	0.314* (0.181)	0.232* (0.131)	0.263** (0.129)
WPFNW	-0.072 (0.082)	-0.016 (0.057)	0.005 (0.049)	-0.103 (0.128)	-0.103 (0.093)	0.055 (0.091)
POP	0.117*** (0.038)	0.036 (0.027)	0.021 (0.023)	0.103* (0.159)	0.025 (0.049)	-0.019 (0.423)
DUM1 (Clerical)	0.107*** (0.034)	0.081*** (0.024)	0.087*** (0.021)	0.153*** (0.153)	0.135*** (0.039)	0.138*** (0.038)
DUM2 (mfg)	-0.226*** (0.043)	-0.159*** (0.029)	-0.141*** (0.026)	-0.455*** (0.167)	-0.301*** (0.048)	-0.290*** (0.048)
Constant	-1.957 (1.463)	-0.661 (1.006)	-0.432 (0.873)	-0.935 (2.273)	-2.458 (1.645)	-1.732 (1.625)
R^2	.561	.505	.509	.559	.571	.559
n	89	89	89	89	89	89

*** = significant at .01
** = significant at .05
* = significant at .10

All variables (except dummy) in log form
Standard errors in parentheses

participation by unmarried women in all age groups. City size is significant for the youngest group. For married women the pattern is very similar, with education and industrial-occupational mix being the most important explanatory factors.

While the regression results presented in this chapter are disappointing when taken as tests of the standard theory of occupational choice, they do offer some insights into factors which encouraged participation by employed women in clerical occupations. For both periods and for all demographic groups, the most important variables are education and the dummy variables which reflect the industrial-occupational mix. Thus, demand factors are seen to play a key role in determining the participation by employed women in clerical occupations. Education, as measured by school attendance, is the most important supply side variable. No positive response to wage variables was observed for either period or for any demographic group.

Summary

This chapter's finding of no positive association between clerical wages and female participation in clerical employment in cross sections is consistent with the secular pattern of rising participation and falling relative wages that was discussed in chapter 4. Throughout this period the earnings received by women employed in office work fell relative to earnings of women in other jobs. Despite this earnings decline, women's participation in the clerical labor force increased dramatically. Indeed, it would seem that the supply of women to the clerical labor force outstripped demand throughout most of this period, resulting in downward pressure on wages. There were reductions in the private human capital investment required to enter clerical occupations because of routinization of office production and because of public funding of commercial education. This meant that the relative returns to human capital of clerical workers probably did not fall as precipitously as did their relative earnings. Nevertheless, the pattern of long term participation increase with declining relative wages suggests that other factors were vitally important in drawing increasing numbers of women into clerical jobs.

The cross-sectional analysis in this chapter indicates that educational level and job availability were the most important factors for explaining variation among cities in the proportion of the female labor force in clerical occupations. For no demographic group was participation in clerical employment positively associated with relative earnings. Though caution must be exercised in drawing conclusions about individual behavior from city level associations, it would appear that educated young women accepted employment in offices whenever such jobs were available, and that they were more concerned with factors other than earnings.

These cross-sectional findings and the movements over time in relative wages and participation suggest that for the rapidly expanding group of educated young women seeking jobs in this period, the non-pecuniary attractions of clerical work compensated for falling relative earnings. Women workers were available in abundance whenever employers were willing to open clerical positions to them.

8

Conclusions

The two most fundamental facts about the female labor force in the U.S. are: (1) the rapid increase in participation that has taken place in the past century and (2) the high degree of concentration of female employment in sex segregated occupations. Any comprehensive study of women's role in the labor force must deal with both of these facts and try to come to terms with the relationship between labor force participation and occupational structure.

The current study has provided an economic history of women's role in the U.S. non-agricultural labor force from 1870 to 1930. Until very recently there were few economic studies of women's labor force participation in this period; most work has concentrated on the post World War II period when increased participation by married women was the largest cause of labor force growth. Little research has focused on the actions of single women. However, for the 60 years covered by this study, young single women made up the overwhelming majority of female gainful workers; and increased labor force participation by single women constituted the greatest share of the growth in the female labor force. A very large percentage of these women entered the expanding field of clerical employment, which was rapidly being opened to women.

This study has set forth an analysis that relates increased participation by single women to changes within the household. The decline in the importance of the family economy, in which all members made economic decisions in consideration of the economic well-being of the family unit rather than the individual, signalled greater economic independence for young women and increased their tendency to work for pay in the years prior to marriage. We might speculate that the decline in family size, the increased availability of market-produced consumer goods, and the increased use of technology in the smaller urban home reduced the demand by families for the services of their daughters in household production.

The period was characterized throughout by a secular increase in the educational level attained by the population. Although women made up less than half of all young persons attending school, they were always more than half of all high school graduates. This phenomenon may have been due to the lower opportunity cost for girls. Since young men could obtain good jobs with less than a high school education, there was a greater incentive for them to drop out prior to graduation. For young women, particularly those whose social class and aspirations precluded domestic service or factory work, the employment prospects were much less bright.

The decline of the family economy coupled with rising levels of education produced an increase in the supply of young, unmarried, native-born, white women with relatively high levels of education. These women were willing and able to accept paid employment, but many of them belonged to or aspired to social strata in which factory or domestic employment for women was not regarded as an acceptable option. Before clerical occupations were opened to women, teaching was virtually the only occupation available to educated women with middle class aspirations.

It is difficult to predict what sorts of adjustments would have taken place in the labor market to accomodate this new supply of workers if clerical occupations had not expanded in such a manner as to offer acceptable employment. Beginning in 1880 there was rapid expansion in the demand for clerical labor. This increase in demand was associated with rising demand for products that used clerical labor as an input, with institutional changes that increased the demand for record keeping, and with the decline in the cost of clerical output as a result of technological innovation in office production. The most notable of the technological advances in the office was the typewriter, but there were a myriad of other innovations (mechanical and organizational) that reduced the unit cost of clerical output.

These technological advances did not merely expand the demand for clerical labor. They transformed the work processes in such a way as to increase the demand for a different kind of labor than had previously been employed in offices. The new techniques of office production caused a change in the nature of the skills required of clerical labor. Prior to the development of the modern, mechanized office, the skills required of clerical workers had been specific to the individual firm. Many clerical jobs were entry points to job ladders with managerial functions attached. In such a situation it is to be expected that the firm was very concerned with worker turnover and sought to hire clerical workers who were expected to have a long work life with the firm. With increased mechanization and routinization of clerical tasks, the skills required of clerical workers became much more firm-general. This stimulated employers to hire for such jobs the young, educated women who had high expected turnover and desired clean, high status employment. The rapid development of a system of commercial education (both public and private) facilitated the change in the sex composition of the growing clerical work force.

Both demand for female clerical labor and supply of educated young women expanded during this period. It is unclear whether demand or supply side factors were more important for increasing female participation in office work, but the timing of the growth of the relevant magnitudes provides a possible explanation. The pattern of secular growth in women's labor force participation and in women's educational attainment was relatively smooth throughout the period. Women's participation in clerical employment grew much more rapidly and shows a more volatile pattern. The peaks and troughs in the series do not always coincide, the most notable discrepancy being in the differences between the first two decades of this century. Women's non-agricultural labor force participation expanded most rapidly from 1900 to 1910 while the most rapid growth in female clerical employment took place from 1910 to 1920, especially during the war years. This evidence on timing suggests that while the long term growth in female clerical employment was undoubtedly related to the secular increase in female labor supply, the short term fluctuations were more clearly related to demand factors, especially to technological advances.

Appendix A

Nine Occupational Categories of Major Female Employment

In his U.S. census monograph, *Comparative Occupation Statistics for the United States, 1870 to 1940*, Alba M. Edwards grouped data from previous censuses into the occupational categories used in the 1930 tabulation. For the analysis in chapter 2, Edwards' data were used to develop nine occupational categories in which most female gainful workers were employed during the period 1870–1930.

Table A.1 lists the occupations which make up each category. Table A.2 presents the number of detailed occupations in each category and shows how the nine catogories relate to the total number of detailed occupations listed by Edwards. Table A.3 presents numbers of women employed in each category at each date.

TABLE A.1

OCCUPATIONS WHICH MAKE UP NINE CATEGORIES
OF MAJOR FEMALE EMPLOYMENT

1. Clothing manufacturing

        operatives and laborers in factories
        dressmakers and apprentices
        tailors and tailoresses

2. Textile manufacturing

        operatives and laborers in factories

3. Telephone operators

4. Saleswomen and clerks in stores

5. Teachers and professions

        teachers
        college presidents and professors

6. Trained nurses

7. Laundry workers

8. Servants, etc.

        housekeepers and stewards
        cooks
        other servants
        waiters and waitresses
        charwomen and cleaners
        porters, domestic and personal
        porters, professional service

9. Clerical occupations

        bookkeepers, cashiers and accountants
        clerks (except "clerks in stores")
        stenographers and typists

Source: Alba M. Edwards, Comparative Occupation Statistics for the
         U.S., 1870-1930, U.S. Bureau of the Census (Washington, DC:
         G.P.O., 1943), pp. 122-129.

TABLE A.2

NUMBER OF DETAILED OCCUPATIONS IN EDWARDS STUDY
AND IN NINE CATEGORIES OF MAJOR FEMALE EMPLOYMENT

	1870	1880	1890	1900	1910	1920	1930
Number of detailed occupations in Edwards Study	115	116	123	123	396	408	436
Number of detailed occupations in 9 categories of major female employment	20	22	24	24	58	58	58
Percent of all detailed occupations in nine categories	17.4	19.0	19.5	19.5	14.7	14.2	13.3
Number of detailed occupations in nine categories							
1. Clothing manufacturing	4	6	7	7	17	17	17
2. Textile manufacturing	8	8	8	8	23	23	23
3. Telephone operators	-	-	-	1	1	1	1
4. Saleswomen and clerks in stores	1	1	1	1	2	2	2
5. Teachers and professors	1	1	1	1	2	2	2
6. Trained nurses	1	1	1	1	1	1	1
7. Laundry workers	1	1	1	1	3	3	3
8. Servants, etc.	1	1	2	2	6	6	7
9. Clerical occupations	3	3	3	3	3	3	3

Source: Edwards, pp. 122-129.

TABLE A.3

WOMEN IN NINE CATEGORIES OF MAJOR FEMALE EMPLOYMENT, 1870–1930

	1870	1880	1890	1900	1910	1920	1930
(in thousands)							
1. Clothing manufacturing	197	352	597	699	865	613	575
2. Textile manufacturing	109	187	235	293	403	471	452
3. Telephone operators	–	–	–	16	88	178	235
4. Saleswomen and clerks in stores	9	31	98	180	362	527	706
5. Teachers and professors	85	153	244	325	481	649	880
6. Trained nurses	1	1	4	11	77	144	289
7. Laundry workers	58	108	217	335	597	468	519
8. Servants, etc.	902	970	1303	1431	1596	1359	2144
9. Clerical occupations	2	7	73	214	573	1396	1964

Appendix B

The Urban Sample

At every census date from 1870 to 1930 the U.S. Censuses of Population and Manufactures published considerable amounts of detailed information about the largest cities. In general, information on demographic structure, occupational structure, school attendance, and manufacturing-industrial structure was available. Earnings data sufficiently detailed to construct manufacturing and clerical earnings by sex were available in only two of these years, 1890 and 1930. Demographic and employment data were collected for all years from 1870 through 1930, but because of the availability of earnings data, cross-sectional analysis was limited to 1890 and 1930.

Wages, 1890

The *1890 Census of Manufactures* published data on total wages paid and number employed in manufacturing establishments in 165 cities for the following occupational categories: (1) officers, firm members, and clerks; (2) operatives, skilled and unskilled; and (3) pieceworkers. The data were presented separately for males over 15, females over 15, and children.[1] These data were used to construct average annual earnings for males, females, and children in manufacturing occupations and for males and females in clerical occupations. This was done by simply dividing the total annual wage bill by the number employed in each category. Annual clerical earnings were taken to be the total wages paid to "officers, firm members and clerks," divided by the number employed in that category. It is likely that the figure for male clerical wages overstates the actual earnings of males in clerical occupations because there were larger numbers of males who were officers of firms. There is undoubtedly much less bias in the computed female clerical earnings

TABLE B.1

AVERAGE ANNUAL EARNINGS, BY SEX,
IN 56 U.S. CITIES, 1890

	Average Annual Earnings in Clerical Occupations		Average Annual Composite Wages	
	Males	Females	Males	Females
Albany, NY	951.01	524.87	595.86	283.09
Allegheny, PA	997.80	416.82	592.6?	231.87
Atlanta, GA	853.42	454.28	483.62	258.21
Baltimore, MD	859.01	425.76	514.62	213.92
Boston, MA	978.88	487.74	702.10	328.55
Brooklyn, NY	1002.18	463.39	677.75	289.98
Buffalo, NY	994.17	450.91	560.07	218.43
Cambridge, MA	878.58	362.67	617.54	291.17
Camden, NJ	892.16	389.59	626.43	229.71
Charleston, SC	748.10	336.11	479.69	221.41
Chicago, IL	1065.25	531.16	632.05	328.23
Cincinnati, OH	972.75	445.06	571.03	249.69
Cleveland, OH	1062.74	476.07	603.08	265.04
Columbus, OH	948.58	429.68	553.92	279.97
Dayton, OH	857.32	436.66	544.49	251.95
Denver, CO	1332.80	753.20	836.17	461.17
Des Moines, IA	895.56	406.57	571.4?	279.57
Detroit, MI	965.49	427.06	543.4?	248.20
Evansville, IN	880.58	422.43	498.52	203.48
Fall River, MA	1098.92	414.51	442.79	306.79
Grand Rapids, MI	955.67	432.73	524.05	254.89
Hartford, CT	1056.14	426.59	662.38	328.70
Indianapolis, IN	941.25	467.95	563.44	216.50
Jersey City, NJ	1184.68	363.94	669.12	298.15
Kansas City, MO	969.98	586.59	683.12	336.97
Los Angeles, CA	1130.22	616.62	782.83	350.68
Louisville, KY	882.43	450.58	524.24	248.32
Lowell, MA	1035.77	413.11	489.51	279.21
Lynn, MA	909.23	467.15	636.81	392.88
Milwaukee, WI	928.57	415.77	548.91	197.31
Minneapolis, MN	970.37	478.34	582.23	326.50
Nashville, TN	838.25	385.73	514.41	254.22
Newark, NJ	1183.38	459.34	652.06	291.33
New Haven, CT	1031.54	461.86	641.19	275.68

TABLE B.1
Continued

	Average Annual Earnings in Clerical Occupations		Average Annual Composite Wages	
	Males	Females	Males	Females
New Orleans, LA	939.20	513.67	531.86	187.30
New York, NY	1205.48	578.03	762.83	353.32
Omaha, NB	1109.94	548.43	699.45	331.64
Paterson, NJ	1155.07	418.38	583.30	305.45
Philadelphia, PA	925.70	433.12	606.97	301.48
Pittsburgh, PA	1195.79	427.67	640.34	276.04
Providence, RI	1096.17	439.05	594.33	294.73
Reading, PA	919.06	523.03	474.50	223.71
Richmond, VA	928.76	377.23	457.76	193.92
Rochester, NY	1044.01	462.77	601.34	265.49
S. Joseph, MO	871.50	503.32	556.55	258.96
St. Louis, MO	1101.55	462.16	638.16	269.07
St. Paul, MN	918.71	460.98	600.08	335.15
San Francisco, CA	988.69	606.64	724.21	321.59
Scranton, PA	1193.07	319.39	524.16	163.29
Syracuse, NY	966.82	403.87	555.23	210.21
Toledo, OH	892.43	421.24	560.75	247.45
Trenton, NJ	1032.98	456.70	606.20	267.49
Troy, NY	1043.94	623.64	570.89	231.69
Washington, DC	818.46	509.02	652.71	482.56
Wilmington, DE	1007.87	474.76	570.61	286.86
Worcester, MA	1113.29	501.51	596.18	287.40

because there were very few female officers of manufacturing firms. Annual earnings in manufacturing jobs were constructed as:

$$\text{WAGEMFG} = \frac{(O \cdot WO) + (P \cdot WP)}{(O + P)}$$

where

O   =   number of operatives
WO   =   total wages paid to operatives
P   =   number of pieceworkers
WP   =   total wages paid to pieceworkers.

A composite annual earnings figure was constructed for males and females in each city by weighting the occupational earnings as constructed above by the numbers reported employed in these occupations in the Census of Population. Thus,

$$\text{FWAGE} = \frac{(FCW \cdot FWAGECW) + (FMFG \cdot FWAGEMFG)}{(FCW + FMFG)}$$

where

FWAGECW   =   average annual earnings of women in clerical occupations as computed from data in the manufacturing census

FWAGEMFG   =   annual earnings of women in manufacturing occupations as computed from data in the manufacturing census

FCW   =   number of female clerical workers as reported in the population census

FMFG   =   number of female manufacturing workers as reported in the population census.

A similar calculation was performed to produce a composite average annual earnings figure for males. In table B.1, clerical earnings and the composite earnings figures are presented for the 56 cities included in the 1890 urban sample.

Wages, 1930

The creation of earnings figures for males and females in cities in 1930 is a much more complex undertaking because the *1930 Census of Manufactures* did not provide separate wage data for clerks and did not break down manufacturing earnings and employment by sex.

TABLE B.2

AVERAGE ANNUAL EARNINGS, BY SEX,
IN 89 U.S. CITIES, 1930

	Clerical		Manufacturing		Composite Real Earnings	
	Male	Female	Male	Female	Male	Female
	(1)	(2)	(3)	(4)	(5)	(6)
Albany, NY	1500.08	1048.22	1559.50	887.75	1744.10	963.71
Atlanta, GA	1265.22	1079.31	1065.40	738.88	1445.67	930.18
Baltimore, MD	1116.22	900.90	1304.25	618.43	1146.55	986.22
Birmingham, AL	1428.87	1149.21	1197.69	788.45	1203.72	702.54
Boston, MA	1447.46	1181.25	1580.06	989.53	1124.89	960.81
Bridgeport, CT	1490.38	1070.76	1418.95	914.97	1474.47	1043.15
Buffalo, NY	1283.45	994.63	1544.23	921.70	1461.69	998.34
Cambridge, MA	1490.38	1070.76	1445.09	919.98	1409.02	901.82
Camden, NJ	1500.08	1048.22	1318.05	865.15	1382.65	953.29
Canton, OH	1515.95	1048.00	1827.29	874.04	1364.27	946.93
Chattanooga, TN	1428.87	1149.21	1056.36	730.72	1816.48	990.89
Chicago, IL	1431.38	1257.28	1639.43	1146.18	1081.75	880.56
Cincinnati, OH	1282.14	1076.09	1514.72	648.09	1607.35	1221.21
Cleveland, OH	1336.59	1200.26	1728.59	890.75	1502.28	890.92
Columbus, OH	1501.63	1130.97	1539.26	757.03	1751.98	1098.94
Dallas, TX	1527.47	1251.52	1277.11	795.19	1460.80	933.97
Dayton, OH	1515.95	1048.00	1671.03	799.30	1368.61	1128.96
Denver, CO	1551.88	1127.31	1381.92	716.22	1851.03	1044.60
Des Moines, IA	1402.94	956.83	1424.00	940.86	1495.60	1068.96
Detroit, MI	1784.27	1268.92	1841.05	1008.51	1438.52	965.53
Duluth, MN	1402.94	956.83	1409.65	995.71	1976.54	1265.57
Elizabeth, NJ	1500.08	1048.22	1556.45	1021.63	1341.30	920.51
El Paso, TX	1490.38	1070.76	1092.45	680.90	1532.32	1025.09
Erie, PA	1500.08	1048.22	1608.81	947.29	1101.66	934.33
Evansville, IN	1515.95	1048.00	1128.28	863.47	1645.90	1035.66
Fall River, MA	1490.38	1070.76	1051.10	680.06	1116.04	887.52
Fort Wayne, IN	1515.95	1048.00	1476.09	1129.64	1107.45	745.05
Fort Worth, TX	1527.47	1251.52	1277.11	795.19	1459.52	1075.59
Grand Rapids, MI	1515.95	1048.00	1522.30	833.90	1404.00	992.90
Hartford, CT	1490.38	1070.76	1563.17	1018.58	1426.06	903.55
Houston, TX	1527.47	1251.52	1289.49	804.53	1596.29	1085.28
Indianapolis, IN	1175.98	1099.96	1375.81	1052.90	1377.01	1148.48
Jacksonville, FL	1518.67	1157.54	1182.34	754.02	1319.04	1057.79
Jersey City, NJ	1600.00	1110.01	1604.23	1052.99	1189.94	970.55
Kansas City, KS	1402.94	956.83	1449.61	957.78	1691.47	1148.67
Kansas City, MO	1397.83	1178.78	1457.94	897.55	1483.00	983.90
Knoxville, TN	1428.87	1419.21	996.13	689.06	1458.66	1106.50
Long Beach, CA	1513.66	1235.70	1516.64	941.14	1037.18	839.07
Los Angeles, CA	1527.48	1301.91	1576.98	985.78	1514.70	1155.98
Louisville, KY	1428.41	1086.58	1210.81	733.39	1593.50	1218.98

	Clerical		Manufacturing		Composite Real Earnings	
	Male	Female	Male	Female	Male	Female
	(1)	(2)	(3)	(4)	(5)	(6)
Lowell, MA	1490.38	1070.76	1171.52	745.83	1161.35	856.87
Lynn, MA	1490.38	1070.76	1545.11	983.66	1114.76	761.04
Memphis, TN	1428.87	1149.21	1089.69	753.78	1555.55	1027.17
Miami, FL	1518.67	1157.54	1413.83	901.65	1124.50	988.75
Milwaukee, WI	1342.68	1072.72	1559.57	979.85	1542.07	1167.30
Minneapolis, MN	1343.19	1033.73	1364.76	975.19	1641.27	1100.49
Nashville, TN	1428.87	1149.21	1115.56	771.67	1374.25	1024.96
Newark, NJ	1588.64	1098.73	1550.95	1018.03	1109.19	931.95
New Bedford, MA	1490.38	1070.76	1175.04	748.07	1452.15	986.89
New Haven, CT	1490.38	1070.76	1406.90	926.29	1104.71	729.17
New Orleans, LA	1322.11	1126.06	1078.43	602.04	1459.40	1023.67
New York, NY	1436.31	1259.39	1847.96	1003.99	1066.48	813.92
Norfolk, VA	1518.67	1157.54	1291.77	929.55	1687.58	1108.86
Oakland, CA	1574.56	1196.73	1435.38	890.71	1323.05	1043.76
Oklahoma City,OK	1527.47	1251.52	1411.30	849.05	1463.34	1106.70
Omaha, NB	1402.94	956.83	1394.83	961.89	1537.07	1266.21
Paterson, NJ	1500.08	1048.22	1504.88	987.79	1330.17	912.44
Peoria, IL	1515.95	1048.00	1330.25	930.02	1482.18	989.78
Philadelphia,PA	1477.02	1179.49	1557.12	924.93	1334.02	992.07
Pittsburgh, PA	1538.31	1157.75	1550.52	909.05	1490.34	1003.25
Portland, OR	1513.66	1235.70	1392.62	797.02	1624.76	1141.29
Providence, RI	1229.11	1009.24	1298.81	933.73	1313.67	1024.32
Reading, PA	1500.08	1048.22	1396.63	822.36	1244.38	927.46
Richmond, VA	1518.67	1157.54	1137.24	754.75	1404.02	868.99
Rochester, NY	1458.04	1090.39	1591.39	903.27	1252.82	974.82
St. Louis, MO	1133.22	1082.56	1387.73	812.71	1612.02	1013.93
St. Paul. MN	1363.42	902.68	1415.33	988.12	1451.09	1030.13
Salt Lake City,UT	1427.87	1081.09	1413.56	759.75	1530.82	1013.17
San Antonio, TX	1527.47	1251.52	1058.74	659.89	1402.27	984.18
San Diego, CA	1513.66	1235.70	1449.60	899.54	1122.00	934.46
San Francisco, CA	1676.13	1366.06	1618.47	996.94	1441.36	1112.27
Scranton, PA	1500.08	1048.22	1275.92	747.90	1539.46	1187.75
Seattle, WA	1457.86	1170.67	1511.84	836.44	1353.14	907.34
Somerville, MA	1490.38	1070.76	1451.75	924.23	1402.43	1004.53
South Bend, IN	1515.95	1048.00	1473.47	1127.64	1502.83	1045.50
Spokane, WA	1513.66	1235.70	1348.84	746.26	1517.40	1119.75
Springfield, MA	1490.38	1070.76	1480.51	942.53	1286.55	1026.77
Syracuse, NY	1500.08	1048.22	1579.73	899.27	1477.49	1014.22
Tacoma, WA	1513.66	1235.70	1380.70	763.89	1611.17	1018.14

TABLE B.2
Continued

	Clerical		Manufacturing		Composite Real Earnings	
	Male	Female	Male	Female	Male	Female
	(1)	(2)	(3)	(4)	(5)	(6)
Tampa, FL	1518.67	1157.54	1175.85	749.89	1365.71	1035.28
Toledo, OH	1510.07	1108.11	1597.43	764.09	1235.67	846.90
Trenton, NJ	1500.08	1048.22	1441.43	946.13	1511.43	913.14
Tulsa, OK	1527.47	1251.52	1639.28	986.20	1450.64	988.74
Utica, NY	1500.08	1048.22	1273.37	724.87	1607.76	1208.29
Wichita, KS	1402.94	956.83	1392.69	920.18	1374.56	880.35
Wilmington, DE	1518.67	1157.54	1407.44	897.58	1365.62	927.89
Worcester, MA	1490.38	1070.76	1547.15	984.96	1326.50	970.83
Yonkers, NY	1500.08	1048.22	1480.15	842.58	1536.12	1022.57
Youngstown, OH	1515.95	1048.00	1833.57	877.04	1514.01	977.60

Earnings in Manufacturing. Earnings for workers in manufacturing were constructed using the method followed by Erika Schoenberg and Paul Douglas in their study of relationships between earnings and employment in 41 cities in 1929.[2] For 1930, the *Census of Manufactures* provided only total wages paid and total employees with no information by sex.[3] Schoenberg and Douglas developed a corrected average earnings figure for male-equivalent workers by using data by state on female/male earnings ratios. These ratios were developed by Schoenberg and Douglas from a series of surveys made by the Bureau of Labor Statistics for 1929.[4] The use of these ratios requires the assumption that the sex ratio of earnings was the same for each city as it was for the state in which the city was located. Additionally, we must assume that the ratio of male manufacturing workers to female manufacturing workers was the same in the Census of Manufacturing as was reported in the Census of Population. If these assumptions are made, then the state sex ratios in earnings from 1929 can be put together with the wage payment and employment figures in the 1930 Censuses of Manufactures and Population to produce the average annual earnings estimates presented in columns 3 and 4 of table B.2.

Earnings of Clerical Workers. In 1931 the U.S. Personnel Classification Board published a detailed survey of wages paid to clerical workers in private industry in urban areas. Those workers included in the survey were clerical workers in jobs equivalent to government job categories CAF-1 and CAF-2. These jobs (listed in table B.3) involved the more routine clerical tasks and were dominated by female employees. Therefore, women made up an average of 72% of the CAF-1 category and 63% of the CAF-2 category. From the *1930 Census of Population* we know that women made up 52% of all persons reported as clerical workers in 1930. The jobs in the CAF-1 and CAF-2 categories were then the lower paid, routine clerical positions most commonly filled by women. For this reason the clerical wages computed using this source will tend to underestimate male clerical wages by a significant amount while female clerical wage estimates are more likely to be accurate. Because our computed male clerical earnings are overestimates in 1890 and underestimates in 1930, they cannot be used to make judgments about movements in men's clerical earnings over time. However, it is likely that for each cross section the variation across cities in the estimated figures approximates the variation in the actual figures. The clerical earnings estimated for women from this source are more likely to reflect accurately the actual levels of earnings of females in all clerical jobs because the occupations surveyed were those most likely to be filled by women.

TABLE B.3

OCCUPATIONS INCLUDED IN CAF-1 AND CAF-2 CATEGORIES
IN 1929

GRADE CAF-1   Adding machine operator.

Duplicating machine operator.

Addressing machine operator.

Card punch operator.

Routine typist.

Telephone operator.

File clerk.

Under clerk.

****

GRADE CAF-2   Routine stenographer.

Routine stenographer-clerk.

Dictating machine operator.

Calculating machine operator.

Tabulating machine operator.

Bookkeeping machine operator.

Routine bookkeeper.

Junior clerk.

****

Source: U.S. Personnel Classification Board, Salaries for Routine
Clerical Work in Private Industry, 1929 (Washington, DC:
G.P.O., 1931), p.5.

TABLE B.4

LABOR FORCE PARTICIPATION BY WHITE WOMEN AND PROPORTION OF
EMPLOYED WHITE WOMEN IN CLERICAL OCCUPATIONS IN 56 CITIES
1890

	Labor Force Participation Rate (White Women ages 10+)	Proportion of Employed White Women In Clerical Occupations
Albany, NY	21.8	3.4
Allegheny, PA	20.1	3.3
Atlanta, GA	16.2	5.4
Baltimore, MD	22.2	2.1
Boston, MA	30.0	5.6
Brooklyn, NY	21.8	3.4
Buffalo, NY	19.6	4.9
Cambridge, MA	25.7	5.5
Camden, NJ	19.5	3.8
Charleston, SC	16.2	2.3
Chicago, IL	21.6	6.5
Cincinnati, OH	24.3	3.5
Cleveland, OH	19.4	4.2
Columbus, OH	16.5	5.0
Dayton, OH	19.1	4.1
Denver, CO	21.7	6.2
Des Moines, IA	18.6	8.2
Detroit, MI	21.1	5.2
Evansville, IN	22.3	3.1
Fall River, MA	41.0	0.7
Grand Rapids, MI	19.7	6.2
Hartford, CT	26.0	3.9
Indianapolis, IN	19.7	6.6
Jersey City, NJ	20.4	3.5
Kansas City, MO	19.8	7.4
Los Angeles, CA	17.6	4.0
Louisville, KY	20.7	4.4
Lowell, MA	44.3	2.0
Lynn, MA	30.8	5.0
Milwaukee, WI	20.6	4.3
Minneapolis, MN	25.9	5.4
Nashville, TN	15.9	4.1
Newark, NJ	21.2	3.2
New Haven, CT	24.5	4.1
New Orleans, LA	17.7	1.9
New York, NY	28.6	2.5

TABLE B.4
Continued

	Labor Force Participation Rate (White Women ages 10+)	Proportion of Employed White Women In Clerical Occupations
Omaha, NB	24.7	8.4
Paterson, NJ	29.6	1.3
Philadelphia, PA	27.1	2.4
Pittsburgh, PA	17.5	2.9
Providence, RI	29.8	3.7
Reading, PA	19.3	2.4
Richmond, VA	17.5	4.1
Rochester, NY	26.9	4.8
St. Joseph, MO	20.0	5.0
St. Louis, MO	20.9	4.0
St. Paul, MN	24.7	5.7
San Francisco, CA	21.5	3.5
Scranton, PA	22.1	3.1
Syracuse, NY	23.3	6.1
Toledo, OH	19.4	5.8
Trenton, NJ	20.7	2.9
Troy, NY	31.3	1.3
Washington, DC	20.4	12.9
Wilmington, DE	19.0	3.7
Worcester, MA	23.9	3.4

Detailed data on clerical wages was provided by the Personnel Classification Board (PCB) for 32 large cities; 30 of these are included in the urban sample for 1930. In addition, clerical wages were provided by region for urban areas not included among the 32 cities chosen for detailed study. For cities in the sample that were not surveyed separately by the PCB, the regional figures were used. The average annual clerical earnings as derived from this source are presented in columns 1 and 2 of table B.2

Composite Earnings. Composite earnings figures for females and males in each city were constructed in the same manner as that employed for 1890. The result is a weighted average of clerical and manufacturing wages. The resulting earnings figure was deflated by a food price index presented by Schoenberg and Douglas for 1929. Since the index was only available for the 41 cities in their study, it was assumed that the relevant index for other cities was the one that applied to similar size cities in the same state or region. The deflated annual earnings figures for males and females are in columns 5 and 6 of table B.3.

Participation Rates for Women in the Total Labor Force and the Clerical Labor Force, 1890 and 1930

Table B.4 presents data on labor force participation by white women and on participation by employed white women in clerical occupations for cities included in the urban sample in 1890. Table B.5 gives the same data for 1930.

Clerical employment is defined as the total employed in the following categories: bookkeepers, cashiers, and accountants; clerks (not in stores); stenographers and typists. For 1890, corrections in the census data on clerical employment were made to adjust for the inclusion of storeclerks in the general category clerks and bookkeepers. This was accomplished by adopting the adjustments made by Alba Edwards in the national figures and then applying his estimated ratio of storeclerks to total clerks for cities in the sample.[5]

Value Added in Manufacturing, 1890 and 1930

The variable used in the equations in chapter 3 to control for the availability of manufacturing employment for women is based on value added in those manufacturing industries which were the largest employers of women. In 1890 these industries were: clothing, textiles, leather, and tobacco. In 1930 they were: food processing, clothing and

TABLE B.5

LABOR FORCE PARTICIPATION BY WHITE WOMEN AND PROPORTION
OF EMPLOYED WHITE WOMEN IN CLERICAL OCCUPATIONS
IN 89 CITIES, 1930

	Labor Force Participation Rate (White Women ages 10+)	Proportion of Employed White Women In Clerical Occupations
Albany, NY	28.9	30.4
Atlanta, GA	28.9	40.6
Baltimore, MD	25.3	26.6
Birmingham, AL	21.1	36.5
Boston, MA	32.1	27.8
Bridgeport, CT	28.3	23.8
Buffalo, NY	29.0	27.3
Cambridge, MA	34.1	27.5
Camden, NJ	24.9	22.6
Canton, OH	20.4	25.6
Chattanooga, TN	26.3	25.8
Chicago, IL	27.9	35.1
Cincinnati, OH	26.7	25.9
Cleveland, OH	26.0	27.0
Columbus, OH	27.1	27.8
Dallas, TX	21.9	33.0
Dayton, OH	26.0	27.4
Denver, CO	29.5	27.6
Des Moines, IA	29.2	35.7
Detroit, MI	22.7	29.7
Duluth, MN	25.9	25.0
Elizabeth, NJ	25.4	33.2
El Paso, TX	26.9	15.6
Erie, PA	22.2	23.0
Evansville, IN	24.5	19.5
Fall River, MA	35.9	7.9
Fort Wayne, IN	26.5	25.4
Grand Rapids, MI	25.1	25.5
Hartford, CT	33.2	36.8
Houston, TX	29.7	28.4
Indianapolis, IN	27.5	30.4
Jacksonville, FL	24.4	34.3
Jersey City, NJ	27.2	38.0
Kansas City, KS	27.7	26.4
Kansas City, MO	30.3	34.2
Knoxville, TN	26.2	20.1
Long Beach, CA	22.7	20.2
Los Angeles, CA	20.0	27.5

TABLE B.5
Continued

	Labor Force Participation Rate (White Women ages 10+)	Proportion of Employed White Women In Clerical Occupations
Louisville, KY	25.7	29.0
Lowell, MA	32.0	13.6
Lynn, MA	31.5	23.9
Memphis, TN	25.1	35.1
Miami, FL	22.5	25.4
Milwaukee, WI	26.4	26.9
Minneapolis, MN	31.7	28.7
Nashville, TN	25.6	32.8
Newark, NJ	28.0	29.7
New Bedford, MA	38.3	8.8
New Haven, CT	28.6	25.8
New Orleans, LA	23.8	28.6
New York, NY	28.4	32.8
Norfolk, VA	20.7	34.5
Oakland, CA	25.2	29.2
Oklahoma City, OK	26.5	31.4
Omaha, NB	27.9	31.8
Paterson, NJ	28.6	18.0
Peoria, IL	28.0	25.7
Philadelphia, PA	27.7	27.2
Pittsburgh, PA	24.6	27.9
Portland, OR	30.0	25.9
Providence, RI	32.4	21.5
Reading, PA	29.8	13.8
Richmond, VA	29.1	33.9
Rochester, NY	29.2	25.5
St. Louis, MO	27.9	29.4
St. Paul, MN	28.9	30.4
Salt Lake City, UT	23.8	26.8
San Antonio, TX	24.6	19.0
San Diego, CA	25.6	19.8
San Francisco, CA	32.1	32.9
Scranton, PA	23.8	21.7
Seattle, WA	29.9	27.5
Somerville, MA	27.9	36.5
South Bend, IN	26.0	25.7
Spokane, WA	27.1	24.0
Springfield, MA	29.9	28.4
Syracuse, NY	26.8	27.0
Tacoma, WA	23.5	20.8
Tampa, FL	30.1	14.3
Toledo, OH	24.2	25.7
Trenton, NJ	25.9	20.7

TABLE B.5
Continued

	Labor Force Participation Rate (White Women ages 10+)	Proportion of Employed White Women In Clerical Occupations
Tulsa, OK	26.7	32.8
Utica, NY	29.4	18.4
Wichita, KS	26.9	25.6
Wilmington, DE	24.5	29.7
Worcester, MA	28.1	23.2
Yonkers, NY	27.5	29.0
Youngstown, OH	18.4	26.1

textiles, paper, leather, and tobacco. The value added figures were divided by the population in the area to control for city size. For 1890, the *Census of Manufactures* provided manufacturing value added breakdowns for all cities in the sample. For 1930, data provided was more variable. City level data was available for some in the sample; for others, value added data was only available for the county or industrial area. For 72 cities it was possible to collect the relevant value added data for either the city or for the county or industrial area in which the city was located. These 72 cities were used to estimate the 1930 equations in chapter 3. The value added variable was not used in the regression analysis in chapter 7; there the original sample of 89 cities was used for 1930.

Notes

Chapter 2

1. Gainful workers are all persons who reported themselves as having an occupation. The terms labor force and gainful workers are used interchangeably throughout this book.

2. Alba M. Edwards, *Comparative Occupation Statistics for the United States, 1870 to 1940*, U.S. Bureau of the Census (Washington, DC: Government Printing Office, 1943), p.89.

3. Robert W. Smuts, "The Female Labor Force: A Case Study in the Interpretation of Historical Statistics," *Journal of the American Statistical Association* 55 (March 1960) 71–79.

4. See, for example, Joseph A. Hill, *Women in Gainful Occupations, 1870 to 1920*, Census Monographs 9 (Washington, DC: Government Printing Office, 1929), p. 28.

5. U.S. Bureau of the Census, *1930 Census: Abstract*, pp. 330–331.

6. A $=$ Change in female gainful workers (ages 15+) 1920–1930 $=$ 3,012,242.
   B $=$ Change in married female gainful workers (25-44) 1920–1930 $=$ 719,391.
   B/A $=$ 23.88 $=$ percent of total increase in female gainful workers due to increase in married women gainful workers ages 25–44.

7. A $=$ Total female gainful workers (ages 15+) 1930 $=$ 10,632,227.
   B $=$ Total never-married native white female gainful workers (ages 15+) $=$ 4,662,496.
   B/A $=$ 43.85 $=$ percent of female gainful workers who were never married, native-born white women.
   C $=$ Total female (ages 15+) 1930 $=$ 42,837,149.
   D $=$ Never married, native-born white women (ages 15+) 1930 $=$ 9,498,027.
   D/C $=$ 22.17 $=$ percent of women (ages 15+) who were native-born white, never married.

8. Hill, *Women in Gainful Occupations,* p.28

9. Edwards, *Comparative Occupation Statistics* pp. 100-156.

10. Hill, *Women in Gainful Occupations* p. 36.

11. See Valerie K. Oppenheimer, *The Female Labor Force in the United States* (Berkeley: University of California Population Monograph Series no. 5, 1970), pp. 66–77, and Mary H. Stevenson, "Relative Wages and Sex Segregation by Occupation," in Cynthia B. Lloyd, *Sex, Discrimination and the Division of Labor* (New York: Columbia University Press, 1975), pp. 175–200.

12. Barbara Bergmann, "Occupational Segregation, Wages and Profits When Employers Discriminate by Race or Sex," *Eastern Economic Journal* 1, no. 2/3 (April/July 1974): 103–110.

13. 13.5% employed in clothing manufacturing
    7.4   employed in textile manufacturing
    61.7 employed in servant class
    4.0   employed in laundry work
    ─────
    86.6%

14. See for example, Oppenheimer, *Female Labor Force,* pp. 26, 120; Stevenson, "Relative Wages and Sex Segregation by Occupation," and U.S. President, *Economic Report of the President,* 1973 (Washington, DC: Government Printing Office, 1973), pp. 89–112.

15. Oppenheimer, *Female Labor Force* pp. 70–71.

16. Edward Gross, "*Plus ça change...,*" *Social Problems* 16. (1968): 202.

17. For an example of this using 1950 data, see Oppenheimer, *Female Labor Force,* p. 67.

18. Edwards, *Comparative Occupation Statistics for the United States, 1870 to 1940,* pp. 105, 123.

19. Edwards, *Comparative Occupation Statistics,* pp. 107, 125.

20. U.S. Bureau of the Census, *1930 Census: Abstract,* pp. 330–331.

21. C.H. Garland, "Women as Telegraphists," *Economic Journal* 6 (June 1901): 251–261.

22. Robert W. Smuts, *Women and Work in America* (New York: Columbia University Press, 1959), p. 22.

23. Edwards, *Comparative Occupation Statistics,* pp. 111, 128.

24. Oppenheimer, *Female Labor Force* p. 77.

25. U.S. Department of Labor, *Employment and Earnings,* (Jan. 1980), p. 172.

26. A = 8,379,675 = change in female non-agricultural labor force 1870–1930.
   B = 32,262,693 = change in total non-agricultural labor force 1870–1930.
   A/B = 26% = % of increase in total non-agricultural labor force due to increase in female non-agricultural labor force.

Chapter 3

1. U.S. Department of Labor and U.S. Department of Health, Education and Welfare, *Employment and Training Report of the President* (Washington, D.C.: G.P.O., 1979) p. 234.

2. T. Aldrich Finegan, "Participation of Married Women in the Labor Force," in Cynthia B. Loyd, *Sex, Discrimination and the Division of Labor* (New York: Columbia University Press, 1975), p. 28.

3. Lionel Robbins, "On the Elasticity of Demand for Income in Terms of Effort," *Economica* 10 (June 1930): 123–129.

4. Jacob Mincer, "Labor Force Participation of Married Women; A Study in Labor Supply," in National Bureau of Economic Research, *Aspects of Labor Economics* (Princeton: N.B.E.R., 1962), pp. 63–106.

5. Glen G. Cain, *Married Women in the Labor Force: An Economic Analysis* (Chicago: University of Chicago Press, 1966).

6. There have been many studies which use this basic model to analyze female labor force participation in the post World War II period. For the most comprehensive study, see William G. Bowen and T. Aldrich Finegan, *The Economics of Labor Force Participation* (Princeton: Princeton University Press, 1966).

7. Erika Schoenberg and Paul H. Douglas, "Studies in the Supply Curve of Labor," *Journal of Political Economy* 45 (February 1937): 45–79.

8. Clarence D. Long, *The Labor Force Under Changing Income and Employment* (Princeton: Princeton University Press, 1958), p. 118.

9. Claudia Goldin, "Female Labor Force Participation: The Origin of Black and White Differences, 1870 and 1880, "*Journal of Economic History* 38, no. 1 (March 1977): 87–103.

10. Martha Norby Fraundorf, "The Labor Force Participation of Turn-of-the-Century Married Women," *Journal of Economic History* 39, no. 2 (June 1979): 401–418.

11. *Employment and Training Report of the President*, 1979, p. 292.

12. Valerie K. Oppenheimer, *The Female Labor Force in the United States* (Berkeley: University of California Population Monograph Series no. 5, 1970), pp. 12–13.

13. Bowen and Finegan, *Economics of Labor Force Participation*, chapter 8 and appendix 13-A.

14. Bowen and Finegan, *The Economics of Labor Force Participation,* p. 267.

15. Schoenberg and Douglas, "Studies in Supply Curve", p. 50.

16. Paul H. Douglas, *The Theory of Wages* (New York: Macmillan Co., 1934), p. 290.

17. Historical researchers on the family economy have produced a large number of articles in recent years, many of them published in the *Journal of Family History.* Two recent collections which contain articles on family economic decisions in nineteenth-century America are: Tamara K. Hareven, ed., *Transitions: The Family and the Life Course in Historical Perspective* (New York: Academic Press, 1978) and Tamara K. Hareven and Maris A. Vinovskis, ed., *Family and Population in Nineteenth Century America* (Princeton: Princeton University Press, 1978). In *Women, Work and Family* (New York: Holt, Rinehart & Winston, 1978) Louise A. Tilly and Joan W. Scott have surveyed much of the family economy research for Britain and France and have attempted to present a general framework for examining the relationships among women's work, industrialization, and family structure.

18. Claudia Goldin, "Household and Market Production of Families in a Late Nineteenth Century City," *Explorations in Economic History* 16, no. 2 (April 1979): 111–131. Also relevant is Claudia Goldin, "The Work and Wages of Single Women, 1870 to 1920, " *Journal of Economic History* 40, no. 1 (March 1980): 81–88.

19. Michael R. Haines, "Industrial Work and Family Life Cycle, 1889/90," in Paul Uselding, ed., *Research in Economic History* (New York: Academic Press, 1979).

20. Leslie Woodcock Tentler, *Wage Earning Women: Industrial Work and Family Life in the United States,* 1900-1930 (New York: Oxford University Press, 1979), chapter 4, p. 92.

21. John Modell, F. Furstenberg, and T. Hershberg, "Social Change and Transitions to Adulthood in Historical Perspective," *Journal of Family History* 1, no. 1 (Autumn 1976): 7–31.

22. See, for example, previously cited works by Mincer and by Bowen and Finegan, and see Michael L. Wachter, "A Labor Supply Model for Secondary Workers," *Review of Economics and Statistics* 54, no. 2 (May 1972).

23. For a summary discussion of nineteenth-century attitudes toward market work by women, see Robert W. Smuts, *Women and Work in America,* chapter 4.

24. William H. Chafe, *The American Woman, Her Changing Social Economic and Political Roles, 1920-1970* (New York: Oxford University Press, 1972), p. 50.

25. Mincer, "Labor Force Participation," p. 72, and Finegan, "Participation of Married Women," p. 30.

26. Smuts, *Women and Work,* p. 113.

27. *Employment and Training Report of the President, 1979*, p. 295, and Jacob Mincer, "Labor Force Participation and Unemployment: A Review of Recent Evidence," in R.A. Gordon and M.S. Gordan, eds. *Prosperity and Unemployment* (New York: Wiley, 1966), pp. 73–112.

28. Bowen and Finegan, *Economics of Labor Force Participation*, chapter 15.

29. Schoenberg and Douglas, "Studies in Supply Curve of Labor," p. 79.

Chapter 4

1. Charles Dickens, *Bleak House* (1853) (Boston: Houghton Mifflin, 1956).

2. Charles Dickens, *David Copperfield* (1850) (New York: Macmillan & Co., 1928).

3. Herman Melville, "Bartleby, the Scrivener" in *The Piazza Tales* (1856), (London: Constable & Co., 1923).

4. David Lockwood, *The Black-Coated Worker* (London: George Allen and Unwin, 1958), pp. 19–35.

5. Bruce Bliven, *The Wonderful Writing Machine* (New York: Random House, 1954), pp. 6–7.

6. Lockwood, *Black-Coated Worker*, pp. 21–22.

7. Houlston's Industrial Library, no. 7, *The Clerk: a Sketch in Outline of His Duties and Discipline* (London, 1878), p. 13. Quoted in Lockwood, *Black-Coated Worker*, p. 20.

8. Richard N. Current, *The Typewriter and the Men Who Made It* (Urbana, Ill.: University of Illinois Press, 1954), pp. 20, 68.

9. Current, *Typewriter and Men Who Made It*, p. 68.

10. Daniel J. Boorstin, *The Americans: The Democratic Experience* (New York: Vintage Books, 1973), p. 399.

11. Bliven, *Wonderful Writing Machine*, p. 74 and Current, *Typewriter and Men Who Made It*, p. 116.

12. Current, *Typewriter and Men Who Made It*, p. 117.

13. *Asher and Adams Pictoral Album of American Industry, 1876*, (New York: Rutledge Books, 1976), p. 61.

14. Bliven, *Wonderful Writing Machine*, p. 68.

15. Current, *Typewriter and Men Who Made It*, p. 112.

16. Bliven, *Wonderful Writing Machine*, p. 95.

17. Bliven, *Wonderful Writing Machine*, pp. 112, 71-72.

18. Julius Ensign Rockwell, "The Teaching Practice and Literature of Shorthand," *Circular of Information*, no. 2, 1884, pp. 19-159, and "Shorthand Instruction and Practice," *Circular of Information*, no. 1, 1893, pp. 7-205 (Washington, D.C.: G.P.O.).

19. Boorstin, *Americans: Democratic Experience, p. 409.*

20. *Typewriter Trade Journal* (September 1904), p. 5, and Bliven, *Wonderful Writing Machine*, pp. 132, 133, and Boorstin, *Americans: Democratic Experience*, p. 172.

21. C. Wright Mills, *White Collar* (New York: Oxford University Press, 1951), p. 193.

22. *Office Management*, vol. 19 of *Modern Business* (Alexander Hamilton Institute, 1919), p. 48.

23. B.G. Orchard, *The Clerks of Liverpool* (1871), quoted in Lockwood, *Black-Coated Worker*, p. 19.

24. Women's Educational and Industrial Union of Boston, *The Public Schools and Women in Office Service* (Boston: Women's Educational and Industrial Union, 1914), p. 76.

25. U.S. Bureau of the Census, *1900 Census, Special Report on Occupations*, p. 7. *1910 Census of Population*, vol. 4 *Occupations*, p. 94. *1920 Census of Population*, vol. 5, *Occupations*, p. 43. *1930 Census of Population*, vol. 5, *Occupations*, p. 49.

26. Mills, *White Collar*, p. 193.

27. Glen Cain, Richard B. Freeman, and W. Lee Hanson, *Labor Market Analysis of Engineers and Technical Workers* (Baltimore: Johns Hopkins University Press, 1973), p. 27.

28. It is possible for the output effect to result in reduced hiring of one input in the unusual case of an "inferior" input. Charles E. Ferguson, *The Neoclassical Theory of Production and Distribution* (New York: Cambridge University Press, 1969), chapter 9.

29. Robert E. Gallman and Edward S. Howle, "Trends in the Structure of the American Economy Since 1840," in Robert E. Fogel and Stanley L. Engerman, *Reinterpretation of American Economic History* (New York: Harper & Row, 1971), pp. 26–27.

30. Simon Kuznets, *Modern Economic Growth: Rate, Structure and Spread* (New Haven: Yale University Press, 1966), p. 113.

31. Kuznets, *Modern Economic Growth* p. 112.

32. Gallman and Howle, "Trends in Structure of the American Economy," p. 29.

33. Alba M. Edwards, *Comparative Occupation Statistics for the United States, 1870–1940* (Washington, DC: G.P.O., 1943), pp. 104–155.

34. Type II growth is equal to the pure effect of differential industrial growth (holding employment constant at the earlier level) plus an interaction term:

$$\text{Type II change} = \begin{array}{c}\text{pure effect of}\\ \text{differential}\\ \text{industrial growth}\end{array} + \begin{array}{c}\text{interaction between Type I}\\ \text{change and pure differential}\\ \text{industrial growth effect}\end{array}$$

$$\left[E_{t+n} \cdot \Delta\!\left(\frac{E_i}{E}\right) \cdot \left(\frac{C_i}{E_i}\right)_t \right] / \Delta C = \left[E_t \cdot \Delta\!\left(\frac{E_i}{E}\right) \cdot \left(\frac{C_i}{E_i}\right)_t \right] / \Delta C + \left[\Delta E \cdot \Delta\!\left(\frac{E_i}{E}\right) \cdot \left(\frac{C_i}{E_i}\right)_t \right] / \Delta C$$

35. Type III growth is equal to the pure effect of changes in the percentage clerical (holding total employment and industries' shares of employment constant at the earlier levels) plus all interactions between changes in the percentage clerical, the size of the labor force and differential industrial growth:

$$\text{Type III change} = \begin{array}{c}\text{pure effect of intra-industry}\\ \text{clerical growth}\end{array} + \text{interaction effects}$$

$$\left[E_{t-n} \cdot \left(\frac{E_i}{E}\right)_{t+n} \cdot \Delta\!\left(\frac{C_i}{E_i}\right) \right] / \Delta C = \left[E_t \cdot \left(\frac{E_i}{E}\right)_t \cdot \Delta\!\left(\frac{C_i}{E_i}\right) \right] / \Delta C + \left[\Delta E \cdot \left(\frac{E_i}{E}\right)_t \cdot \left(\frac{C_i}{E_i}\right) \right] / \Delta C$$

$$+ \left[E_i \cdot \Delta\!\left(\frac{E_i}{E}\right) \cdot \Delta\!\left(\frac{C_i}{E_i}\right) \right] / \Delta C$$

$$+ \left[\Delta E \cdot \Delta\!\left(\frac{E_i}{E}\right) \cdot \Delta\!\left(\frac{C_i}{E_i}\right) \right] / \Delta C$$

36. For discussion of the relationship between the organization of firms and the need for information, see Alfred D. Chandler, Jr., *Strategy and Structure: Chapters in the History of the American Industrial Enterprise* (Cambridge, Ma.: M.I.T. Press, 1962), pp. 145–153.

37. See discussions of output and input trends by Kuznets, *Modern Economic Growth,* and Gallman and Howle, "Trends in Structure of American Economy," earlier in this chapter.

38. Kuznets, *Modern Economic Growth,* pp. 150–151.

39. Thomas C. Cochran, *200 Years of American Business* (New York: Basic Books, 1977), pp. 88–89.

40. Cochran, *200 Years of American Business,* pp. 140–141.

41. David F. Hawkins, "The Development of Modern Financial Reporting Practices Among American Manufacturing Corporations," in James P. Baughman, *The History of American Management* (Englewood Cliffs, NJ: Prentice-Hall, 1969), pp. 108–116.

42. Cochran, *200 Years of American Business,* p. 136.

43. Ross Robertson, *History of the American Economy,* 2nd ed. (New York: Harcourt, Brace and World, 1964), pp. 420–421.

44. Robertson, *History of American Economy*, p. 425.

45. Robert Lincoln O'Brien, *Atlantic Monthly* (1904) quoted in Bliven, *Wonderful Writing Machine*, p. 134.

46. William G. Bowen and T. Aldrich Finegan, *The Economics of Labor Force Participation* (Princeton: Princeton University Press, 1969).

Chapter 5

1. U.S. Department of Labor, *Employment and Earnings* (Jan. 1980), p. 172.

2. "Stenographers," in *Typewriter Trade Journal* (October 1904), p. 5.

3. U.S. Bureau of the Census, *Current Population Reports, The Social and Economic Status of the Black Population in the U.S.* (Washington, DC: G.P.O., 1974), p. 55.

4. Janet M. Hooks, *Women's Occupations Through Seven Decades*, U.S. Department of Labor, Women's Bureau, *Bulletin* no. 218 (Washington, DC: G.P.O., 1947), p.77.

5. M.C. Elmer, *A Study of Women in Clerical and Secretarial Work in Minneapolis, Minnesota* (Minneapolis, Minn.: Women's Occupational Bureau, 1925).

6. Harriet A. Byrne, "The Age Factor as It Relates to Women in Business and the Professions," U.S. Department of Labor, Women's Bureau, *Bulletin* no. 117 (Washington, DC: G.P.O., 1934), pp. 8, 10–11.

7. Ethel Erickson, "The Employment of Women in Offices," U.S. Department of Labor, Women's Bureau, *Bulletin* no. 120 (Washington, DC: G.P.O., 1934), p. 13.

8. This demand centered explanation is similar to the explanation offered for the growth of participation by married women in the overall labor force after 1940 by Valerie K. Oppenheimer, *The Female Labor Force in the United States* (Berkeley: University of California Population Monograph Series, no. 5, 1970), pp. 177–181.

9. "Women in Business," *Fortune Magazine* 12, no. 1 (July 1935): 53.

10. Alba M. Edwards, *Comparative Occupation Statistics for the United States, 1870 to 1940*. U.S. Bureau of the Census (Washington, DC: G.P.O., 1943), p. 153.

11. Summarized from Bruce Bliven, *The Wonderful Writing Machine* (New York: Random House, 1954), chapters 1 and 5.

12. Richard N. Current, *The Typewriter and the Men Who Made It* (Urbana, Ill.: University of Illinois Press, 1954), p. 286.

13. Women's Educational and Industrial Union of Boston, *The Public Schools and Women in Office Service* (Boston: Women's Educational and Industrial Union, 1914, pp. 15–16.

14. Joseph A. Hill, *Women in Gainful Occupations,* 1870 to 1920, Census Monographs 9 (Washington, DC: G.P.O., 1929), p. 58.

15. See, for example, Ericksen, "Employment of Women in Offices," p. 1 and Women's Educational and Industrial Union of Boston, *The Public Schools and Women in Office Service,* p. 101.

16. See discussion of clerical technology in chapter 4.

Chapter 6

1. Leslie Woodcock Tentler, *Wage-Earning Women: Industrial Work and Family Life in the United States, 1900-1930.* (New York: Oxford University Press, 1979), p. 96.

2. Alice Kessler Harris, "Stratifying by Sex," in Richard C. Edwards, Michael Reich, and David M. Gordon, *Labor Market Segmentation* (Lexington, Mass.: D.C. Heath and Co., 1975), p. 229. Cindy S. Aron, "To Barter Their Souls for Gold: Female Clerks in Federal Government Offices, 1862-1890," (Paper presented at the OAH Conference on Quantitative Women's History, July 1979).

3. Richard N. Current, *The Typewriter and the Men Who Made It* (Urbana, Ill.: University of Illinois Press, 1954), pp. 117-118.

4. Margery Davies, "Woman's Place Is at the Typewriter: The Feminization of the Clerical Labor Force" in Edwards, Reich, and Gordon, *Labor Market Segmentation,* p. 283.

5. For a history of commercial education in the United States see Janice H. Weiss, "Educating for Clerical Work: A History of Commerical Education in the United States since 1850," (Ed.D. diss., Harvard University, 1978).

6. Women's Educational and Industrial Union of Boston, *The Public Schools and Women in Office Service* (Boston: Women's Educational and Industrial Union, 1914), p. 13.

7. Ethel Erickson, "The Employment of Women in Offices," U.S. Department of Labor, Women's Bureau, *Bulletin* no. 117 (Washington, D.C.: G.P.O., 1934), p. 1.

8. See Tentler, *Wage Earning Women,* pp. 39-44 for description of hazardous work environment in manufacturing.

9. For a discussion of women clerical workers in literature see C. Wright Mills, *White Collar* (New York: Oxford University Press, 1951). pp. 200-204.

10. See Tentler, *Wage Earning Women,* chapter 1 for a survey of studies of women's wages in the early twentieth century.

11. Paul Douglas, *Real Wages in the United States, 1890-1926* (Boston: Houghton-Mifflin, 1930), pp. 367-368.

12. Aron, "To Barter Souls for Gold," p. 15.

13. Current, *Typewriter and Men Who Made It,* p. 118.

14. Robert W. Smuts, *Women and Work in America* (New York: Schochen Books, 1959), p. 90.

15. Rhode Island Bureau of Industrial Statistics, *Third Annual Report, 1890* (Providence, 1890), pp. 145–146.

16. Amy Maher, *Wage Rates, Earnings, and Fluctuations of Employment, Ohio, 1914–1926* (Toledo: Information Bureau on Women's Work, 1928), pp. 44–47.

17. Margaret Elliot and Grace E. Manson, "Earnings of Women in Business and the Professions," *Michigan Business Studies,* 3, no. 1, Sept. 1930 (University of Michigan).

18. Grace L. Coyle, "Women in the Clerical Occupations,"   *The Annals of the American Academy of Political and Social Science* 143 (May 1929): 181–182.

19. Smuts, *Women and Work in America,* p. 34.

20. Davis, "Woman's Place is at the Typewriter," pp. 282, 283.

21. Elizabeth Faulkner Baker, *Technology and Women's Work* (New York: Columbia University Press, 1964), pp. 72, 214.

22. Lance Davis et al., *American Economic Growth* (New York: Columbia University Press, 1964), pp. 238–239.

23. Lee Galloway, *Office Management; Its Principles and Practice* (New York: Ronald Press, 1919), p. 84.

24. Baker, *Technology and Women's Work,* p. 73.

25. Galloway, *Office Management; Its Principles and Practice,* p. 157.

26. *Typewriter Trade Journal,* vol. 6, no. 5 (October 1904).

27. Davies, "Women's Place Is at the Typewriter," p. 282.

28. Judith Smith, "The 'New Woman' Knows How to Type: Some Connections Between Sexual Ideology and Clerical Work, 1900–1930," (Paper presented at the Berkshire Conference on Women's History, October 1974).

29. "Women in Business," *Fortune Magazine,* p. 53.

30. Maher, *Wage Rates, Earnings and Fluctuations of Employment,* p. 69.

31. U.S. Personnel Classification Board, *Salaries For Routine Clerical Work in Private Industry, 1929* (Washington, D.C.: G.P.O., 1931), pp. 10–11.

32. Life Office Management Association, *Clerical Salaries in the Life Insurance Business* (Fort Wayne, Ind.: Life Office Management Assn., 1932) Computed from figures, pp. 87–96. This study differentiated clerical work into 63 job classes.

33. The sexual division of labor varies widely across cultures and time periods, but the existing division is usually defended as "natural." For a discussion see Ester Boserup, *Women's Role in Economic Development* (New York: St. Martin's Press, 1970), pp. 15–19.

34. "Women in Business," p. 53.

35. Cindy Aron, "Womanpower in the Federal Government," (paper presented at the Social Science History Association Meetings, November 1979).

36. Janet M. Hooks, *Women's Occupations Through Seven Decades,* U.S. Department of Labor, Women's Bureau, *Bulletin* no. 218 (Washington, D.C.: G.P.O., 1947), p. 75.

37. Gary Becker, *Human Capital* (New York: Columbia University Press, 1964), pp. 11–59.

38. For a discussion of this model and an evaluation of its usefulness for understanding the current labor market position of women, see Cynthia B. Lloyd and Beth T. Niemi, *The Economics of Sex Differentials* (New York: Columbia University Press, 1979), pp. 122–147.

39. Women's Educational and Industrial Union of Boston, *The Public Schools and Women in Office Service,* p. 78.

40. National Industrial Conference Board, *Clerical Salaries in the United States, 1926,* (New York: NICB, 1927), p. 31.

41. J.W. Schultze, *The American Office; Its Organization, Management and Records* (New York: Ronald Printing Co., 1914), p. 96.

42. National Industrial Conference Board, *Clerical Salaries in the United States,* 1926, p. 11.

43. F.G. Nichols, *A New Conception of Office Practice, Based on Investigation of Actual Office Requirements* (Cambridge: Harvard University Press, 1927), p. 49.

Chapter 7

1. Theodore W. Schultz, "Capital Formation by Education," *Journal of Political Economy* 68 (December 1960): 571.

2. Glen Cain, Richard Freeman, and W. Lee Hansen, *Labor Market Analysis of Engineers and Technical Workers* (Baltimore: Johns Hopkins Press, 1973), pp. 34–35.

3. Cain, Freeman, and Hansen, *Labor Market Analysis of Engineers and Technical Workers,* chapter 4.

4. John F. O'Connell, "The Labor Market for Engineers," *Journal of Human Resources* 7, no. 1 (Winter 1972): 82-85.

Appendix B

1. United States Bureau of the Census, *1890 Census of Manufactures*, part II, *Statistics of Cities*, table 3.

2. Erika H. Schoenberg and Paul H. Douglas, "Studies in the Supply Curve of Labor: The Relation in 1929 Between Average Earnings in American Cities and the Proportions Seeking Employment," *Journal of Political Economy* 45 (February 1937).

3. United States Bureau of the Census, *1930 Census of Manufactures*, 3, *Reports by States*.

4. Schoenberg and Douglas, "Studies in the Supply Curve of Labor," p. 57.

5. Alba M. Edwards, *Comparative Occupation Statistics for the U.S., 1870-1930* (U.S. Bureau of the Census, 1943), pp. 149-150.

Bibliography

Government Publications

United States Bureau of the Census. *1870 Census, Compendium.*
_____.*1880 Census, Compendium.*
_____.*1890 Census of Manufactures,* part II, *Statistics of Cities.*
_____.*1890 Census of Population,* vol. 1.
_____.*1900 Census of Population,* vol. 2, part 2.
_____.*1900 Census, Special Report on Occupations.*
_____.*1910 Census, Abstract.*
_____.*1910 Census of Population,* vol. 4, *Occupation Statistics.*
_____.*1920 Census, Abstract.*
_____.*1920 Census of Population,* vol. 4, *Occupation Statistics.*
_____.*1930 Census, Abstract.*
_____.*1930 Census of Manufactures,* vol. 3, *Reports by States.*
_____.*1930 Census of Population,* vol. 4, *Occupations by States.*
_____.*1930 Census of Population,* vol. 5, *General Report on Occupations.*
_____.*1930 Census, Unemployment Returns,* vol. 1, *Returns by Classes.*
_____.*Comparative Occupation Statistics for the United States, 1870 to 1940,* by Alba M. Edwards. Washington, DC: G.P.O., 1943.
_____.*Women in Gainful Occupations, 1870 to 1920* by Joseph A. Hill. Census Monographs, no. 9. Washington, DC: G.P.O., 1929.
_____.*Historical Statistics of the U.S. from Colonial Times to the Present.* Washington, DC: G.P.O., 1957.
United States Bureau of Education. *Bulletin.* Washington, DC: G.P.O., 1919–1931.
_____.*Circular of Information,* no. 2. "The Teaching Practice and Literature of Shorthand," by Julius Ensign Rockwell. Washington, DC: G.P.O., 1884.
_____.*Circular of Information,* no. 1. "Shorthand Instruction and Practice," by Julius Ensign Rockwell. Washington, DC: G.P.O., 1893.
U.S. Department of Labor and U.S. Department of Health, Education and Welfare. *Employment and Training Report of the President.* Washington, D.C.: G.P.O., 1979.
United States Department of Labor, Women's Bureau. *Bulletin* no. 95. "Bookkeepers, Stenographers and Office Clerks in Ohio, 1914–1929," by Amy Maher. Washington, DC: G.P.O., 1932.
_____.*Bulletin* no. 117. "The Age Factor As it Relates to Women in Business and the Professions," by Harriet Byrne. Washington, DC: G.P.O., 1934.

_____.*Bulletin* no. 218. "Women's Occupations Through Seven Decades," by Janet M. Hooks. Washington, DC: G.P.O., 1947.

_____.*Bulletin* 120. "The Employment of Women in Offices," by Ethel Erickson. Washington, DC: G.P.O., 1934.

United States Bureau of Labor Statistics. *Bulletin* no. 613. "Average Annual Wage and Salary Payments in Ohio, 1916–1930," by Fred C. Croxton, Frederick E. Croxton, and Frank C. Croxton. Washington, DC: G.P.O., 1935.

United States Office of Education. *Biennial Surveys of Education, 1950–1952.* U.S. Department of Health, Education and Welfare. Washington, DC: G.P.O., 1955.

United States Personnel Classification Board. *Salaries for Routine Clerical Work in Private Industry, 1929.* Washington, DC: G.P.O., 1931.

United States President. *Economic Report of the President.* Washington, DC: G.P.O., 1973.

Books

Asher and Adams Pictoral Album of American Industry, 1876. New York: Rutledge Books, 1976.

Baker, Elizabeth Faulkner. *Technology and Women's Work.* New York: Columbia University Press, 1964.

Becker, Gary. *Human Capital.* New York: Columbia University Press, 1964.

Blaxall, Martha, and Reagan, Barbara B., Editors. *Women and the Workplace, the Implications of Occupational Segregation.* Special issue of *Signs: Journal of Women in Culture and Society,* vol. 1, part II, 1976.

✓Bliven, Bruce. *The Wonderful Writing Machine.* New York: Random House, 1954.

Boorstin, Daniel J. *The Americans: The Democratic Experience.* New York: Vintage Books, 1973.

Boserup, Ester. *Women's Role in Economic Development.* New York: St. Martin's Press, 1970.

Bowen, William G., and Finegan, T. Aldrich. *The Economics of Labor Force Participation.* Princeton: Princeton University Press, 1966.

Cain, Glen G. *Married Women in the Labor Force: An Economic Analysis.* Chicago: University of Chicago Press, 1966.

Cain, Glen G.; Freeman, Richard B.; and Hanson, W. Lee. *Labor Market Analysis of Engineers and Technical Workers.* Baltimore: Johns Hopkins University Press, 1973.

Chafe, William H. *The American Women, Her Changing Social Economic and Political Roles, 1920–1970.* New York: Oxford University Press, 1972.

Chandler, Alfred D., Jr. *Strategy and Structure: Chapters in the History of American Industrial Enterprise.* Cambridge, Ma.: M.I.T. Press, 1962.

Cochran, Thomas C. *200 Years of American Business.* New York: Basic Books, 1977.

✓Current, Richard N. *The Typewriter and the Men Who Made It.* Urbana: University of Illinois Press, 1954.

Davis, Lance *et. al. American Economic Growth.* New York: Harper and Row, 1971.

Dickens, Charles. *Bleak House.* Boston: Houghton Mifflin, 1956.

_____.*David Copperfield.* New York: Macmillan & Co., 1928.

Douglas, Paul. *Real Wages in the United States, 1890–1926.* Boston: Houghton Mifflin, 1930.

_____.*The Theory of Wages.* New York: Macmillan & Co., 1934.

Easterlin, Richard A. *Population Labor Force and Long Swings in Economic Growth.* New York: National Bureau of Economic Research, 1968.

Elmer, M. C. *A Study of Women in Clerical and Secretarial Work in Minneapolis, Minnesota.* Minneapolis: Women's Occupational Bureau, 1925.

Ferguson, Charles E. *The Neoclassical Theory of Production and Distribution.* New York: Oxford University Press, 1969.

Galloway, Lee. *Office Management; Its Principles and Practice.* New York: Ronald Press, 1919.

✓ Hareven, Tamara K., ed. *Transitions: The Family and the Life Course in Historical Perspective.* New York: Academic Press, 1978.

Hareven, Tamara K., and Vinovskis, Maris A., eds. *Family and Population in Nineteenth Century America.* Princeton: Princeton University Press, 1978.

Knepper, Edwin G. *History of Business Education in United States.* Bowling Green, Ohio, 1941.

Kuznets, Simon. *Modern Economic Growth: Rate, Structure and Spread.* New Haven: Yale University Press, 1966.

Lloyd, Cynthia B., and Niemi, Beth T. *The Economics of Sex Differentials.* New York: Columbia University Press, 1979.

Lockwood, David. *The Black-Coated Worker.* London: George Allen and Unwin, 1958.

Long, Clarence D. *The Labor Force Under Changing Income and Employment.* Princeton: Princeton University Press, 1958.

Maher, Amy. *Wage Rates Earnings, and Fluctuations of Employment, Ohio 1914-1926.* Toledo: Information Bureau on Women's Work, 1928.

Melville, Herman. "Bartleby, the Scrivener" in *The Piazza Tales.* London: Constable & Co., 1923.

Mills, C. Wright. *White Collar.* New York: Oxford University Press, 1951.

National Industrial Conference Board. *Clerical Salaries in the United States, 1926.* New York: NICB, 1927.

Nichols, F. G. *A New Conception of Office Practice, Based on Investigation of Actual Office Requirements.* Cambridge: Harvard University Press, 1927.

Office Management. Vol. 19 of *Modern Business.* Alexander Hamilton Institute, 1919.

Oppenheimer, Valerie K. *The Female Labor Force in the United States.* Berkeley: University of California Population Monograph Series no. 5, 1970.

Schultze, J. W. *The American Office: Its Organization, Management and Records.* New York: Ronald Printing Co., 1914.

Smuts, Robert W. *Women and Work in America.* New York: Columbia University Press, 1959.

Tentler, Leslie, Woodcock. *Wage Earning Women: Industrial Work and Family Life in the United States, 1900-1930.* New York: Oxford University Press, 1979.

Tilly, Louise A., and Scott, Joan W. *Women, Work and Family.* New York: Holt, Rinehart and Winston, 1978.

Weiss, Janice H. "Educating for Clerical Work: A History of Commercial Education in the United States Since 1850." Ed.D. dissertation, Harvard University, 1978.

Women's Educational and Industrial Union of Boston. *The Public Schools and Women in Office Service.* Boston: Women's Educational and Industrial Union, 1914.

Woody, Thomas. *A History of Women's Education in the United States.* New York: Science Press, 1929.

Articles and Papers

Aron, Cindy S. "To Barter their Souls for Gold: Female Clerks in Federal Government Offices, 1862-1890." *Journal of American History* vol. 67 (March 1981).

_____."Womanpower in the Federal Government." *Journal of Social History,* forthcoming.

Becker, Gary. "A Theory of the Allocation of Time." *The Economic Journal* 75 (September 1975).

Coyle, Grace L. "Women in the Clerical Occupations." *The Annals of the American Academy of Political and Social Science* 143 (May 1929).

✓ Davies, Margery. "Woman's Place is at the Typewriter: The Feminization of the Clerical Labor Force." In Richard C. Edwards, Michael Reich, and David M. Gordon, *Labor Market Segmentation.* Lexington: D.C. Heath and Co., 1975.

Fabricant, Solomon. "The Changing Industrial Distribution of Gainful Workers: Comments on the Decennial Statistics 1870-1940." In National Bureau of Economic Research, *Conference on Research in Income and Wealth* 11. New York: NBER, 1949.

Finegan, T. Aldrich. "Participation of Married Women in the Labor Force." In Cynthia B. Lloyd, *Sex, Discrimination and the Division of Labor.* New York: Columbia University Press, 1975.

Fraundorf, Martha Norby. "The Labor Force Participation of Turn-of-the-Century Married Women." *Journal of Economic History* 39 (June 1979).

Gallman, Robert E., and Howle, Edward S. "Trends in the Structure of the American Economy Since 1840." In Robert E. Fogel and Stanley L. Engerman, *Reinterpretation of American Economic History.* New York: Harper and Row, 1971.

Garland, C. H. "Women as Telegraphists." *Economic Journal* 6 (June 1901).

Goldin, Claudia. "Female Labor Force Participation: The Origin of Black and White Differences, 1870 and 1880." *Journal of Economic History* 38, no. 1 (March 1977).

_____. "Household and Market Production of Families in a Late Nineteenth Century City." *Explorations in Economic History* 16 (April 1979).

_____.The Work and Wages of Single Women, 1870 to 1920." *Jounal of Economic History* 40 (March 1980).

Gross, Edward. *"Plus ça change...:* The Sexual Structure of Occupations over Time." *Social Problems* 16 (Fall 1968).

Haines, Michael R. "Industrial Work and Family Life Cycle, 1889/90." In Paul Uselding, ed. *Research in Economic History.* New York: Academic Press, 1979.

James, Estelle. "Income and Employment Effects of Women's Liberation." In Cynthia Lloyd, *Sex, Discrimination and the Division of Labor.* New York: Columbia University Press, 1975.

Miller, Ann R. "Components of Labor Force Growth." *Journal of Economic History* 22 (March 1962).

Mincer, Jacob. "Labor Force Participation and Unemployment: a Review of Recent Evidence." In R. A. Gordon and M. S. Gordon, eds. *Prosperity and Unemployment.* New York: Wiley, 1966.

_____."Labor Force Participation by Married Women: A Study in Supply Labor." In National Bureau of Economic Research, *Aspects of Labor Economics.* Princeton: Princeton University Press, 1962.

Modell, John; Furstenberg, F.; and Hershberg, T. "Social Change and Transitions to Adulthood in Historical Perspective." *Journal of Family History* 1 (Autumn 1976).

O'Connell, John F. "The Labor Market for Engineers." *Journal of Human Resources* 7 (Winter 1972).

Robbins, Lionel. "On the Elasticity of Demand for Income in Terms of Effort." *Economica* 10 (June 1930).

Schoenberg, Erika, and Douglas, Paul H. "Studies in the Supply Curve of Labor." *Journal of Political Economy* 45 (February 1937).

Schultz, Theodore. "Capital Formation by Education," *Journal of Political Economy* 68 (December 1960).

Smith, Judith. "The 'New Woman' Knows How to Type: Some Connections Between Sexual Ideology and Clerical Work, 1900–1930." Paper presented at the Berkshire Conference on Women's History, 1974.

Smuts, Robert W. "The Female Labor Force: A Case Study in the Interpretation of Historical Statistics." *Journal of the American Statistical Association* 55 (March 1960).

Stevenson, Mary H. "Relative Wages and Sex Segregation by Occupation." In Cynthia B. Lloyd, *Sex, Discrimination and the Division of Labor*. New York: Columbia University Press, 1975.

Typewriter Trade Journal. New York, Chicago, 1904.

Wachter, Michael L. "A Labor Supply Model for Secondary Workers." *Review of Economics and Statistics* 54 (May 1972).

"Women in Business." *Fortune Magazine* 12 (July 1935).

Index